George Reynolds

A Dictionary of the Book of Mormon

Comprising its biographical, geographical and other proper names.

Pronouncing vocabulary.

George Reynolds

A Dictionary of the Book of Mormon
Comprising its biographical, geographical and other proper names. Pronouncing vocabulary.

ISBN/EAN: 9783337298074

Printed in Europe, USA, Canada, Australia, Japan

Cover: Foto ©Lupo / pixelio.de

More available books at **www.hansebooks.com**

A DICTIONARY

OF THE

BOOK OF MORMON,

COMPRISING ITS

BIOGRAPHICAL, GEOGRAPHICAL AND

OTHER PROPER NAMES.

BY ELDER GEORGE REYNOLDS.

Author of " The Story of the Book of Mormon," "The Myth of the Manuscript Found," Etc., Etc.

1891
SALT LAKE CITY, UTAH
JOS. HYRUM PARRY

PREFACE.

The increasing interest taken in the study of the Book of Mormon and in the history of the peoples whose origin, progress and destruction it narrates, encourages the author of this little work to think that this addition to the literature of the subject will not be like one born out of due time, but will be received as an acceptable aid to the study of its sacred pages. To the members of the Theological Classes of the Church of Jesus Christ of Latter-day Saints, whether of the quorums of the Priesthood, of the Sunday Schools, Church Schools or Improvement Associations, we particularly submit this book—the first of its kind—believing it will afford them material help in their investigations of Book of Mormon subjects, and their study of Nephite and Jaredite history; and we trust it will not be without value to every one who takes an interest in the races who rose, flourished and vanished in Ancient America.

PREFACE.

This Dictionary contains the name of every person and place mentioned in the Book of Mormon, with a few other subjects of interest referred to therein.

With the hope that it may not be altogether unproductive of good, or of increasing true knowledge with regard to the handworkings of God in the history of the nations of the earth, this little volume is respectfully submitted to all who love the truth.

GEO. REYNOLDS.

JANUARY, 1, 1892.

ERRATA.

Page 11—Title and elsewhere for Ablon read Ahlon.

Page 31—Line 10, insert "to" between people and assent.

Pages 47, 48—Title and elsewhere for Amalekiah, read Amalickiah.

Page 77—line 9, for seemed read seems.

" 100—lines 8 and 9, for Coriantum read Coriantumr.

" 119—Add Figs under title of Fruits.

" 191—line 3, for elder Pahoran read Nephihah

" 191—line 7, for younger read elder.

" 225—line 17, for Anti Lehi-Nephi read Anti-

" 236— " 18, i Nephi-Lehi

" 225—line 24, for Gulf of Arabia read Gulf of Akaba.

" 265—line 21, for Ness read Neas.

" 268—lines 19, 25, for Laman read Lemuel.

" 281—Transpose lines 6 and 7.

" 303—Title, for Nuem, read Neum.

" 319— " " Remlia, read Remalia.

A DICTIONARY

OF THE

BOOK OF MORMON.

NOTE.—The name of a person or place printed in *Italics* directs attention to the matter under that particular heading for further information, and obviates the necessity of references, such as (See Alma).

AARON. One of the sons of the Nephite King, *Mosiah II*, generally supposed to have been the eldest, as it is said that the sovereignty of the people rightly belonged to him on the death of his father, but he refused this great honor on purpose to fulfil a mission to the Lamanites, upon which he and his brothers had set their hearts. Aaron was born in the land of Zarahemla, probably not earlier than B. C. 126, as his father would then have been about thirty years old. During his youth he was wayward and uncontrollable, and joined with those who persecuted the people of God. In fact he and his brothers and the younger *Alma* were leaders among those who harassed the church. The conduct of the young princes in this regard cannot be ascribed to the corrupting influence of lives of pomp and luxury spent at their father's court, for that was a model of simplicity and frugality, and the king himself labored with his hands to lighten the burdens of the people.

suitable that he ruled his people for a lengthy period. It is only reasonable to judge that the king of such a people as the Lamanites then were, would be a type of the race—brutal, bloodthirsty and merciless.

AARON. One of the royal race of the Jaredites. He was the son of Heth, a descendant of Jared. In the days of his grandfather, Hearthom, who was the reigning monarch, the kingdom was taken away from him and he was kept a prisoner all his days. His son Heth, his grandson Aaron, and Aaron's son Amnigaddah were also kept in captivity all their lives by the triumphant party. In the days of Aaron's great-grandson, Com, the kingdom was reconquered for the dynasty of which Aaron was a member. At a rough guess we should imagine that Aaron lived about a thousand years before Christ.

AARON, CITY OF. When Alma was first cast out of Ammonihah he turned his face toward a city called Aaron (Alma viii: 13). It is natural to suppose that Aaron was not far distant from Ammonihah; at any rate, not on the other side of the continent. Yet the only other time when a city called Aaron is referred to, it is spoken of as joining the land of Moroni, which was the frontier district in the extreme southeast of the lands possessed by the Nephites. Our only way out of this difficulty is to suggest that there were two cities called Aaron; not at all an unlikely thing when we reflect how important a personage Aaron, the son of Mosiah, was among his people. When chosen to be king he declined this great honor and the republic was established. It requires no stretch of the imagination to believe that a free and grateful people would name more than one city in honor of this self-denying prince.

The only mention made of the first of these two cities is that Alma bent his way "towards the city which was called Aaron." (B. C. 82.) Of the

secondcity of Aaron we learn that it was north of Moroni, on the Atlantic slope; between these two places the Nephites built (B. C. 72) a third city and called it Nephihah (Alma 50: 14).

AARON, BORDERS OF. The only time that this place is mentioned is in Alma 50: 14, when the building of the city of Nephihah is spoken of. It is stated that the Nephites also began a foundation for a city between the city of Moroni and the city of Aaron, joining the borders of Aaron and Moroni; and they called the name of the city or the land, Nephihah.

ABEL. The son of Adam. He is mentioned once by name in the Book of Mormon (Helaman 6: 27), when his murder by his brother Cain is referred to.

ABINADI. A Nephite prophet, whom the Lord raised up in the land of Lehi-Nephi to reprove the wicked people of King Noah for their sins. As near as we can tell he delivered his prophecies about 150 B. C. At his first appearance he announced as the word of the Lord that if the people did not repent of their iniquities they should be brought into bondage and none should deliver them except the Lord, and He would be slow to hear their prayers in the days of their tribulations. The people did not repent, but sought the life of Abinadi and his words were fulfilled in the days of Noah's son, Limhi. Two years later he reappeared in disguise, so that the people knew him not, and pronounced yet greater woes upon the unrepentant Noah and his subjects. Slavery of the most oppressive kind, famine, pestilence and death were to be their lot, and but a few years passed before Abinadi's prophecies were fulfilled. For his bold denunciations of their abominations he was taken by the priests of the king with whom he had a long controversy on the principle of the atonement and other laws of God, which ended in his being condemned to death.

In accordance with this sentence he was burned at the stake in the City of Lehi-Nephi. One man only. Alma the elder, of whom we leave record, pleaded with Noah in behalf of Abinadi, and this, so incensed the smul-degraded king that he sought to take Alma's life. Alma, however, escaped and in his place of retreat made a record of the teachings and acts of Abinadi, and to that record we are indebted for some of the most precious gospel teachings in the Book of Mormon.

ABINADOM. A Nephite prophet and historian, who lived in the third century before Christ. He received the plates of Nephi from his father, Chemish, who was a descendant of Jacob, the brother of the first Mosiah, his son, Amaleki took charge of them. Either he or his son, conveyed the sacred records from the land of Nephi to Zarahemla, in the great migration of the Nephites under Mosiah, but the record does not show whether he died in the land of Nephi before this movement took place or after. His record is a very short one. From it we learn that he was a warrior, and had seen many wars between the Nephites and Lamanites, and that in those wars he, with his own sword, had taken the lives of many of the enemy in the defence of his brethren. These disastrous wars were undoubtedly one of the causes that led to the removal of the righteous portion of the Nephites from Nephi to Zarahemla. Abinadom concludes his brief record with the following statement: "And I know of no revelation, save that which has been written, neither prophecy; wherefore, that which is sufficient is written. And I make an end."

ABISH. A Lamanite woman of the land of Ishmael, who was a servant-maid to the queen of King Lamoni, at the time that Ammon the son of Mosiah, carried the gospel to that people. (B. C. 91.) Abish herself, had been converted to the Lord

---

many years previously through a remarkable vision which had been granted to her father, but of this conversion she had never spoken. When Lamoni and all his court, including Ammon, were overcome by the power of God that they fell to the earth, Abish understood by what power they were affected. In the hope of convincing the people of the divinity of Ammon's message, she joyously ran from house to house and told all she met, what had happened. While she was thus engaged a multitude gathered at the palace. They viewed with many conflicting emotions the monarch, his wife, and retainers all lying as if dead, with Ammon, the Nephite, also lying in their midst. A great dispute arose, some argued for good, some for evil, and the contention would doubtless have ended in bloodshed had not Abish returned. She was greatly grieved at the turn matters had taken. In the hope of raising the queen from the ground Abish took her by the hand. No sooner did she do so than the queen revived and arose. The latter uttered many expressions of love and gratitude to the Saviour and pleaded for His mercy for her subjects. She next took her husband by the hand, when he arose also, and seeing the contention he rebuked the people and began to teach them the truths of the Gospel. Here commenced the great work of conversion among the Lamanites which eventually terminated in the salvation of many thousand souls. Abish is mentioned in the book of Mormon only in connection with this incident.

ABLOM. A place on the Atlantic seaboard of the Northern Continent, east of the hill Cumorah. The Lord in a dream warned Omer, king of the Jaredites, to flee from his native land, at the time his kingdom was overthrown by Akish and his friends. This he did, and after a long journey settled at Ablom Nimrah, a son of Akish with a number of adherents, afterwards joined Omer at Ablom After many years Omer was re-

stored to his kingdom and returned to his own land.

ABRAHAM. The father of the faithful. As in the Bible so in the Book of Mormon, God is frequently spoken of as the God of Abraham. Most of the references to Abraham in the latter book are doctrinal and but few historical; mention is however made of his paying tithes to Melchizedek.

ADAM. The great father of the human family. His name is mentioned about two dozen times in the Book of Mormon; almost always in connection with the creation, or with the doctrine of the fall and the atonement.

AGOSH, PLAINS OF. A place, locality unknown, in North America, where a great battle was fought in the final war among the Jaredites. The commanders of the contending armies were the Coriantumr and Lib. After a victory by were latter, in the wilderness of Akish, he pursued Coriantumr as far as the plains of Agosh, when another battle was fought in which Coriantumr was victorious and Lib was slain. Shiz, the brother of Lib, assumed command in the place of his brother and attacked and defeated Coriantumr. Probably about B. C. 600; but this is only conjectural.

AHA. A Nephite military officer of the days of the republic. He was the son of Zoram and brother of Lehi. He accompanied his father and brother when they went to Alma, the younger, to inquire the will of the Lord with regard to what course the Nephite army should take in the pursuit of the Lamanites who had destroyed the city of Ammonihah (B. C. 81). Having received the word of the Lord, Zoram and his two sons proceeded to carry it out. They followed and overtook the Lamanites in the great wilderness south of Manti and east of the upper waters of the river Sidon. Here a severe battle took place, which ended in the Lamanite forces being scattered and driven into the wilderness; while all the Nephite

captives were delivered and taken back to their own lands.

AHAH. A wicked king of the Jaredites, who reigned in the latter days of that nation. His father's name was Seth, owing to internal commotions, was brought into captivity and thus remained all his life But Ahah obtained the kingdom, and reigned over the people until his death. He did all manner of iniquity by which he caused the shedding of much blood, but providentially his reign was a short one. He was succeeded on the throne by his son Ethum.

AHAZ. The eleventh king of Judah. His name only appears in the Book of Mormon in quotations from 7th and 14th chapters of Isaiah. (II Nephi, chap. 17 and 24).

AIATH. A place named by Isaiah (10:28), and quoted in II Nephi, 20:28. Possibly another name for Ai.

AKISH. One of the most subtle and cruel of the early Jaredites. Nothing more is known of his descent than that he was the son of Kimnor. The history of Akish is one with which are associated deeds of cruelty, treachery and iniquity that are securely paralleled in the annals of any nation. When the Jaredites first reached this continent they were a righteous, God-fearing, though somewhat unstable people. They, however, made one great mistake, they desired to be ruled by a king. Their prophet-leaders told them that this thing would lend to captivity, but they insisted, and Orihah, who had destroyed the city of Jared, was chosen as their first monarch. The words of their prophets were quickly fulfilled, and bloodshed and internal commotions soon disgraced the history of this favored people. Orihah was succeeded by Kib, who was dethroned by Corihor, his afterwards restored. In the succeeding reign, that of Shule, the kingdom was rent in twain, but when he died he was succeeded by his son Omer, who, we have reason to believe, was a good man. The example of the kings and princes had thus far, as a rule, been pernicious, and tended to encourage the people in lives of wickedness.

Omer had a son named Jared, an ambitious, unscrupulous man. He rebelled against his father and by his flatteries induced half the people to join his standard. He established himself in a land named Heth, and when he felt sufficiently strong he gave battle to and defeated the forces of his father, whom he took prisoner and held in captivity; and, it is said, Omer remained in this condition half his days. So long, indeed, was the time that Jared kept him prisoner that sons begotten by him during his captivity grew up to manhood before he was released. Two of these young men, named Esrom and Coriantumr, became very angry at the way their father was treated, and they raised an army and attacked their brother Jared by night. This attack appears to have been an utter surprise to Jared, for his army was entirely destroyed, and he himself would have been slain had he not humbly pleaded with his brothers that his life might be spared, he promising that he would surrender the kingdom to his father. On this condition his life was granted him.

Now Jared, though he had made this promise when his life was in peril, still longed for the glories and power of the kingly authority; and his sorrow and unrest could not be hid from those near him. Among those who noticed his deep-seated grief was a daughter, who, was exceeding fair, and was apparently as unscrupulous as her father. Whether it was because she really had affection for her father, or, like him, languished for the pomp and magnificence of the court life she no longer possessed that caused her to submit to him a plan by which he might regain the kingdom, cannot be told; perhaps, also, she loved the man whom she suggested as the instrument to be

used in the fulfillment of her ambition—possibly all three, for our motives are seldom single; our actions, in other words, are generally the result of a combination of motives.

The young lady's plan was this: She reminded her father that when their ancestors came across the great waters they brought with them records of the doings of mankind in the ages before the flood. And in those records was an account of how men by secret plans and combinations obtained kingdoms and great glory. She suggested that her father acquire a knowledge of these unholy methods and use them to regain the throne. She further proposed that he send for a friend of Omer's named Akish, the son of Kimnor, and she, being graceful as well as beautiful, would dance so entrancingly before him that he would desire her to wife. If she did not love Akish, she simply sold herself to gratify her father's and possibly her own ambition.

Her advice was listened to, her suggestions carried out. The old oaths and bloody mysteries were searched out, the plan laid, Akish invited, the suggestive dance danced. Akish's passions inflamed and the maiden asked in marriage. The proposal was received with favor, but terrible conditions were attached, such that would have appalled any honorable man. It was that Akish should obtain for Jared the head of his father, the king, and to enable him to carry out this murderous design Jared proposed that he administer to his friends the old oaths that had come down from the days of Cain, the first murderer.

Akish accepted this terrible responsibility. He gathered his associates at the house of Jared and there made them all swear by the God of heaven, and by the heavens, by the earth and by their heads, that whoso should vary from what he desired should lose his head, and whoso should divulge whatever he made

known should lose his life. He then submitted his plans to them, which they accepted. The plot was so far successful that they overthrew the kingdom of Omer, but did not succeed in obtaining his head. For the Lord was merciful to Omer and warned him to depart out of the land. So taking those of his family who were faithful to him he traveled for a great distance until he reached the shores of the Atlantic Ocean. There he and his companions tarried until the course of events permitted him to return.

Omer being driven from his kingdom, Jared was anointed king, and his daughter was given to Akish to wife. But this did not satisfy Akish; he had learned the power of these secret combinations, and now determined to use them for his own ends. He aspired to the throne, and made up his mind to murder his father-in-law. So he assembled his followers, instructed them in his wishes, and Jared was slain by them as he sat on his throne giving audience to the people; a case of poetical retribution which, though often found in fiction, is seldom met with in real life. Akish was now made king, and under his cruel rule wickedness became almost universal. The secret societies by which he obtained power had corrupted the hearts of all the people. As may be well supposed, with such a condition of society his throne was not a stable one. He became jealous of one of his sons. What cause, if any, he had therefor, we are not told, but he shut him up in prison and slowly starved him to death. This cruel act greatly incensed another of Jared's sons, named Nimrah, and he, gathering a few followers, fled to the land where Omer dwelt.

Now Akish had other sons, and though they had sworn to support him in all his doings, they were not true to their oaths. They found that the hearts of the Jaredites werconsumed with the love of gain, and they bribed the greater portion

of the people to join them in a revolt against their father. So corrupt had the people now become that their extinction appears to have been the only remedy; they were past repentance. A war of the most horrible character broke out, which lasted several years, and only ended when nearly every soul was slain. Of the kingdom of Akish, for which he had sinned so much, there remained but thirty souls, all the rest—men, women and children—had been swept by bloody hands into untimely graves. The people of Akish having been thus destroyed, Omer, with his friends, returned from his captivity, and reigned over the feeble remnant of a wasted people.

AKISH, WILDERNESS OF. A place in North America, apparently not far from the Atlantic coast, where a severe battle was fought in the last great war which ended in the extinction of the Jaredite race. The conflict was between the armies of Gilead and Coriantumr in which many thousands were slain. It appears to have been indecisive, as Gilead remained in the wilderness and Coriantumr lay siege thereto. But one night Gilead unexpectedly sallied forth and slew a part of the army of his enemy, they being drunken. This, for the time being, gave him the advantage. In a later campaign, after Gilead had been assassinated, a battle was fought between Coriantumr and Lib in which the latter was victorious, and the former fled to the wilderness of Akish, but being pursued by Lib, he continued his retreat to the plains of Agosh where another desperate conflict occurred.

ALMA, the elder, was an Israelite of the tribe of Manasseh, a direct descendant of Nephi, the son of Lehi. He was born in the land of Lehi-Nephi, or a region contiguous, 173 years before the advent of the Redeemer, when Zeniff was king in that portion of the South American Continent. He is first introduced to the readers of the Book

of Mormon shortly before the martyrdom of the prophet Abinadi, as a young man associated with the apostate and iniquitous priesthood of king Noah, the son of Zeniff. Unlike his soul-seared associates, his heart was pricked by the warnings and teachings of Abinadi, for he knew that his denunciations of the prevailing wickedness were true. Inspired with this knowledge, he very courageously went to the tyrant Noah, and pleaded for the prophet's life. His appeal in behalf of the devoted servant of the Lord was ineffectual; the infuriated and besotted king would not hearken to Alma's appeal for justice and mercy, but to the contrary he ordered the young priest to be cast out from his anger, he sent his servants to slay him. Alma, however, successfully hid from his pursuers, and, during his concealment, wrote the words he had heard Abinadi speak, which teachings now form one of the most important of the doctrinal portions of the Book of Mormon.

The power, the importance, the efficiency of Abinadi's teachings had sunk deep in the heart of Alma; he not only realized their truth, but he comprehended their saving value. The next lesson they impressed upon his mind was the necessity of his immediate and thorough repentance, combined with unfaltering faith in the Savior, who was to come to redeem mankind. In much tribulation he sought the Lord with all his powers and therefore. Father vouchsafed to him an abundant, soul-satisfying answer. From this time Alma began to preach privately to the people the words of Gospel truth. To do this he received power from on high. We have no account of the time of his ordination, whether when a lad he had received the holy priesthood under the hands of some one of God's servants, before the days that Noah led his people into iniquity and corrupted the priesthood, or, whether at this time he was ministered to by

messengers from Heaven. Perhaps both; but the time and place is but a secondary consideration, the important fact remains, that he was commissioned by God to officiate in His name, which commission he ever after magnified to the salvation of his fellow-men. Alma's preaching of God's holy word was not without fruit. Many received the truth with joy. These gathered to a convenient spot on the borders of the wilderness, but not far from their city. This place was called Mormon. It was admirably suited for a hiding place, having formerly been infested by ravenous beasts, and was dreaded and avoided by the people. Near by was a thicket of small trees, in which the Gospel believers could hide should they be pursued by the king's servants; here also was a fountain of pure water, most excellently adapted for the purposes of baptism. Here, in the midst of the luxuriance of tropical vegetation, and by the side of the inviting stream, did Alma proclaim the principles of everlasting life; here the people entered into covenant to serve the Great Father of all; here were the repentant believers baptized unto Christ, for the remission of sins, and here was the Church of the First Born organized, the holy priesthood ordained, and the work of God founded in power.

Alma and another servant of the Lord, named Helam, were the first to enter the water, and when there, Alma lifted his voice in prayer and besought the Lord for His Holy Spirit. This blessing having been bestowed, he proceeded with the sacred ordinance. Addressing his companion, he said, "Helam, I baptize thee, having authority from the Almighty God, as a testimony that ye have entered into a covenant to serve Him until you are dead as to the mortal body; and may the Spirit of the Lord be poured out upon you; and may He grant unto you eternal life, through the redemption of Christ whom He has prepared from the foundation of the

world." Alma having said these words, both he
and Helam were buried in the water, whence they
came forth rejoicing, being filled with the Holy
Spirit. Others, to the number of two hundred
and four souls, followed Helam into the waters of
baptism, but in all these cases Alma did not again
bury himself beneath the liquid wave, but only
the repentant believers. From this time we may
date the organization of the Church of Jesus
Christ in that land, and henceforth its members
assembled for worship and testimony once a
week.

Notwithstanding the care and circumspection
with which the members of the Church acted,
Noah soon discovered that there was some secret
movement among his subjects, and by the help
of his spies he discovered what was taking place
at Mormon. Making the tyrant's usual excuse,
that the Christians were in rebellion against him,
he sent his armies to capture and destroy them.
But a greater than he stretched forth His arm to
preserve His people. The Lord warned Alma of
the king's intentions, and in obedience to the Divine
direction, he assembled his people, some 450 souls,
gathered his flocks and herds, loaded up his grain,
provisions and other supplies, and departed into
the untrodden wilderness.

Being strengthened by the Lord, notwithstanding that they were impelled by their flocks
and families, the pilgrims traveled with sufficient rapidity to escape the pursuing forces of
king Noah, who were reluctantly compelled to
return to the land of Nephi without having accomplished the object of the expedition. At the
end of eight days Alma's company ceased their
flight, and settled in a very beautiful and pleasant
land where there was an abundant supply of pure
water. We have no direct information with
regard to the course taken by this colony, but it is
evident, from the details of their later history,

the days when they both belonged to king Noah's
priesthood, and with the venom so often conspicuous in apostates, the latter soon commenced
to persecute those who were faithful to the Lord.
He placed task-masters over them, he imposed inhuman burdens upon them, and otherwise afflicted
them grievously.

In their affliction the people of Alma cried
unremittingly to Heaven for deliverance, but even
their prayers were an annoyance to their task-
masters, and they were forbidden to lift up their
voices in supplication to the Lord; but the ty-
rants could not prevent them from pouring out
their hearts to Him who knoweth the inmost
thoughts of all men. He answered in His own
way; He did not bring them immediate deliverance, but He strengthened their backs to bear the
heavy burdens placed upon them, and, strong in
the faith of their ultimate release from this bondage, they toiled on with cheerfulness and patience.

In His due time the Lord delivered them. Having revealed His intentions to Alma, that the people might make ready, He caused a deep sleep to
come upon the Lamanite guards and task-masters.
The hour to strike for liberty had arrived, but it
was obtained at a heavy cost, that of their homes
and possessions. Under the guidance of Alma
they departed into the wilderness At eventide
they rested in a beautiful valley which they called
Alma; but they did not tarry there. The next day
they pushed farther into the wilderness, and continued their journey until they arrived at the land
of Zarahemla, which they reached in twelve days'
travel from the valley of Alma. Their arrival
amongst their Nephite kindred was the occasion
of great joy both to them and to the people of
king Mosiah, which joy was intensified by the
fact that Limhi and his subjects had also arrived
in safety at the home of their forefathers a short
time previously, thus uniting all the Nephite

that the new settlement lay somewhere between
the lands of Nephi and Zarahemla, though possibly somewhat aside from the most direct route.
We think it far from improbable that it was
situated at the head waters of some one of the
numerous tributaries to the Amazon that take
their rise on the eastern slopes of the Andes.

The colonists, whose industry is especially referred to by the inspired historian, immediately
set to work to till the soil and build a city. The
city, with the surrounding territory, they named
the city and land of Helam. Now that they were
established as a separate people, independent of
both Lamanite and Nephite princes, they desired a
form of temporal government such as Alma as their
king. This honor he declined. He rehearsed to
them the history of their fathers; he pictured to
them the infamies of king Noah's reign; he showed
them how a wicked ruler could lead his subjects
into all manner of evil, and how such things led
to bondage; and, on the other hand, how much
better it was to have the Lord as their King and
Ruler, and to be guided by His servants under His
inspiration. This counsel the people wisely accepted. Alma, though not bearing the title of
king, acted as their leader, as their high priest and
prophet, and as the mouthpiece of God to them
whenever His holy word was graciously given
them. In this happy state the people of Helam
continued for some years, the Lord greatly pros-
pering them and crowning their labors with abundant increase.

How long these blissful days lasted is not defined in the sacred record of the Book of Mormon;
but as the Lord chastens those whom He loves, so,
after a time, He permitted the Lamanites to discover their secluded and happy home, and to bring
them into bondage.

It so happened that a Lamanite army corps
(that had been pursuing a body of fugitive Ne-

people (except the few apostates with Amulon)
in one land and under one king.

Alma and his people must have dwelt in the
land of Helam quite a number of years, as he is
called a young man at the time of Abinadi's
martyrdom, and at the time he led his people into
the land of Zarahemla he was more than fifty
years old, possibly several years older.

On the arrival of Alma in the land of Zarahemla, king Mosiah gave him charge of the
spiritual concerns of the Nephites. He became
the high priest to the whole nation. In this
capacity he gathered the people together, and in
words of power and plainness he reminded them
of their duties to Heaven Nor had he unwilling
hearers; numbers hearkened to his words, renewed
their covenants with God, went down into the
waters of baptism, and recommenced a life of godli-
ness and faith. From place to place Alma bent his
way, preaching, counseling, reproving, comforting,
instructing, as the Holy Spirit led Through these
labors seven branches of
the Church, were established in the land of Zarahemla, while great prosperity attended the faithful As years rolled by, the hearts of those who
loved the Lord were pained by the unbelief and
wickedness of the rising generation. Many of
these not only rejected the truth themselves, but
persecuted and reviled those who were righteous.
This unholy crusade received great strength and
assumed great effrontery owing to the fact that
the four sons of king Mosiah, and the son of the
high priest Alma, were their ringleaders. Vain were
the exhortations of these holy men to their wayward sons; they rebelled against their fathers'
admonitions, and set their authority at defiance
Great was Alma's grief. The Lord of Hosts was
his only resource In much sorrow, but with
much faith, he earnestly and unceasingly prayed
for his loved but rebellious son. The Lord heard

phites under Limhi, the son of Noah, who had
broken away from their bondage in the land of
Nephi,) lost themselves in the wilderness. While
traveling hither and thither, not knowing which
way to go, they came across a body of men who
had once been the priests of king Noah, but who
had fled from the face of their fellows to escape the
just indignation their continued iniquities had
aroused. These priests, at the instigation of
Amulon, their leader, joined the Lamanite troops,
and unitedly endeavored to get back to the land
of Nephi. While thus engaged, they wandered
near the city of Alma.

When the people of Alma first perceived the
approach of this body of men, they were occupied
in tilling the soil around their city, into which they
immediately fled in great fear. In this perilous
hour the faith and courage of Alma were conspicuous. He gathered his people around him,
called upon them to east aside their unsaintly
fears, and to remember the God who had ever
delivered those who trusted in Him. The words
of their leader had the desired effect; the people
silenced their fears and called mightily upon the
Lord to soften the hearts of the Lamanites that
they might spare their lives and those of their
wives and little ones Then, with the assurance
in their hearts that God would hearken unto their
prayers, Alma and his brethren went forth out
of their city and delivered themselves up to their
former foes.

The Lamanites were in a dilemma, therefore
they were profuse in promises. They were willing
to grant the people of Helam their lives and liberty
if they would show them the way to the land
of Nephi. Having obtained this information and
reached home in safety, they broke their promises
and made Amulon king over a wide district
of country, including the land of Helam.

Alma and Amulon had known each other in

His faithful servant's petitions, sent His angel to
stay the young man's mad career and bring him
to a knowledge of the truth There, overpowered
by the presence and message of the angel, he was
struck dumb and paralyzed. When the news of
this visitation reached his father, he was greatly
rejoiced, for he knew it was the power of God.
He gathered his people to witness the miracle, and
assembled the priests that they might join him in
prayer and fasting for his son's perfect restoration. Their prayers were heard, not only were
the natural powers of the body restored, but Alma
became a changed man, and from thenceforth was
a valiant soldier of the cross—a body, a comfort,
and a joy to his father, who was now beginning
to feel the effects of advancing years.

Before his death, Alma, who had ordained his
son a high priest, gave the latter charge concerning all the affairs of the Church, and then, full
of years and honor he departed this life.) His
death took place (B C 91) when he was eighty-
two years old, five hundred and nine years having passed from the time Lehi and his family left
Jerusalem.

ALMA, the younger, was born either in
the land of Mormon, when his devout and intrepid
father was there organizing the Church of Christ,
or after the little colony of Christians had removed to the land of Zarahemla. From personal
observation made in one of his discourses, we are
inclined to think it was in the latter place. With
his father he came to the land of Zarahemla, and
there, as the son of the presiding high priest of the
entire Church, he became the associate and companion of the sons of the king. Their course was
one too often pursued by the children of the great.
They took pleasure in evil-doing; they laid no
faith in the revelations of God, while they ridiculed,
mocked and persecuted those who had. We can
well understand the anxiety, the distress, the

sorrow this course caused their God-fearing
parents, we can realize how frequent and how
fervent were the prayers offered by the king, the
high priest, and the people for those misguided
youths. And their prayers prevailed before God.

It came to pass that as Alma and the sons of
king Mosiah were going about to destroy the
Church and to lead astray the people of the Lord,
that an angel descended in a cloud and stopped
them on the way. When he spoke his voice was as
thunder, and caused the whole earth to tremble
beneath their feet. Naturally this manifestation
of the power of God spread terror and dismay in
the hearts of those who witnessed it; simulta-
neously they fell to the ground, and so confused
and terrified were they, that they failed to understand the words of the holy messenger. "Arise,
Alma, and stand forth," he cried; and when Alma
arose, his eyes were open to see who stood before
him. "Why persecutest thou the Church of God?"
he was asked. "for the Lord hath said, This is my
Church, and I will establish it; and nothing shall
overthrow it, save it is the transgression of my
people. If thou wilt of thyself be destroyed, seek
no more to destroy the Church of God." Besides
this, the angel spoke to him of his father's fervent
prayers in his behalf, and that because of those
prayers of faith he was sent to convince him of
the power of God. He also recounted to him the
captivity of his fathers in the lands of Helam and
Nephi, and of their miraculous deliverance therefrom, but Alma heard none of these latter sayings,
for the terrors of the first salutation had overpowered him.

Alma, hereft of the presence of the angel, dismayed and soul-stricken, sank to the ground.
When his companions gathered around him, they
found he could not move, neither could he speak;
outwardly he was dead to the world; but the
torments of the damned had taken hold of his

daunted or dismayed, for he had joy in preaching
the word, and in the conversion of many from
their ungodliness. So conspicuous as a champion
of the cause of God did he become, that Mosiah
considered him the most proper person to whom
to confide the custody of the sacred plates, and to
act as the recorder of the nation's doings and progress, still more, when Aaron, the son of Mosiah,
declined to succeed his father on the Nephite
throne, and it was wisely determined by the people that they would be ruled by judges for the future. Alma was chosen by the united voice of his
countrymen to be their first chief judge. He was
also their presiding high priest, he having been
consecrated to this exalted position by his father,
who, shortly before his death, gave him charge of
the affairs of the Church throughout all the land.
(B. C. 91.)

Five hundred and nine years had now passed
away since Lehi left Jerusalem, during which
time the Nephites had been ruled by kings, the successors of the first Nephi. A wonderful but blood-
less revolution now took place—the monarchy was
merged into a republic; but so wise had been the
steps taken by Mosiah, so equitably had he arranged the laws, that the change was made without popular tumult or disorder in the affairs of the
state. Indeed the change was hailed with unbounded satisfaction by the people, who greatly rejoiced in the more extended liberties now guaranteed to them. In Alma, as their first chief judge,
they had a man admirably adapted for the situation; he had the confidence of the people, inasmuch
as he was the Lord's mouthpiece to them, besides
his worth and abilities claimed their trust and
respect; he was a man of great talent, courage,
faith and energy, an unwearied worker for good,
and, as a judge judged righteous judgment in the
midst of the people. Still his position was not one
of unmixed delights—apostates from the Church,

soul, and in the most bitter pain and mental anguish he lay racked with the remembrance of all
his past sins. The thought of standing before the
bar of God to be judged for his iniquities overwhelmed him with horror; he would have rejoiced in annihilation; he desired to become extinct, both body and soul, without being brought
before his abused Creator. Thus he continued for
three days and three nights to suffer the pains of
hell, which to his tortured conscience must have
seemed an eternity.

When his companions found that he could
neither speak nor move, they carried him to his
father, and related to him all that had happened.
Strange as it must have seemed to them, the elder
Alma's heart was filled with joy and praise when
he looked upon the body of his much-loved son,
for he realized it was God's power that had
wrought all this, and that his long-continued
prayers had been answered. In his joy he
gathered the people to witness this mighty manifestation of the goodness and might of Jehovah.
He assembled the priests, sought their co-opera-
tion, and unitedly, in God's own way, they
prayed and fasted for the stricken youth. For
two days they continued their supplications, at
the end of which time Alma stood upon his feet
and spoke. He comforted them by declaring, "I
have repented of my sins, and have been redeemed
of the Lord; behold I am born of the Spirit."

In later years Alma, in relating to his son
Helaman the details of his conversion, thus des-
cribes the causes that led him to bear this testimony. He says: "Behold, I remembered also to
have heard my father prophesy unto the people
concerning the coming of one Jesus Christ, a Son
of God, to atone for the sins of the world. Now,
as my mind caught hold upon this thought, I
cried within my heart, O Jesus, thou Son of God,
have mercy on me, who art in the gall of bitter-

pride and unbelief in its members, assaults and invasions from the national enemies, all combined to
require his undiminished energies and undaunted
faith. But above and beyond all, as compensa-
tion for these trials and annoyances, he had the
right to receive the word of the Lord, which was
given to him as he needed or his people inquired.

The first year of Alma's judgeship was troubled
by the apostasy of Nehor, a man of many personal
attractions and great persuasiveness of manner,
who went about among the people preaching a
kind of universalism—that all men should be saved;
he also established priestcraft, making a lucrative
business of spreading his pernicious ideas. His
success in turning the hearts of the people was unfortunately quite extensive, and the cause of many
of the troubles that afterwards afflicted the Nephites. The individual career of Nehor, however,
was short; he met an aged servant of the Lord
named Gideon, and because the latter would not
accept his dogmas, but withstood him with the
words of God, Nehor drew his sword and slew the
venerable disciple. For this offence he was
brought before Alma, and, being tried by the law
of the land, was found guilty and condemned to
death.

Notwithstanding the development of those
follies, and departures from the strictness of Gospel
law apparently incidental to great worldly prosperity, there was continued peace in the land until
the fifth year of Alma's judgeship, when a great
division took place among the people, owing to
the more corrupt portion wishing to restore the
monarchy, and make a man after their own heart,
named Amlici, king. The movement grew to so
much importance that it was referred to the decision of the whole people, who gathered in large
bodies all over the land, and expressed their
wishes for or against Amlici's elevation to the
throne in the way prescribed by the law. The

ness, and art encircled about by the everlasting
chains of death. And now, behold, when I
thought this, I could remember my pains no more;
yea, I was harrowed up by the memory of my
sins no more. And oh, what joy, and what mar-
vellous light I did behold; yea, my soul was filled
with joy as exceeding as was my pain; yea, I say
unto you, my son, there could be nothing so exquisite and so bitter as my pain. Yea, and again
I say unto you, my son, that on the other hand,
there can be nothing so exquisite and sweet as
was my joy; yea, methought I saw, even as our
father Lehi saw, God sitting upon his throne,
surrounded with numberless concourses of angels,
in the attitude of singing and praising their God;
yea, and my soul did long to be there."

From that time to the end of his mortal career,
Alma labored without ceasing to bring souls to
Christ, and to guide his fellow men in the paths of
salvation.

We have now to present Alma as the foremost man of his age and nation, the presiding
high priest and chief judge of a mighty people; a great prophet, filled with the spirit of his
calling; an unceasing missionary, an undaunted
soldier of the cross, a lucid expounder of the principles of the everlasting Gospel; a proficient or-
ganizer of men, a distinguished warrior and a triumphant general. While in his conversion, extended missionary journeyings, and elaborate discourses on saving truths, we are reminded of Saul
of Tarsus, recollections of Joshua, the son of
Nun, are vividly brought before us when we consider him as the great leader and prophet of his
people, and the victorious commander-in-chief of
their armies.

The change in the life of Alma brought down
upon him the persecutions of the wicked, for
others treated him as he before-time had treated
the Saints. But in none of these things was he

result was that Amlici's ambitious schemes were
defeated by the voice of the majority, and the
liberties of the republic were preserved.

This should have ended the matter, but it did
not; the turbulent minority, incited by Amlici,
would not accept this constitutional decision.
They assembled and crowned their favorite as
king of the Nephites, and he at once began to prepare for war, that he might force the rest of the
people's consent to his government. Nor was Alma
idle; he also made ready for the impending contest.
He gathered his people and armed them with all
the weapons known to Nephite warfare. The
two armies met near a hill called Amnihu, on the
east bank of the river Sidon. There a bloody
battle followed, in which Amlici's forces were disastrously defeated with a loss of 12,532 men,
while the victors had to mourn the loss of 6,562
warriors slain. After pursuing the defeated
monarchists as far as he was able, Alma rested his
troops in the valley of Gideon. He there took the
precaution to send out four officers with their
companies to watch the movements and learn the
intentions of the retreating foe. These officers
were named Zeram, Amnor, Manti and Limher.
On the morrow these scouts returned in great
haste, and reported that the Amlicites had joined
a vast host of Lamanites in the land Minon,
where unitedly they were slaying the Nephite
population and ravaging their possessions; at the
same time they were pushing rapidly towards the
Nephite capital with the intent of capturing it
before Alma's army could return. Alma at once
headed his troops for Zarahemla, and with all
haste marched towards it. He reached the crossing of the Sidon without meeting the enemy, but
while attempting to pass to the western bank he
was confronted by the allied armies. A terrible
battle ensued; the Nephites were taken somewhat
at a disadvantage, but being men of faith, they

fervently sought Heaven's aid, and in the increased fervor this faith inspired, they advanced to the combat. With Alma at their head, the advance-guard forded the river and broke upon the enemy who stood awaiting them. By the fury of their charge they drove in the ranks of the enemy, and as they pushed onward they cleared the ground by throwing the bodies of their fallen foes into the Sidon, thus making an opening for the main body to obtain a foothold. In this charge Alma met Amlici face to face, and they fought desperately. In the midst of this hand-to-hand combat, Alma lifted his heart on high, and prayed for renewed strength that he might not be overpowered, but live to do more good to his people. His prayers were answered, and thereby he gained new vigor in battle with and eventually slay Amlici. Amlici slain, Alma led the attack to where the king of the Lamanites fought. But that monarch retired before the impetuous valor of the high priest, and commanded his guards to close in upon his assailant. The order was promptly obeyed, but it did not succeed. Alma and his guards bore down upon them with such fury that the few of the monarch's warriors who escaped made a hasty retreat. Pushing steadily on, Alma kept driving the allies before him, until his whole army had crossed the Sidon. There the enemy, no longer able to meet his welbordered advance, broke in all directions, and retreated into the wilderness that lay to the north and west. They were hotly pursued by the Nephites as long as the latter's strength permitted, and were met on all quarters by patriots rallying to the call of the commonwealth, who slew them by thousands. A remnant eventually reached that part of the wilderness known as Hermounts. There many died of their wounds and were devoured by the wild beasts and vultures with which that region abounded.

To the Nephites was left the sad task of bury-

was in the hands of a corrupt clique of judges and lawyers, who stirred up sedition, tumult and rioting, that they might make money out of the suits that followed such disturbances. Further than this, they were secretly plotting to overthrow the government, and rob the people of their highly prized liberties. Among such a people Alma labored in vain, for no would listen, none would obey, none offered him rest and food, but scorn and mockery were his reward, and he was spat upon, maltreated and cast out of the city for his pains. Weary in body and sick at heart because of the iniquity of the people, after many fruitless efforts, fervent prayers and long fastings, Alma left the city to seek some other people more worthy of salvation's priceless gifts. He bent his way towards the city of Auron; but as he journeyed thitherward, an angel of the Lord (that same that beforetime had been the agent in his conversion to God,) stood before him and blessed him. He told him to lift up his heart and rejoice, for because of his faithfulness he had great cause to do so. The angel then directed Alma to return to the sin-cursed city he had just left, and proclaim unto its godless citizens the awful message that "Except they repent the Lord will destroy them."

Speedily the prophet obeyed the angel's words. By another road he drew near the doomed city, which he entered by its south gate. As he passed in he was an hungered, and asked a man whom he met, "Will you give to an humble servant of God something to eat?" With joy the man took him to his home and fed, clothed and lodged him. Furthermore, Amulek, for such was his name (for he also had received a visit from a holy angel, who had informed him of the high priest's coming and directed him to receive him into his house. And Alma blessed Amulek and all his household, and tarried and recruited

ing the innumbered dead, many of whom were women and children who had become victims to the ravages of the foe.

A few days after this decisive battle, another invading Lamanite army was reported. This one advanced along the east bank of the Sidon. It appears to have been the plan of their military commanders to invade the Nephite territory with two separate armies, both traveling northward toward the city of Zarahemla, but on opposite sides of the Sidon. That advancing on the west side moved the most rapidly, and was met, conquered and dispersed by Alma, while the other afterwards met the same fate at the hands of one of his lieutenants, Alma himself having been too seriously wounded in one of the preceding battles to permit him to lead his troops in person.

The great losses sustained by the Nephites in war, not of warriors alone, but of women and children, together with the vast amount of their property destroyed, had the effect of humbling them and softening their wayward hearts, so that many thousands, during the next few years, were added to the church by baptism. But the recollection of their former disasters was gradually worn away by time and prosperity. Three years later we find great inequality in the Church—some poor and some rich, the more powerful abusing and oppressing their weaker brethren. This course proved a great stumbling-block to those who were not numbered with the Church, as well as being the cause of much sorrow and ill-feeling among its members. Finding that no man could properly attend to the duties of his many offices, Alma determined to resign the chief judgeship, and devote his entire time to his duties as the earthly head of the Church. Preparatory to his resignation, he selected one of the leading elders, named Nephihah, to be his successor as chief judge. This choice was confirmed by the people. (B. C. 83.)

under the generous hospitality which his home afforded. But his rest was not to be a lengthened one; the people waxed stronger in sin; the cup of their iniquity was nearly full. "Go," came the word of the Lord, "Go forth, and take with thee my servant Amulek, and prophesy unto this people, saying, Repent ye, for thus saith the Lord, except ye repent, I will visit this people in mine anger; yea, I will not turn my fierce anger away" Filled with the Holy Ghost, these servants of Israel's God went forth and valiantly delivered their terrible message. From place to place they went, raising their Jonah-like cry. The heathen Ninevites hearkened and repented; the sin-stained Israelites of Ammonihah laughed, scorned, mocked and turned contemptuously away. A few indeed received the word, but that only increased the anger of the majority, who, led and egged on by their still more depraved rulers and teachers, persecuted the prophets and martyred the believers.

The account given of the teachings of Alma and Amulek, their disputations with Zeezrom and other lawyers and rulers in Ammonihah, is given at length in the Book of Mormon, and, in consequence thereof, we have handed down to us some of the plainest, yet profoundest teachings on the atonement, the resurrection, the powers of the priesthood, etc., that are to be had among mankind. We cannot follow them here through all the varied incidents that led to the final catastrophe. Faithfully the prophets warned Ammonihah of its approaching desolation; scornfully and incredulously the hardened people hurled back their words of warning with distance. The few that believed, of which the crafty, hair-splitting Zeezrom was the most notable example, were cast out of the city, while Alma and Amulek were bound with strong cords, and, under false accusations of having reviled the laws, they were cast into prison. Alma consigned Alma and his companion to a prison

The cares of the state having thus been removed from his shoulders, Alma commenced his ministerial labors at Zarahemla, the chief city of the nation, and thence proceeded throughout the land. As often happens in other nations, the capital was the centre of pride, vanity, envy, hypocrisy and class distinctions. These evils Alma severely rebuked, at the same time he guided the minds of the people to the contemplation and understanding of the beauties and saving powers of redemption's wondrous plan, whilst he exhorted all to become members of Christ's holy Church. His call was heeded by many; the Church was set in order; the unworthy were disfellowshiped; elders, priests and other officers were ordained to preside and watch over the Saints. This being accomplished, Alma took his journey eastward, across the river Sidon, to the city of Gideon, where he happily found the Church in a prosperous condition. Alma's teachings to this people were full of prophecies concerning the coming of the Messiah, which show how clearly he read his faithful fellow servants understood the details of the advent and life of the promised Redeemer. Having established the Church in Gideon, Alma returned to Zarahemla to rest and recruit for a short time before visiting other portions of the land.

At the commencement of the next year (B. C. 82), Alma turned his face westward, He first visited the land of Melek, where his labors were crowned with abundant blessings. Having satisfied himself with the good that he had accomplished, he traveled three days' journey on the north of the land of Melek." to a great and corrupt city called Ammonihah. Here he found a godless people, filled with the falsehoods of Nehor, and living in the committal of all manner of abominations without repentance, because they cherished the flattering lie as the foundation of their creed, that all men would be saved. The city

cell, the infuriated people hunted up the wives and the little ones of the believers whom they had cast out, with such as had accepted the truth who still remained in the city, and, gathering them in a body, they burned them in one great martyr's fire. Into the flames they also cast the records that contained the holy Scriptures, as though they imagined in their blind fury that they could thereby destroy the truths that were so odious to them. In the refinement of their devilish cruelty they brought Alma and Amulek to the place of martyrdom, that they might be witnesses of the agonies of the suffering innocents, and listen to the crackling and the roaring of the flames. With jeers, with mouthings and derisive gestures, they called upon the prophets to rescue their dying converts. Amulek's noble heart was pained beyond endurance; he besought Alma to exercise the power of God that was in them, and to save the victims from the consuming flames. But Alma replied, "The Spirit constraineth me that I must not stretch forth mine hand, for behold the Lord receiveth them up unto Himself in glory; and he doth suffer that the people may do this thing, according to the hardness of their hearts, that the judgments which he shall exercise upon them in his wrath may be just; and the blood of the innocent shall stand as a witness against them at the last day." Then Amulek said, "Perhaps they will burn us also." To which Alma responded, "Be it according to the will of the Lord. But, behold, we are not finished; therefore they burn us not."

When the fire had burned low, and the precious fuel of human bodies and sacred records was consumed, the chief judge of the city came to the two prophets as they stood bound, and mocked and jeered. He smote them on the cheeks, and sneeringly asked them if they would preach again that his people should be cast into a lake of fire and brimstone, seeing that they had no power to save those who had been burned, neither had God exercised His power in their behalf. But neither answered him a word. Then he smote them again and remanded them to prison.

After they had been confined three days, they were visited by many judges and lawyers, priests and teachers, after the order of Nehor, who came to exult in the misery of their prisoners. They cross-questioned and badgered them, but neither would reply. They came again the next day, and went through the same performance. They mocked at, they smote, they spat upon the two disciples. They tantalized them with outrageous and blasphemous questions, such as the nature of their peculiar faith inspired. Patiently and silently all this was borne; day after day was it repeated; harder and harder grew the hearts of the Ammonihahites towards their prisoners; fiercer and stronger grew their hatred. They stripped Alma and Amulek of their clothes, and, when naked, bound them with strong ropes. They withheld food and drink from them, and in various ways they tortured their bodies, and sought to aggravate, tantalize and harrow up their minds. On the 12th day of the tenth month of the tenth year of the Judges (B. C 82), the chief judge and his followers again went to the prison. According to his usual custom he smote the brethren, saying as he did so, "If ye have the power of God, deliver yourselves from these bonds, and then we will believe that the Lord will destroy this people according to your words." This impious challenge the crowd one by one repeated as they passed by the prophets, and smote them in imitation of their leader. Thus each individual assumed the responsibility of the defiance cast at the Almighty, and virtually said, "Our blood be upon our own heads." The hour of God's power had now come—the challenge had been accepted.

routed, retreated to their own lands, and there was continued peace throughout the continent for three years.

During this period of peace, Alma and his fellow priesthood preached God's holy word in the power and demonstration of the Spirit, and with much success. Great prosperity came to the Church throughout all the lands of the Nephites. At this happy time "there was no inequality among them, the Lord did pour out His Spirit on all the face of the land," as Alma supposed, to prepare the hearts of His people for the coming of Christ. With this object full in view, he labored and rejoiced, preached, blessed and prophesied, never tiring in his energies, and feeling sorrowful only because of the hard-heartedness and spiritual blindness of some of the people. In one most glorious event he had unspeakable joy: The companions of his youth, the sons of king Mosiah, returned from a fourteen years' mission among the Lamanites, during which time, after many sore trials and great tribulation, they, by the grace of the Father, had brought many thousands of that benighted race to a knowledge of the principles of the everlasting Gospel.

Alma was traveling south on one of his missionary journeys from the land of Zarahemla to the land of Manti, when he met Ammon and his brethren coming from the land of Nephi. On hearing the story of their mission, he at once returned home with them to Zarahemla. Here the condition of affairs among the Lamanites was rehearsed to the chief judge, who laid the whole subject before the Christian Lamanites, might be done by common consent. The Nephites decided to give the land of Jershon (which lay south of the land Bountiful) to these people for an inheritance. With this cheering news Ammon, accompanied by Alma, returned into the southern wilder-

The prophets in the majesty of their calling, rose to their feet; they were endowed with the strength of Jehovah; like burned thread the cords that bound them were snapped asunder, and they stood free and unshackled before the error-stricken mob. To rush from the prison was the first impulse of the God-defying followers of Nehor; in their fear all else was forgotten. Some fell to the earth, others, impelled by the mob behind, stumbled and fell over their prostrate bodies, until they became one confused, inextricable mass, blocking each other's way, struggling, yelling, cursing, pleading, fighting; frantically, but vainly, endeavoring to reach the outer gate. At this moment of supreme horror an earthquake rent the prison walls; they trembled, then tottered, then fell on the struggling mass of humanity below, burying in one vast, unconsecrated grave, rulers and judges, lawyers and officers, priests and teachers. Not one was left of all the impious mob, who a few moments before defied Heaven and challenged Jehovah's might. Alma and Amulek stood in the midst of the ruins unhurt. Straightway they left the scene of desolation and went into the city. Here the horrified people fled from them as a herd of goats flee from before two young lions.

Alma and Amulek, being so commanded, left the doomed city and passed over to the land of Sidom. Here they found the Saints who had been cast out of Ammonihah. To them they told the sad, though glorious story of their martyred kin, and with many words of wisdom and consolation they encouraged them to lives of devotion to Christ. Here also they found Zeezrom, the lawyer, racked in spirit with the recollection of his former infamies, and tortured in body by the heats of a burning fever. At his request the two servants of the Most High visited him. They found he had repented in much tribulation for the past,

ness, to the place where his people were awaiting the decision of the Nephites. Here they were ministered to and comforted by Alma and others, after which they resumed their march to the land designated for their future abode.

We pass over the next few years of Alma's life, during which period he was laboring with his usual zeal and devotion, to the latter portion of the seventeenth year of the judges (B. C. 75). It was then that Korihor, the anti-Christ, appeared. His pernicious doctrines savor much of certain classes of modern religious delusion, but his main arguments were directed against the advent and atonement of the Redeemer. From land to land he journeyed among the Nephites, spreading his false theories and notions. But as he claimed that as he taught so he believed, the law could not touch him, for it was strictly forbidden in the Nephite constitution that any one should be punished on account of his belief; freedom of conscience was guaranteed to all. At last, not knowing what to do with him, as he was fomenting dissension and endangering the peace of the community, the local officers sent him to Alma and the chief judge, for them to decide in the matter. When brought before these officers he continued, with great swelling words of blasphemy, to ridicule the holy principles of the Gospel, and to revile the servants of God, falsely accusing them, among other things, of glutting themselves out of the labors of the people. In Alma's answer to this charge we have a pleasing insight into his private life. He said: "Thou knowest that we do not glut ourselves upon the labors of this people, for behold, I have labored, even from the commencement of the reign of the judges until now, with mine own hands for my support, notwithstanding my many travels around about the land to declare the word of God unto my people; and notwithstanding the many labors I have performed in the

and that faith had developed in his heart. Alma then exercised the power of his calling. Appealing to Heaven, he cried "O Lord, our God, have mercy on this man, and heal him according to his faith, which is in Christ." Zeezrom thereupon leaped upon his feet; his fever had left; he was made whole by the grace of God, whilst the people wondered and were astonished at this manifestation of God's goodness. Zeezrom was then baptized by Alma, and became a zealous, faithful advocate of divine law.

The more complete organization of the Church in Sidom was the next work accomplished by Alma, which, having been satisfactorily attended to, and the proper officers of the priesthood having been ordained and appointed, Alma, accompanied by his faithful friend Amulek, returned to his home in Zarahemla.

Next year Ammonihah was destroyed. Less than four months had elapsed since the two inspired followers of the Lamb left it to its fate, when the Lamanites fell upon it like a whirlwind in its suddenness, and as an avalanche in its utter desolation. For one day the fierce flames consumed the walls and towers of Ammonihah. The great city was no more; the word of the Lord had been fully accomplished; not one of its children remained. A desolation and a desert remained, where dogs, vultures and wild beasts struggled for the carcasses of the slain. Having resigned the office of chief judge, Alma no longer led the armies of Nephi. A righteous man named Zoram was their commander. Without delay he gathered his forces, and prepared to meet the invading Lamanites. Knowing that Alma was the mouthpiece of God, he and his two sons went to the high priest, and inquired how the campaign should be conducted. That word was given, its instructions were carried out, victory perched upon the Nephite banners, and the Lamanites, utterly

Church, I have not so much as received even one senine for my labor; neither has any of my brethren, save it were in the judgment seat, and then we have received only according to law for our time."

Korihor continued to withstand the prophet, until, in compliance with his impious importunities, a sign was given him—a most unwelcome and unexpected sign to him—he was struck dumb by the power of God. He was cast out from the face of society, a wanderer and a vagabond, begging from door to door for bread to sustain life. While thus dragging out a miserable existence, he was run over and trodden to death in a city of the Zoramites.

The Zoramites were a dangerous body of dissenters, who also taught that which was not of Christ. They deluded themselves with the idea that they were the peculiar objects of Heaven's favor, born to be saved, predestined to eternal glory, while the rest of the world were the rejected; the fore-ordained damned. This consoling creed, to the corrupt and crime-stained, was rapidly growing and gaining influence at the time of Korihor's death, and became the next object of Alma's ever-watchful care. Accompanied by Amulek, Zeezrom, three of the sons of king Mosiah, and two of his own sons, he went over to the regions inhabited by these apostates. This mission was one of the most important of his life, and, like that to Ammonihah, was but partially successful. As soon as Alma discovered the gross iniquity of this people, and the peculiarities of their forms of worship, he held a council meeting with his fellow-missionaries, and, having prayed fervently to the Lord, "that he clasped his hands upon them, they were filled with the Holy Ghost. And after that, they did separate themselves one from another; taking no thought for themselves what they should eat, or what they should drink, or what they should put on." And in all these things the Lord provided for them. The missionaries labored dilligently; they visited the people in their homes; they preached in their synagogues; they proclaimed the truth in their streets; but the flattering errors of their false faith had so thoroughly taken possession of them that they rejected the truth, and persecuted and even attempted to slay some of Alma's companions. However, this rejection was not universal; a number of the poorer and more humble Zoramites accepted the Divine message, in consequence of which they were shortly after driven from their homes and out of their country by their more numerous, more influential, and also more corrupt fellow-citizens.

When Alma and his associates had done all the good that seemed to them practicable, they retired to the land of Jershon, where the Ammonites dwelt; thither the believing Zoramites followed when they were expatriated by their fellow-countrymen. In Jershon they were kindly received by its inhabitants and welcomed as brethren. Here Alma again administered to them. Having done this, he and most of his co-laborers returned to Zarahemla.

Alma was now growing old. Notwithstanding his unceasing efforts and fervent prayers, the Nephites were again backsliding into iniquity. To every Nephite city, and to every Nephite land he went or sent, to revive the Gospel fires in the souls of the inhabitants. But many became offended because of the strictness of the Gospel's laws, which forbade not only sin itself, but the very appearance of sin. As this feeling grew, Alma's heart became exceedingly sorrowful and he mourned the depravity of his people. Like many of the ancient patriarchs, when they felt that their mortal career was drawing to a close, he

called his sons to him, and gave them his last charge and blessing; speaking to each as the spirit of instruction and prophecy inspired. To Helaman his eldest, he transferred the custody of the sacred plates, with many words of warning and caution regarding them. With hearts strengthened and renewed by the inspiration of his fervent admonitions, his sons went forth among the people; nor could Alma himself rest while there was a soul to save or a wrong to make right. He also went forth once again, in the spirit of his holy calling, and raised his voice in advocacy of the principles of the everlasting gospel.

Another bloody war now commenced, one that before its close drew out the whole strength of both Nephite and Lamanite. The youthful, but brilliant and God-fearing Moroni, took charge of the armies of Nephi. He, not willing to trust to his own powers, sent to Alma for the Divine word to direct his movements. As was his wont, the high priest was favored with the revelation of heaven's will, which being conveyed to Moroni, was in faith implicitly followed. We need not enter into the details of the terrible battle that ensued: victory crowned the inspired general's efforts, and with the account of this battle the record of Alma closes.

It was in the nineteenth year of the Judges (B. C. 73), that Alma took his beloved son, Helaman, and after having discovered, through divers questions, the strength and integrity of his faith, he prophesied to him of many important events which should transpire in the distant future, especially with regard to the destruction of the Nephites. This prophecy he commanded him to record on the plates, but not to reveal to any one. Alma then blessed Helaman, also his other sons; indeed he blessed all who should stand firm in the truth of Christ from that time forth. Shortly after this he departed out of the land of Zara-

hemla, as if to go to the land of Melek, and was never heard of more. Of his death and burial no men were witnesses. Then the saying went abroad throughout the Church that the Lord had taken him, as He heretofore had taken Moses. This event occurred exactly one hundred years from the time of the elder Alma's birth.

ALMA, VALLEY OF. A valley one day's travel north of the City of Helam on the road to Zarahemla. When the people of Alma escaped from the Lamanites in the land of Helam they pitched their tents in this valley and gave unto it this name, because Alma (the elder) was their leader. Here they all—men, women and children—poured out their thanks to God for their deliverance. But they were not permitted to tarry in this valley. The Lord commanded Alma to hasten and depart, for their Lamanite oppressors were pursuing them, but that He would here stop them. After twelve days' journey from this place Alma and his people reached the land of Zarahemla.

AMALEKI. The son of Abinadom and a descendant of Jacob, the son of Lehi. He was one of the custodians of the sacred records of the Nephites, and was born in the days of the first Mosiah, but whether in the land of Nephi or of Zarahemla does not appear. If in Nephi then he transported the plates from that land to Zarahemla in the great migration of the Nephites under Mosiah, and it is quite likely that he did so, for it is he that gives the account of this vast movement. Having no children, at his death he transferred the holy things of which he had charge to king Benjamin. He lived about B. C. 200.

AMALEKI. A descendant of Zarahemla, and one of the brothers of Ammon, the leader of the company of sixteen picked men who, by king Mosiah's permission. visited the land of Lehi-Nephi (B. C. 122) to discover what had become of the

---

company of Nephite colonists who had returned there, under the leadership of Zeniff, during the reign of the first Mosiah, as near as can be told some 75 or 80 years previously. Amaleki, with two other brothers of Ammon (Helem and Hem), was chosen by Ammon, when they approached the city of Lehi-Nephi, to go with him in advance of the rest of the company and find out how matters stood in that region. They were captured by the guards of King Limhi and cast into prison, but were liberated two days afterwards when it was found that they were Nephites.

AMALEKITES. A sect of Nephite apostates whose origin is not given. Many of them were after the order of Nehor. Very early in the days of the republic they had affiliated with the Lamanites and with them built a large city, not far from the waters of Mormon, which they called Jerusalem. They were exceedingly crafty and hard-hearted, and in all the ministrations of the sons of Mosiah among them only one was converted. They led in the massacres of the Christian Lamanites or people of Anti-Nephi-Lehi; and in later years the Lamanite generals were in the habit of placing them in high command in their armies, because of their greater force of character, their intense hatred to their former brethren, and their more wicked and murderous disposition. In the sacred record they are generally associated with the Zoramites and Amulonites.

AMALEKIAH. A Nephite traitor and apostate in the days of the Republic, and afterwards king of the Lamanites. He was descended from Zoram, the servant of Laban.

We judge from the conspicuous military ability shown by Amalekiah that his early training was that of a soldier, as no one would be more likely to be chosen by the disaffected monarchists as their leader than a brilliant and ambitious officer in the national army. It appears that in

the 19th year of the judges (B. C. 73), one of those frequently occurring outbreaks in favor of a change in the form of the Nephite government took place. The hallowed glories of Mosiah's reign were still bright in the hearts of many, while others, by ambition led, intrigued for the restoration of the kingly power, that they might find place and profit at the court. The plan for a revolution was laid, the king—men gathered in armed array and Amalekiah was chosen as their general; but they were disappointed, the masses did not join their standard in the expected numbers. On the other hand, Moroni, the Nephite commander, gathered so great a force for the defence of the commonwealth, that retreat was considered the better part of wisdom; but his followers being out-generaled by Moroni, Amalekiah fled to the court of the king of the Lamanites.

The king received him with much honor. It is altogether probable that the monarch also was of an apostate Nephite family. Seven or eight years previously the Christian Lamanites with the king at their head had been ruthlessly driven from their homes by their unbelieving fellow countrymen, led by members of the various Nephite apostate orders who had taken up their residence amongst the Lamanites. A leader of one of these sects would naturally work his way to the front when the rightful king and his family sought refuge in the land of Zarahemla. What makes this idea more probable is that Amalekiah afterwards married the widowed queen, a thing he was much more likely to do if she were a fair Nephite than a dark-skinned daughter of Laman. On the first favorable opportunity Amalekiah commenced to rekindle the fires of hatred in the bosoms of the Lamanites toward his former friends. At first he was not successful; the recollection of their recent defeats was too fresh in the memory of the multitude. The king issued a war proclamation,

but it was disregarded. Much as his subjects feared the imperial power, they dreaded a renewal of war more. Many gathered to resist the royal mandate. The king, unused to such objections, raised an army to quell the advocates of peace, and placed it under the command of the ambitious Amalickiah.

The peace-men had chosen an officer named Lehonti for their king and leader, and he had assembled his followers at a mountain called Antipas. Thither Amalickiah marched, but with no intention of provoking a conflict; he was working for the good feelings of the entire Lamanite people. On his arrival he entered into a secret correspondence with Lehonti, in which he agreed to surrender his forces on condition that he should be appointed second in command of the united armies. The plan succeeded. Amalickiah surrendered to Lehonti and assumed the second position. Lehonti now lived in the way of his ambition; it was but a little thing to remove him; he died by slow poison administered by Amalickiah's direction.

Amalickiah now assumed supreme command, and at the head of his forces marched towards the Lamanite capital. The king, supposing that the approaching hosts had been raised to carry the war into Zarahemla, came out of the royal city to greet and congratulate him. As the monarch drew near he was treacherously slain by some of the creatures of the subtle general, who at the same time raised the hue and cry that the king's own servants were the authors of the vile deed. Amalickiah assumed all the airs of grief, affliction and righteous indignation that he thought would best suit his purpose. He next made apparently desperate, but purposely ineffectual, efforts to capture those who were charged with the crime, and so adroitly did he carry out his schemes, that before long he gained the operations of the queen, whom he married, and was recognized by the Lamanites as their king. Amalickiah now cherished the stupendous design of subjugating the Nephites and ruling supply and alone from ocean to ocean. To accomplish this iniquitous purpose, he dispatched emissaries in all directions, whose mission was to stir up the angry passions of the populace against the Nephites. When this base object was sufficiently accomplished, and the deluded people had become clamorous for war, he raised an immense army, armed and equipped with an excellence never before known among the Lamanites. This force he placed under the command of Zoramite officers, and ordered its advance into the western possessions of the Nephites, Ammonihah and Noah.

This war was a disastrous one to the Lamanites. It failed in all its objects, and cost them many lives. Great was the anger of Amalickiah at this miscarriage of his schemes; he cursed God and swore he would yet drink the blood of Moroni. But it was not until B. C. 57, that he was able to carry out his ambitious projects. He then commenced an invasion of the country of the Nephites with an army which, for equipment and discipline, had never been equaled in the annals of the Lamanites. While other officers commanded in the west and south he personally led the troops intended for the subjugation of the Nephite Atlantic provinces. In this invasion he was eminently successful; for he had chosen a time for his operations when the Nephite commonwealth was rent by internal dissensions, another uprising having taken place in favor of a monarchy. One after another Amalickiah's forces captured the Nephite cities of Moroni, Nephihah, Lehi, Gid. Morianton, Omner, Mulek, and others along the coast, until toward the close of the year he reached the borders of the land Bountiful, driving the forces of the republic before him. At this

ended in Com obtaining power over the remainder of the kingdom.

AMINADAB. A Nephite who, in early life, belonged to the Church of God. From it he turned away, went over to the Lamanites and took up his residence in the city of Lehi-Nephi, where he dwelt B. C. 30.

When the two prophets, Nephi and Lehi, the sons of Helaman, came into the land of Nephi and were there cast into prison, God made use of Aminadab as an instrument in explaining the meaning of the glorious manifestations of His power that then took place. We may therefore infer that Aminadab was not radically a bad man. Whether he was in the prison as an officer, a prisoner, or a stranger led thither by curiosity or by sympathy for the two Nephites, is not explained, but we find him there when the earth shook, when the voice of God was heard from heaven, and the other wonderful and awful manifestations of His presence occurred. Aminadab was apparently the first who was permitted to notice that the faces of the prophets shone with the glory of God, and that they were conversing with angelic beings. To this he drew the attention of the multitude, and when they inquired what these things meant he laid hold of some intelligence sufficient to explain the situation to them, and to instruct them in what they should do to escape the terrible cloud of darkness that overspread them. Further, he instructed them in the principles of faith in the coming Redeemer and of repentance for past misdeeds. It is not unreasonable to suppose that Aminadab was among those who went forth from the prison bearing joyous testimony to what they had seen and heard, through which testimony thousands were brought to a knowledge of, and obedience to the Gospel, and that Aminadab himself again yielded obedience to its laws and remained faithful thereto to the end.

point he was met by Teancum and a corps of veterans renowned for their courage, skill and discipline. The Lamanite leader endeavored to force his way to the isthmus, with the intention of occupying the northern continent. In this he was foiled, for the trained valor of Teancum's warriors was too much for that of Amalickiah's half-savage hordes. All day the fight lasted, and at night the worn-out soldiers of the two armies camped close together, the Lamanites on the sea-beach, and the Nephites on the borders of the land Bountiful.

It was the last night of the old year, according to Nephite reckoning. The great heat and the terrible efforts of the day had overcome both officers and men. The murmur of the Atlantic's waves sounded a soft lullaby in the ears of Amalickiah and his hosts, who, for the first time during the campaign, had suffered a check in their triumphal march. Even Amalickiah slept; but not so with Teancum; he determined by one desperate stroke to put an end to the war; or, if not that, at least to slay the cause of it. Taking one servant with him, he secretly stole out of his own camp into that of the enemy. A deathlike silence reigned in both. Cautiously and unobserved he searched out the royal tent. There lay the foe, there lay his guards, all overcome with resistless fatigue. To draw his javelin, thrust it into the king's heart and then flee, was but the work of a moment, and so adroitly did he fulfil his purpose that Amalickiah died without a struggle or a cry, and it was not until the morning that his guards discovered that the hosts of Laman were without a head. His warriors then hastily retreated to the fortified city of Mulek.

Amalickiah was succeeded on the Lamanitish throne by his brother Ammoron, who continued the war with unrelenting vindictiveness.

AMALICKIAHITES. The followers of

AMINADI. A Nephite, one of the progenitors of the prophet Amulek. We have no record of the time that he lived, but it must have been in the land of Nephi before the Nephites migrated to Zarahemla, as he was at least four generations separated from Amulek. All that is known of him is that he interpreted certain writings written by the finger of God, on the wall of the temple, from which we may conclude that he was a righteous man, probably one holding the holy priesthood.

AMLICI. The first Nephite, in the days of the Judges, who sought to overturn the republic and establish a monarchy, (B. C. 88) Amlici's ambition was to be king of the Nephites, but the people having rejected his pretensions by their votes, his followers consecrated him king. He then raised an army to sustain his claims. A battle was fought near the hill Amnihu on the east of the river Sidon, between his forces and those of the Nephites, commanded by Alma, the younger. The battle was a hotly contested one, in which twelve thousand, five hundred and thirty-two Amlicites and six thousand, five hundred and sixty-two Nephites were slain. The next day the defeated Amlicites joined a body of invading Lamanites in the land Minon, where they unitedly ravaged the country. Alma's troops and the invaders and met them at one of the crossings of the river Sidon. Another desperate battle ensued, during which Alma met Amlici in single combat and slew him. Amlici's followers were defeated and most of them fled to a portion of the northwest wilderness, known as Hermounts, were many died and were devoured by wild beasts. Amlici is represented as being a very cunning and worldly-wise man, and as belonging to the order of Nehor.

AMLICITES. The followers of Amlici. After their dispersion, and their flight to Hermounts,

Amalickiah in his efforts to destroy the Church, to uproot the Nephite commonwealth and establish a monarchy in its stead. Their leader, finding that they were not as numerous as those who wished to maintain the republic, and that many of them doubted the justness of their cause, led those who would follow him towards the land of Nephi, with the intention of joining the Lamanites. Moron, the general of the Nephites, by rapid marches, reached the wilderness, where he intercepted them in their flight, when Amalickiah and a few others escaped to the Lamanites, while the great majority were taken prisoners and carried back to Zarahemla. The Amalickiahites were then given the opportunity to make covenant to sustain the cause of liberty or be put to death. There were but very few who denied the covenant of freedom. (B. C. 73.)

AMARON. A Nephite prophet, son of Omni, and a descendant of Jacob, the younger brother of Nephi. He resided in the land of Nephi, in the third and fourth centuries before Christ. Amaron received the plates of Nephi from his father, and held them from the two hundred and eighty-third to the three hundred and twenty-first year of the Nephite annals, when he transferred them to his brother Chemish. Owing to the increasing wickedness of the Nephite people, the Lord, during Amaron's days, visited them in great judgment, so that the more wicked part were destroyed, but he spared the righteous and delivered them out of the hands of their enemies. Of Amaron's private character the sacred record is silent.

AMGID. A king of the Jaredites, of the dynasty that overthrew the reigning monarch in the days of Hearthom. In Amgid's days a descendant of Hearthom, named Com, having first drawn away half the kingdom, after a lapse of forty-two years went to war with Amgid for the other half. The war lasted many years and

they are no more referred to by the Nephite historians. In fulfillment of the word of the Lord to Nephi, that those who fought against him and his seed should have a mark put upon them, they marked themselves with red on their foreheads as did the Lamanites, but they did not shave their heads as did that race. Of course they did not realize they were fulfilling prophecy when they thus acted or they would not have done so, as it was not their intention to fulfil the words of those from whom they had seceded.

AMMAH. A Christian Nephite elder who accompanied the four sons of Mosiah (B. C. 91) in their mission to the Lamanites. We first read of him preaching to the inhabitants of the village of Ani-Anti, and when rejected by them he, with Aaron and others, went over to the land of Middoni, where he was cast into prison, and with his fellow-laborers suffered all the indignities and hardships there inflicted upon those devoted servants of God. After many days' imprisonment they were delivered through the instrumentality of Ammon and king Lamoni. When the various missionaries recommenced their labors, the regions in which certain ones labored are stated, but no further mention is made of Ammah or his ministrations; yet there is no doubt but that he continued his faithful labors unto the end of this lengthy and most important mission.

AMMARON, was the son of Amos the elder, a descendant of Alma and Nephi. He received the sacred records from his brother Amos, the younger (A. C. 306). Owing to the increasing depravity and vileness of the Nephite people, he was constrained by the Holy Ghost to hide up all the sacred things which had been handed down from generation to generation (A. C. 321). The place in which he hid them is said to have been in the land Antum, in a hill "which shall be called Shim." After he had hidden them up, he informed Mormon, then a child ten years old, of what he had done, and placed the buried treasures in his charge. He instructed Mormon to go when he was about twenty-four years old, to the hill where they were hidden, and take the plates of Nephi and record thereon what he had observed "concerning the people." The remainder of the records, etc., he was to leave where they were. After this we have no information of Ammaron's life. He must have been a very old man, as his father Amos died 126 years before the time that he buried the sacred engravings.

AMMON. A descendant of Zarahemla, (either his son or grandson,) who led a party of sixteen picked men from Zarahemla to Lehi-Nephi in the reign of Mosiah II, in the endeavor to discover what had become of the people of Zeniff. They were unacquainted with the road and wandered for forty days in the wilderness before they reached their destination. Ammon then chose three companions, Amaleki, Helem and Ilem, to go forward and reconnoiter. They were discovered by king Limhi and his guards when near the city and cast into prison, being mistaken for the apostate priests of king Noah. After two days they were again brought before the king, when mutual explanations ensued and Ammon to his joy found that he had reached those for whom he was in search. But Limhi's people were in great distress, and in bondage to the Lamanites. The next day Limhi assembled his people at the temple, that they might all hear of the prosperity of their brethren in Zarahemla, at the recital of which they greatly rejoiced. Limhi and his people also wished to make covenant with God by baptism, but there was no one among them authorized to administer this ordinance, and Ammon would not, considering himself an unworthy servant. Their next study was to escape from their Lamanitish taskmasters, which they shortly afterwards effected with the aid of Ammon and Gideon; Ammon and

his brethren guiding them through the wilderness to the land of Zarahemla (B. C. 112).

AMMON. The most conspicuous of the sons of king Mosiah II, and the ruling spirit in the great mission undertaken by them to convert the Lamanites.

Ammon was born in the land of Zarahemla, probably about 120 B. C. Like his brothers, he was, in early life, headstrong and disobedient, and a persecutor of the Saints. He was brought to an understanding of his perilous position by the intervention of an angel of the Lord, who appeared to a company of young men who were going about molesting the members of the Church of Christ, among whom were Alma, the younger, and Mosiah's four sons. This heavenly manifestation had the effect of entirely changing the course of life of these young men. From this time they bent all the energies of their youth, and the experience of their riper years, to the reparation of the wrongs that they had done, and to the spread of the principles of the Gospel. First, they ministered among the Nephites in the land of Zarahemla, and then determined on the more hazardous task of carrying those same truths to the benighted Lamanites in the land of Nephi. At first there was much opposition to this venture, but Mosiah, their father, having received by revelation assurances of Divine protection, the young men started on their perilous journey (B. C. 91) into the southern wilderness.

They carried with them their bows and arrows and other weapons, not to wage war, but to kill game for their food in the wilderness. Their journey was a tedious one; they lost their way and almost lost heart, and indeed were on the point of returning when they received Divine assurance of their ultimate success. Nerved by this assurance, and with much fasting and prayer, they continued their wanderings, and before long

reached the borders of the Lamanites. Commending themselves to God they there separated, each one trusting to the Lord to guide him to the place where he could best accomplish the purposes of Heaven.

Ammon entered the Lamanite territory at a land called Ishmael. Here Lamoni was the chief ruler, under his father, who was king of all the Lamanites. Ammon was no sooner discovered than he was taken, bound with cords and conducted into the presence of Lamoni. It was the custom of the Lamanites to so use every Nephite they captured, and it rested with the whim of the king whether the captive be slain, imprisoned or sent out of the country. The king's will and pleasure appears to have been the only law in such matters.

Through God's grace, Ammon found favor in the eyes of Lamoni, and, learning that it was his desire to reside among the Lamanites, the king offered him one of his daughters to wife. Ammon courteously declined this intended honor, and begged to be accepted as one of the king's servants, which arrangement pleased Lamoni, and Ammon was placed in that part of the royal household that had charge of the monarch's flocks and herds. Lamoni was rich in livestock, probably the result of the taxation of the people, but even the king's property was not secure from theft. Marauding bands would watch for his numerous cattle as they approached their watering places. Then with yell and prolonged shout they would stampede the herds and drive away all they could, beyond the reach of the king's servants. These would gather up what few animals, if any, they found, and return to the king in the full expectancy of being made to pay for the loss by the forfeit of their lives. They were seldom disappointed, for Lamoni or some of his predecessors had established a uniform unique criminal code with

---

regard to stealing the royal cattle. They had adopted the idea that it was easier and cheaper to make the herdsmen responsible for the losses and punish them therefor, than to hunt out and capture the thieves. It had at least one virtue, it prevented collusion between the robbers and the servants; but it produced much dissatisfaction among Lamoni's subjects.

On the third day of Ammon's service, one of these raids was made on the king's cattle as they were being taken to the waters of Sebus, the common watering place. The cattle fled in all directions, and the dispirited servants, with the fear of death before their eyes, sat down and wept instead of attempting to stay them. Ammon perceived that this was his opportunity. He first reasoned with the servants, then encouraged them, and having sufficiently aroused their feelings, he led them in the attempt to head off the flying herds. With much exertion they succeeded. The cattle were all gathered, but the robbers still waited at the watering place to renew the attack when they drew near enough. Ammon perceiving this, placed the servants at various points on the outside of the flocks and he himself went forward to contend with the robbers. Though they were many, he knew he was more powerful than them all, for God was with him. The idea of one man withstanding so many was supremely ridiculous to the robbers. But as one after another fell before his unerring aim, they were astonished, and dreaded him as something more than human. Enraged at the loss of six of their number, they rushed upon him in a body, determined to crush him with their clubs. Ammon, undaunted, drew his sword and awaited the onslaught. Their leader fell dead at his feet, and as one after another raised their clubs, Ammon struck off their arms until none dared to approach him, but instead retreated in dismay.

Ammon. 59 60 **Ammon.** 61 **Ammon.**

It was a strange procession that returned to the palace. The fears of the herdsmen had been turned to joy, and they marched in triumph into the presence of the king, with the arms of the robbers as testimonials of the truth of the story of Ammon's prowess. Doubtless they did not diminish the telling points in the narrative; the numbers of the band, the courage and strength of the Nephite, were each dilated upon with the vividness of superstitious imagination. When the king had heard their marvelous story his heart was troubled, and he came to the conclusion that Ammon must be the Great Spirit, of whose existence he had an undefined idea. He trembled at the thought that perhaps this Spirit had come to punish him because of the number of his servants whom he had slain for permitting his cattle to be stolen.

Notwithstanding his misgivings, Lamoni desired to see Ammon, who, acting as though nothing particular had happened, was preparing the king's horses and chariots, as the servants had been directed. When he entered the royal presence, the king was too much filled with emotion to speak. More than once Ammon called the king's attention to the fact that he stood before him, as he had been requested, and wished to know what were his commands. But he elicited no response. At last, perceiving the monarch's thoughts, he began to question Lamoni regarding sacred things, and afterwards to expound to him the principles of life and salvation. Lamoni listened and believed. He was conscience-stricken, and with all the strength of his new-born faith, he humbly begged that the Lord would show that same mercy to him and to his people that he had shown to the Nephites. Overcome with the intensity of his feelings he sank to the earth as in a trance. In this state he was carried to his wife, who, with her attendants, anxiously watched over him for two days

and two nights, awaiting his return to consciousness. There was great diversity of opinion among his retainers as to what troubled the king. Some said the power of the Great Spirit was upon him, others that an evil power possessed him, yet others asserted that he was dead, and with remarkable acuteness of smell affirmed, He stinketh. At the end of this time they had resolved to lay him away in the sepulchre, when the queen sent for Ammon and pleaded with him in her husband's behalf. Ammon gave her the joyful assurance: He is not dead, but sleepeth in God, and to-morrow he shall rise again. Then he asked, Believest thou this? She answered, I have no witness, save the word and the word of our servants; nevertheless I believe it shall be according as thou hast said. Then Ammon blessed her, and told her that there had not been such great faithamong all the people of the Nephites.

So the queen lovingly continued her watch by the bedside of her husband until the appointed hour. Lamoni then arose, as Ammon had foretold. His soul was filled with heavenly joy. His first words were of praise to God, his next were blessings on his faithful wife, whose faith he felt or knew. He testified to the coming of the Redeemer, of whose greatness, glory, power and mercy he had learned while in the spirit. His body was too weak for the realities of eternity that filled his heart. Again he sank overpowered to the earth, and the same spirit overcame his wife also. Ammon's rejoicing heart swelled within him as he heard and witnessed these things; he fell upon his knees and poured out his soul in praise and thanksgiving, until he also could not contain the brightness of the glory, the completeness of the joy that overwhelmed him. Unconscious of all earthly things he sank beside the royal pair. The same spirit of unmeasured joy then fell upon all present, with the same results. There was but one exception, a Laman-

...tish woman, named Abish, who had been converted to the Lord many years before, but kept the secret in her own bosom. She comprehended the why and wherefore of this strange scene. She saw the workings of the Almighty through which the unlettered minds of the Lamanites could be brought to an understanding of the plan of salvation. From house to house she went, calling the people to witness what had occurred in the palace. They gathered at her call, but as might naturally be expected, their impressions were very conflicting. Some said one thing, some another; some argued for good, some for evil; to some, Ammon was a god, to others, a demon. One man, whose brother was slain at the waters of Sebus, drew his sword and attempted to slay Ammon, but was struck dead by an unseen power before he could carry his rash intent into action. So fierce was the contention, so angry grew the controversy, that Abish, fearing greater trouble, by an inspiration took hold of the hand of the queen, who thereupon arose to her feet. The queen's first thought was of her husband. She took his hand and raised him up, and ere long all who had been reposing in the spirit stood upon their feet. The king, the queen, the servants, all rejoiced with joy unspeakable. They all bore testimony to God's abundant love and goodness, and some declared that holy angels had visited them. Still the contention was not entirely appeased until Lamoni stood forth and explained to them the Divine mysteries of which they were so ignorant. Many believed, others did not, but Ammon had the indescribable happiness of shortly after establishing a church to the Lord in the midst of the people of the land of Ishmael. Ammon's humility, faith and patience were bringing forth their fruit; while his soul gathered faith and strength in the fulfilment of the promises of the great Jehovah in answer to the pleadings of his faithful, loving father.

anger against their brethren to slay them; therefore get thee out of this land; and blessed are the people of this generation, for I will preserve them.

The word of the Lord thus received was joyfully obeyed. The Ammonites gathered up their flocks and herds and departed into the wilderness that lay between the lands of Nephi and Zarahemla. There they rested while Ammon and his brethren went forward and treated with the Nephites in behalf of the persecuted hosts they had left behind. The people, by united voice, gladly welcomed their co-religionists and set apart the land of Jershon as their inheritance. Thither the Ammonites, with happy feet repaired (B. C. 77), and there Ammon established his home and became their local presiding High Priest.

In later years we have occasional references to Ammon. In B. C. 75, Korihor, the Anti-Christ, endeavored to intrude his soul-destroying doctrines upon the people of Ammon. But they quickly took him, bound him, and carried him before Ammon, who expelled him beyond the borders of Jershon. Later in that same year he accompanied Alma in his memorable mission to the Zoramites in the land of Antionum, returning to his people in Jershon when that mission was ended. He afterwards accompanied Alma to the land of Zarahemla, after which we lose sight of him, as nothing is said of his further labors or death.

Ammon was one of the greatest, most lovable characters of Nephite history. Full of zeal, faith, charity, disinterestedness and love, yet withal a man of good judgment and great wisdom; he left a broad, bright mark in the history of his people, that lasted until the Messiah came and established more completely the perfect law of the Gospel.

AMMON, CHILDREN OF. A people descended from Lot. They are mentioned but once

When the church was satisfactorily established in the land of Ishmael, Lamoni arranged to pay a visit to his father, the great king in the land of Nephi, to whom he was desirous of introducing Ammon. However, the voice of the Lord warned his servant not to go, but instead thereof to proceed to the land of Middoni, where his brother Aaron and other missionaries were suffering in prison. When Lamoni heard of Ammon's intention, and the cause thereof, he decided to accompany him. He felt that he could be of service in delivering the prisoners, as Antiomno, the king of Middoni, was one of his special friends, and likely to grant any favor he might ask. They accordingly started on their errand of mercy, but on their way were surprised to meet Lamoni's father, who grew exceedingly angry when he found Ammon in the company of his son. All the hatred born and nurtured of false tradition boiled up in his breast. He listened impatiently to Lamoni's story of Ammon's visit and its fruits, and when it was finished he broke out in a torrent of abuse towards the Nephite "son of a liar," as he ungraciously styled him, and ordered Lamoni to slay him. Lamoni at once refused to become the murderer of his most loved friend, whereupon the old monarch, in the blind fury of his anger, turned upon his own son, and would have killed him if Ammon had not interposed. Little used to contradiction, much less to direct opposition, the king was not softened by Ammon's interference. Savagely he turned upon him, but youth, strength, dexterity, and above all the protecting care of the Lord, were with Ammon, and he struck the king's sword arm so heavy a blow that it fell useless at his side. Realizing he was now in the power of the man he had so foully abused, he made abundant promises, even to half his kingdom, if his life were spared. This boon Ammon immediately granted, asking only favors for Lamoni and his

in the Book of Mormon (II Nephi, 21; 14), in a quotation from the 11th chapter of Isaiah.

AMMONITES, or PEOPLE OF AMMON. The Christian Lamanites or people of Anti-Nephi-Lehi. The name of Ammonites was given to them by the Nephites because Ammon was the chief instrument in their conversion. When they left their homes in the land of Nephi (B. C. 78) they settled, by permission of the Nephites, in the land of Jershon, which was considered a place of security for them, as it lay far to the north of their former homes, and the great body of the Nephite people inhabited the intervening regions. In Jershon, Ammon became their High Priest. About the year B. C. 76, they were visited by the Anti-Christ Korihor, but they gave no heed to his teachings, and he was, by Ammon's direction, removed beyond their borders. In the next year, many of the persecuted Zoramites found refuge in their territory, and for the protection and aid they afforded them they were threatened with war. To avoid being involved in this strife and being compelled to break their oaths of non-resistance, they moved into the land of Melek, and the armies of the Nephites occupied Jershon (B. C. 74). From time to time they received accessions to their numbers from Lamanite prisoners of war and others who preferred to remain with the Nephites. To them also the servants of the King of the Lamanites repaired in the days of Amalickiah when they were falsely charged with his murder. In later years (B. C. 40), numbers of them emigrated to the northern continent. The two thousand young men who fought so valiantly under Helaman (B. C. 63), in the lengthened war commenced by Amalickiah, were of this people. In process of time they became absorbed into the Nephite race.

AMMONIHAH. The founder of the City of Ammonihah. We have no particulars of his life.

own imprisoned brethren. The king, unused to such generosity and manly love, granted all his requests, and when he proceeded on his journey his mind was filled with reflections regarding Ammon's courage and great love for his son. He was also troubled in his heart concerning certain expressions of Ammon on doctrinal points, which opened up ideas that were entirely new to his mind.

Lamoni and Ammon continued their journey to Middoni, where, by God's grace, they found favor in the eyes of king Antiomno, and by his command the missionaries were released from the horrors of their prison house.

After his release Aaron, with others, visited the old king. Their visit ended in his conversion, and the issuance of a royal proclamation granting full religious liberty to all dwelling within the borders of his dominions. This was followed by a rebellion of the unconverted Lamanites, egged on by Nephite apostates, resulting in two series of massacres of the Christian Lamanites, who unresistingly fell victims to the rage and hate of their unrepentant fellow countrymen. During this period the old king died and he was succeeded by his son Anti-Nephi-Lehi as ruler of the Christian portion of the Lamanites.

Ammon and his brethren were not willing to have the disciples continually harassed and eventually exterminated; they judged that the Lord, having so thoroughly tried the faith of this devoted people, would provide some way of escape. Ammon counseled with the king, and it was thought better to forsake their all so far as worldly possessions were concerned, than to remain and sacrifice their lives. But first they would inquire of the Lord. Ammon did so and the Lord said, Get this people out of this land, that they perish not, for Satan has great hold of the hearts of the Amalekites, who do stir up the Lamanites to

AMMONIHAH, CITY OF. A western city of the Nephites, situated in the same region as the cities of Melek, Noah, and Aaron. It was inhabited almost exclusively by the followers of Nehor, and was notorious for the wickedness of its inhabitants. In the year B. C. 82 it was visited by Alma, but his words were rejected. He left the city to minister elsewhere, but was commanded by an angel to return, which he did, and was entertained by one of its prominent citizens named Amulek. These two together proclaimed to the people of Ammonihah the word of God and the terrible penalty that would follow its rejection. Their words were scorned, their warning ridiculed, and they were cast into prison, while the few that had believed were either driven out of the city or burned at the stake. Alma and Amulek were ultimately delivered by the power of God, when the prison in which they were confined was destroyed by an earthquake, and all except themselves, who were therein, were killed. The two prophets then left the city. Next year, in accordance with the words of Alma, the Lamanites suddenly attacked and utterly destroyed the city by fire. All its people —hale and grandsire, matron and maid—were burned, as they had previously martyred those who believed in the Gospel message delivered by Alma and Amulek. Zeezrom, the lawyer, was a citizen of Ammonihah. After the place where Ammonihah stood had lain desolate for a number of years it was rebuilt and strongly fortified. In B. C. 73 the armies of the Lamanites came against it, but finding how strongly Moroni had fortified it they retired without making an attack.

AMMONIHAH, LAND OF. The country immediately surrounding the city of the same name. It lay between the river Sidon and the Pacific Ocean, but exactly where cannot be determined. It was called after a man named Ammonihah, who was the founder of the city. In the same region were *Melek, Noah*, and *Aaron*, and the great western wilderness. When Alma had made the three days' journey spoken of under head of Melek, he reached Ammonihah. From the text of the passage some conclude that Alma traveled northward from Melek, but to us it conveys the idea that the prophet journeyed three days westward along or near the northern boundary of that land. We are confirmed in this opinion by the statement made in another place regarding Ammonihah's proximity to that portion of the wilderness which ran along the sea shore (*Alma xxii: 27*). In Alma (*xvi: 2*), it is stated: The armies of the Lamanites had come in upon the wilderness side, into the borders of the land, even into the city of Ammonihah. If Ammonihah had been situated three days' journey north of Melek, we suggest that it could not have been near that portion of the wilderness which the Lamanites so easily reached without discovery; for a march due north would have taken them close to, or actually through the lands of *Minon, Noah, Melek* and Zarahemla, the most thickly populated portions of the country; or, to have avoided these, they must have taken a circuitous route of immense length and great danger. Then, when they attempted to retire, their retreat, owing to their great distance from Nephi, would have most assuredly been cut off, as was the case with the Lamanite general *Coriantumr* under these conditions.

AMMONIHAHITES. The people inhabiting the land and city of *Ammonihah.* They were utterly destroyed with their city by the invading hosts of the Lamanites (B. C. 82), in fulfilment of the word of the Lord through Alma and Amulek.

AMMORON. A Nephite traitor and apostate. He was a descendant of *Zoram*, the servant of *Laban*, and the brother of *Amalickiah*, whom he succeeded on the Lamanite throne, (B. C. 68). He was slain by *Teancum*, the Nephite general, in

the city of Moroni, and was succeeded by his son *Tubaloth* (B. C. 61).

Ammoron is not mentioned until the death of his brother; then we are told he left the land of Zarahemla, repaired to the land of Nephi, informed the widowed queen of her loss, and gathered a vast host of men to continue the war, especially on the western border. He determined to carry on hostilities with unabated vigor, for a time taking personal command in the west; but he does not appear to have possessed the military skill and genius of his brother, for during his reign the Nephites reconquered nearly all the territory and recaptured nearly all the cities that had been wrested from them by Amalickiah. Later on in the war, when the Lamanite invaders on the east coast had all been driven to the land of Moroni, Ammoron was with them, and it was in the city of that name that he was slain with a javelin by *Teancum.* Ammoron is brought most prominently before the reader of the Book of Mormon through the insertion of the correspondence that passed between him and Moroni regarding an exchange of prisoners of war. In this correspondence his character is very clearly shown, (Alma, chap. 54).

AMNGADDAH. A Jaredite king, the son of *Aaron*, and the father of *Coriantum.* His father, himself and his son were kept prisoners all their lives by the dynasty that had usurped the throne. In his grandson *Com's* days, the kingdom was recovered.

AMNIHU. A hill on the east of the river Sidon, near which a desperate battle was fought (B. C. 87), between the Nephites and Amlicites, in which more than 19,000 warriors were slain. The Nephites, who were commanded by *Alma*, were the victors.

AMNOR. A Nephite captain, who, with others, was sent out by Alma to watch the Amlicites.

after the battle at *Amnihu.* Next day, they returned and reported that the Amlicites had joined an invading host of Lamanites, and that together they were hastening towards Zarahemla, and ravaging the country (*Amnor*) through which they passed (B. C. 87).

AMORON. A Nephite military officer or messenger, who conveyed to Mormon the tidings of the horrible atrocities committed by the Lamanites on the Nephite prisoners—men, women, and children—captured by them in the tower of Sherrizah. This event took place about the middle of the fourth century after Christ. Amoron's name is mentioned but once, in Mormon's second epistle to his son Moroni.

AMOS, THE ELDER. Amos was the son of Nephi, the son of Nephi, the Apostle. For eighty-four years (from A. C. 110 to A. C. 194) he was the custodian of the sacred records and the other holy things. He lived in the days of the Nephites' greatest prosperity and happiness. The perfect law of righteousness was still their only guide. But before he passed away to his heavenly home, a small cloud had appeared upon the horizon, a harbinger of the approaching devastating hurricane. A few, weary of the uninterrupted bliss, the perfect harmony, the universal love that everywhere prevailed, seceded from the Church and took upon them the name of Lamanites, which ill-boding name had only been known to the Nephites by tradition for more than a hundred years.

There is one thing very noteworthy with regard to the descendants of Alma at this period, it is their longevity. Amos and his two sons (Amos and Amaron) kept the records for the space of two hundred and ten years. This is a testimony to all believers in the Book of Mormon, to the highly beneficial results arising to the body as well as to the soul of every one who gives unvarying, continued obedience to the laws of God.

No people since the deluge, of whom we have any record, lived nearer to the Lord than did the Nephites of this generation; no people have had the average of their earthly life so marvelously prolonged.

AMOS, THE YOUNGER. Amos was the son of the elder *Amos*, and his successor in the custody of the "holy things." So great was his vitality, and so strong was the constitution implanted in him by the virtuous lives of his progenitors, together with his own life of harmony with God's laws, that he retained this sacred trust for the unexampled period of one hundred and twelve years, or from A. C. 194 to A. C. 306, when he placed them in the hands of his brother *Ammaron.*

Amos was a righteous man, but he lived to witness an ever-increasing flood of iniquity break over the land, a phase of evil-doing that arose not from ignorance and false tradition, but from direct and wilful rebellion against God, and apostasy from His laws. In the year A. C. 201, all the second generation, after the appearance of the Redeemer, had passed away, save a few; the people had greatly multiplied and spread over the face of the lands, north and south, and they had become exceedingly rich; they wore costly apparel, which they adorned with ornaments of gold and silver, pearls and precious stones. From this date they no more had their property in common, but, like the rest of the world, every man sought gain, wealth, power and influence for himself and his own. All the old evils arising from selfishness were revived. Soon they began to build churches after their own fashion, and hire preachers who pandered to their lusts, some even began to deny the Savior.

From A. C. 210 to A. C. 230, the people waxed greatly in iniquity and impurity of life. Different dissenting sects multiplied, infidels

abounded. The three remaining disciples were sorely persecuted, notwithstanding that they performed many mighty miracles.

Not only did the wicked persecute these three undying ones, but others of God's people suffered from their unhallowed anger and bitter hatred; but the faithful neither reviled at the reviler nor smote the smiter; they bore these things with patience and fortitude, remembering the pains of their Redeemer.

In the year A. C. 231, there was a great division among the people. The old party lines were again definitely marked. Again the old animosity assumed shape, and Nephite and Lamanite once more became implacable foes. Those who rejected and renounced the Gospel assumed the latter name, and with their eyes open, and a full knowledge of their inexcusable infamy, they taught their children the same base falsehoods that in ages past had caused the undying hatred that reigned in the hearts of the children of Laman and Lemuel towards the seed of their younger brothers. By A. C. 244, the more wicked portion of the people had become exceedingly strong, as well as far more numerous than the righteous. They deluded themselves by building all sorts of churches, with creeds to suit the increasing depravity of the masses.

When 260 years had passed away, the Gadianton bands, with all their secret signs and abominations (through the cunning of Satan) again appeared and increased until, in A. C. 300, they had spread all over the land. By this time, also, the Nephites, having gradually forsaken their first love, had so far sunk in the abyss of iniquity that they had grown as wicked, as proud, as corrupt, as vile, as the Lamanites. All were submerged in one overwhelming flood of infamy, "and there were none that were righteous, save it were the disciples of Jesus."

AMOS. The father of Isaiah, the prophet. He is mentioned twice by Nephi in quotations from Isaiah. (II Nephi, 12: 1, 23: 1.)

AMULEK. A Nephite prophet, son of Giddonah, who was the son of Ishmael, who was a descendant of Aminadi, a descendant of Nephi.

Among the cities built by the Nephites in the northern part of South America was one named Ammonihah, which was situated near the land of Melek, which land lay on the west side of the river Sidon. In this city, eighty-two years before the coming of Christ, dwelt a Nephite named Amulek. He was a man of wealth and great importance, and was blessed with many relatives. One day, in the latter half of the year as he was journeying to see a very near relation, an angel of the Lord appeared unto him and told him to return to his home for he had to feed a holy prophet of God who was exceeding hungry, he having fasted many days on account of the sins of the people of Ammonihah.

This man of God, of whom the angel spoke, was *Alma*, the younger, the presiding High Priest of the Church of Christ. For some time past he had been laboring in the midst of the dwellers in Ammonihah, but they had hardened their hearts against God's word and had cast the prophet out of their city. Sad at heart and bowed down with sorrow, Alma journeyed from that city, but on his way a holy angel met him and with words of encouragement bade him return. Alma was not a man to dally in keeping the word of the Lord. He at once retraced his steps and entered Ammonihah by its south gate. When not far from its portals he was addressed by Amulek, who recognized him as the man of whom the angel had spoken, and took him to his house and nourished him for many days. After a time Alma, accompanied by Amulek, recommenced preaching the principles of life and holiness, but in the meantime the citizens of Ammonihah had grown even more wicked than they were before. No sooner did these brethren raise their voices in their midst than they sought their destruction. They mocked, they ridiculed, they cross-questioned them, they perverted the meaning of their words and cried out that they reviled against their laws that were just and their judges whom they had chosen. But by the spirit of the Lord, Alma and Amulek made bare their evil intentions and severely rebuked their iniquity

Ammonihah at that time was cursed with an abundance of lawyers, who were very expert in the crooked ways of their profession. Among them was a man, whose name was Zeezrom, who, on account of his greater keenness, had a large practice, and especially made himself conspicuous in badgering and seeking to discomfort these two servants of God. But Alma and Amulek, by the power of the Lord, made his lying and perversion of their words manifest to all, to such an extent that Zeezrom himself felt the power of their words and began to tremble exceedingly. Many of the people also began to believe and to repent, but the greater portion thereof, filled with rage because their sins were laid bare with such unsparing hands, bound Alma and his companion and hurried them before the chief justice and with many falsehoods accused them of having reviled their laws, their judges and, indeed, the whole people. Zeezrom, now conscious of the evil he had done, vainly pleaded their cause, but the rabble turned upon him also, and with many indignities cast him and others in whose hearts the germ of faith was planted out of the city, and with stones strove to kill them.

Then followed a scene of horror which in after years had its counterpart in Rome and Smithfield. The infuriated mob, lost to all pity and humanity, dragged the wives and little children of those who had had the gospel preached to them, and in one great fire burned them to death. Not content with

this, in savage spite they took the copies of the Scriptures and hurled them into the flames and burned them also. To add to the refinement of their cruelty they dragged Amulek and his friend from prison, and compelled them to witness the torture of the martyrs who had received the gospel through their instrumentality. Among that throng of cruelly suffering men, women and children we have no record that one flinched or denied the Savior, in whose cause they passed away to a glorious resurrection.

Amulek was exceedingly pained at the horrors of this awful scene and pleaded with Alma that they should exercise the power of God that was in them and save the innocent from their tortures. But Alma would not permit it, saying that the Spirit constrained him, for the Lord received those martyrs to himself in glory.

Now it came to pass that while Alma and Amulek were thus bound, the chief judge came and smote them on the face, and jeered at them for not having delivered the martyrs from the flames; when he had finished he again consigned the prophets to prison. These indignities were repented day after day, not only by the chief judge but by many others; added to which they treated the prisoners with great cruelty; they kept them without food and water that they might hunger and thirst, and stripped them of their clothes and bound them naked in their prison. This continued for some time, until one day the chief judge with many others came and smote the brethren as before, with mocking and ridicule. Then the power of God came upon Alma and Amulek and they rose to their feet and broke the bands that bound them, and cried mightily to the Lord, while their persecutors were stricken with terror. These latter, frantic with fear, attempted to flee from the presence of the prophets, and in their haste fell one upon another and blocked up the way of escape.

At this moment of terror an earthquake rent the prison walls, which swayed and fell in a crumbling, suffocating, crushing mass upon the unholy throng within. Not one escaped; Alma and Amulek alone were preserved in the midst of this awful manifestation of the power of the Almighty.

The citizens, hearing the noise, rushed in crowds to learn of the disaster, but when they saw the ruined heaps of the prison, with the brethren in safety and confronting them, they fled like a flock of frightened sheep before two young lions. Still they would not permit the prophets to remain in their midst, so the latter left and went over into the land of Sidom.

Such crimes as these could not go unpunished by Divine justice. Ammonihah soon felt the force of the wrath of God. It was besieged, captured and made desolate by the armies of the Lamanites, and the very same men who rejoiced in the sufferings of the martyred saints felt the same horrors fall with tenfold fury on their own heads and those of their wives and little ones, for of the horrors of the spoiling of that city we have few counterparts in history.

In the land of Sidom, Alma and Amulek found the saints who had been cast out of Ammonihah. Zeezrom, the lawyer, was also there, sorely sick of a fever, brought on by the anguish of his mind on account of his great sins. While prostrate on his bed, the prophets visited him, comforted him, and having received a confession of his faith in Christ, administered to him, when he was immediately healed. Alma then baptized him, and from that time forth he became a zealous servant of that God whom he had heretofore so often denied and blasphemed.

After Alma had established a prosperous church in the land of Sidom he took Amulek, who had given up all for the Gospel's sake, to the land of Zarahemla. There Amulek dwelt with Alma, as-

sisting him in his labors and ministry. The Lord abundantly blessed their efforts, and the Book of Mormon informs us that they imparted the word of God, without any respect of persons, to the people continually; and there was no inequality among them, and the Lord did pour out His Spirit on all of the land that they might enter into His rest.

Amulek seemed to have henceforth devoted his entire life to the preaching of the gospel. We next hear of him (B. C. 75) being in the land of Melek with Zeezrom, whence Alma took them and other brethren to preach to the Zoramites, a body of Nephite dissenters or apostates who laid inordinate stress upon the idea of their predestination to salvation. Here Amulek preached with great zeal and faith, and did the other Elders, resulting in the repentance of many, who, by their more hardened fellow countrymen, were cruelly persecuted and driven into the land of Jershon, whose inhabitants received them with great kindness and ministered to their wants. Here Alma and his fellow laborers still further instructed them in the principles of eternal life. The wicked Zoramites were highly incensed at the kindness shown to their persecuted brethren by the noble-hearted people of Ammon, and made it a pretext for commencing a war of extermination. This war commenced about eight years after the expulsion of Amulek from Ammonihah.

Amulek has the honor of having some of his sermons handed down to us in detail in the Book of Mormon. From them we judge him to have been a man of liberal education, of great faith, of unswerving integrity and untiring zeal for the truth. He was, from the glimpses of his private life that we glean as we pass along, a man of tender and affectionate disposition, exceedingly fond of his home and family, yet these and all else he readily and joyfully gave up for the riches and

happiness of the Gospel of the Son of God. Of his later ministry and death we are not informed, as the Book of Mormon changes from the history of the labors of the servants of God to an account of the terrible wars between the Nephites and Lamanites, which immediately afterwards deluged the land with blood.

AMULON. One of the most prominent of the degraded priests of king Noah. He undoubtedly took an active part in the martyrdom of the Prophet Abinadi, though not mentioned by name (About B. C. 150). When king Noah was burned to death by his enraged subjects, they would have killed his priests also, but the latter fled before them into the depths of the wilderness. Here the priests hid for a lengthened period, both afraid and ashamed to return to their families. In this dilemma, being without wives, they supplanted and carried off a number of Lamanite maidens, who had gathered to a much-frequented spot in the land of Shemlon, on mirth and pleasure intent. This act led to a war between the Lamanites and the Nephites in the land of Lehi-Nephi, which was soon put to an end when the trouble was understood. Amulon and his associates with their Lamanite wives settled in and commenced to cultivate the land of Amulon. There they were discovered by the Lamanite soldiery who were searching for the people of Limhi, but as they pleaded most abjectly for mercy, in which petitions they were joined by their Lamanite companions, the Lamanites had compassion on them and did not destroy them, because of their wives (B. C. 121). Amulon and his brethren then joined the Lamanites, and soon after the king made Amulon the ruler, under his supreme authority, of the lands of Amulon and Helam. By this appointment Amulon and his associates became the overseers of the people of Alma, and right brutally did they use their authority in oppressing the people of God, until the

day that the Lord delivered them. Amulon and his brethren were also made teachers and educators of the Lamanites by king Laman. These expriests instructed the people in the learning of the Nephites, but they taught them nothing concerning the Lord or the law of Moses. Of Amulon's death we have no record.

AMULON, LAND OF. A portion of the great wilderness lying between the lands of Zarahemla and Nephi, settled by Amulon and his associate priests of Noah. Amulon was made its tributary ruler by the reigning monarch of the Lamanites, whose sovereignty he was compelled to acknowledge. This land afterwards became a stronghold for Nephite apostates. [See Alma chapter 24: 1.]

AMULONITES. The descendants of Amulon and his associates, the corrupt priests of king Noah. They were Nephites on their fathers' side and Lamanites on their mothers', but by association and education were of the latter race. Many of them, however, were displeased with the conduct of their fathers, and took upon them the name of Nephites, and were considered among that people ever after. Of those who remained Amulonites, many became followers of Nehor, and were scattered in the lands of Amulon, Helam and Jerusalem, all of which appear to have been limited districts in the same region of country. In later years the sons of Mosiah and their fellow-missionaries preached to them, but not one received and received the gospel message; to the contrary, they became leaders in the persecutions carried on against the suffering people of Anti-Nephi-Lehi, and were those who, with the Amalekites, slew the greatest number of that unoffending people who suffered martyrdom. In the succeeding war with the Nephites (B. C. 81), when Ammonihah was destroyed, nearly all the Amulonites were killed in the battle in which Zoram, the Nephite general, defeated the Lamanites. The remainder of the Amulonites fled into the east wilderness. where they usurped power over the people of Laman, and in their bitter hatred to the truth caused many of the latter to be burned to death because of their belief in the Gospel. These outrages aroused the Lamanites and they in turn began to hunt the Amulonites and to put them to death. This was in fulfilment of the words of Abinadi, who, as he suffered martyrdom by fire at the hands of Amulon and his associates, told them, What ye shall do unto me, shall be a type of things to come, by which he meant that many should suffer death by fire as he had suffered.

"And he said unto the priests of Noah, that their seed should cause many to be put to death, in the like manner as he was, and that they should be scattered abroad and slain, even as a sheep having no shepherd is driven and slain by wild beasts; and now behold, these words were verified, for they were driven by the Lamanites, and they were hunted, and they were smitten." (Alma ch. 25.)

ANATHOTH. A priest's city, belonging to the tribe of Benjamin, supposed to have been situated about three miles north of Jerusalem. It is only mentioned in the Book of Mormon (II Nephi 20:30) in a quotation from the prophet Isaiah.

ANGOLA. A city occupied by the Nephites under Mormon (A. C. 327-8), when retreating before the forces of the Lamanites. The Nephites made vigorous efforts to fortify it, but did not succeed in preventing its capture by the Lamanites. It is only once mentioned in the Book of Mormon and appears to have been situated near the northern extremity of the Southern Continent.

ANI-ANTI. A Lamanite village in the land of Nephi, in which Aaron, Muloki, Ammah and others proclaimed the gospel; but the people hardened their hearts, and after considerable preaching

Antionum, Land of. 83   **Antipas, Mount.**

Cumorah (A. C. 385). He and his whole command perished.

ANTIONUM, LAND OF. A district of country east of the Sidon, inhabited by the Zoramites (B. C. 75). Thither Alma and his brethren repaired to convince them of their errors. The mission was not altogether successful. Those who believed were driven out of the land and found a refuge among the Ammonites in Jershon. The unconverted Zoramites joined the Lamanites, who, the next year, occupied Antionum with an army. To confront this force the Nephites placed an army in Jershon. The Lamanites did not consider themselves equal to attacking the Nephites, and changed the plan of their campaign. They retired from Antionum into the wilderness, with the intention of invading Manti, in which purpose they were thwarted by Moroni and disastrously defeated by his troops. This land appears to have been of considerable extent, stretching from the great southern wilderness to Jershon on the north; the land of Zarahemla formed its western border, while on the east it extended indefinitely into the great eastern wilderness.

ANTIPARAH. A Nephite city on the southwest border, not far from the Pacific Ocean, which fell into the hands of the Lamanites in the long war inaugurated by Amalickiah. They stationed a powerful garrison there; but afterwards evacuated it to strengthen other Nephite cities which they had captured (B. C. 64). In after years it undoubtedly again fell into the hands of the Lamanites, as at the time of their invasion of the land of Zarahemla, (B. C. 35).

ANTIPAS, MOUNT. A mountain, locality uncertain, but somewhere within the borders of the Lamanites. It was chosen by Lehonti and those who refused to heed the Lamanite king's war proclamation, as their place of rendezvous. They gathered to its summit; Amalickiah, by the

the missionaries departed into the land of Middoni (D. C. 87).

ANIMALS. The animals named in the Book of Mormon are: the Ass, Bear, Bull, Calf, Cow, Dog, Elephant. Goat, Horse, Kid, Lamb, Lion, Mule, Sheep, Sow, Swine, Whale, Wolf. Also the Curelum and Cumom. Many of these are only mentioned in quotations from the Bible.

ANTI-NEPHI-LEHI. The name given by the king of the Lamanites to his son, who succeeded him on the throne, he being also chief of that portion of his race who had become Christians (D. C. 83). He was a brother of Lamoni. The Christian Lamanites became known as the people of Anti-Nephi-Lehi, but when they removed to the lands of the Nephites they were called Ammonites. The unrepentant Lamanites, especially those who were Nephite apostates or their seed, would not recognize the rule of Anti-Nephi-Lehi, but rebelled against him. As the Christian portion of the race would not contend with them, they carried out their rebellious designs and also massacred thousands of the original Lamanites, until, to avoid extinction, the believers in Christ removed in a body to that portion of the land of Zarahemla called Jershon. From this era it would appear that the Nephite apostates and their descendants controlled affairs among the Lamanites. Whether the king, who was slain (D. C. 73) by Amalickiah's men, was of Nephite blood does not appear, though it is presumable that he was, but his three successors—Amalickiah, Ammoron and Tubeloth—unquestionably were. Anti-Nephi-Lehi, if alive, as we have every reason to suppose he was, doubtless accompanied his people to the land of Jershon.

ANTI-NEPHI-LEHI, PEOPLE OF. See Anti-Nephi-Lehi, Ammon. Ammonites.

ANTI-NEPHI-LEHIES. A name given to the people of Anti-Nephi-Lehi, but they are better

Antipus.   84   **Archeantus.**

king's command, followed with an army to compel their obedience. This army was treacherously surrendered by Amalickiah to Lehonti, and the latter took command of both armies. He was soon after killed by slow poison, administered to him by Amalickiah's command, when the last named succeeded to his position (B. C. 73).

ANTIPUS. The commander of the Nephite forces in the extreme southwest, during the war with Amalickiah and Ammoron. He fought stubbornly for several years, against great odds, and was at last slain in battle with the Lamanites, in the wilderness north of the city of Judea (B. C. 65). [See Helaman.]

ANTUM. A land of North America in which was situated a hill called Shim. In this hill Ammaron deposited the sacred records (A. C. 321). Mormon afterwards, by Ammaron's direction, obtained the plates of Nephi from this hiding place and continued the record thereon. On account of his fear that the Lamanites might possess themselves of the records, Mormon, at a later period, removed them all to the Hill Cumorah. The land of Jashon appears to have bordered on the land of Antum; as the city of Jashon is said to have been near the land where Ammaron deposited the records.

ARABIAH. A native of Arabia, in Asia. The name is only used once in the Book of Mormon, (II Nephi, 23 : 20) in a quotation from Isaiah.

ARCHEANTUS. A Nephite officer of rank in the army commanded by Mormon. He was killed in a "sore battle" fought with the Lamanites (probably towards the middle of the fourth century of the Christian era) in which the latter were victorious. He is spoken of by Mormon in his second epistle to his son, in connection with a great number of "choice men" lost in the same disastrous battle.

known as Ammonites, or the people of Ammon, in honor of the son of king Mosiah II, who was the leading spirit in converting them to the truth.

ANTIOMNO. A king of the Lamanites who reigned over the land of Middoni, in the early part of the first century before Christ. It was in his realm that Aaron, the son of Mosiah, and some of his fellow missionaries were imprisoned for many days, and afterwards delivered through the intercession of Ammon and king Lamoni. Antiomno is not again mentioned by name, but as we are informed that among the thousands of the Lamanites converted to the Lord, by the preaching of the sons of Mosiah, were they "who were in the land of Middoni," it is quite probable that their king was also numbered among the converted. Before the coming of Aaron and his associates into their midst the people of Middoni were a hard-hearted and stiff-necked race, and it would be doing no violence to the law of probabilities to imagine that the character of the king was similar to that of his subjects; at any rate he permitted his Nephite prisoners to be treated with much cruelty.

ANTIONAH. A chief ruler among the people of the city of Ammonihah. His inquiry regarding the resurrection, and the immortality of the soul, afforded Alma an opportunity to explain these and other vital principles of the everlasting Gospel. From the manner in which the question is put, we judge that Antionah was, like the majority of the people in Ammoniah, a corrupt man (and the probabilities are that he would not have been elected to that position if he had not been), or at the least very ignorant of the teachings of the servants of God. Whether he repented at Alma's preaching or was destroyed with the unrepentant is not made clear. (B. C. 82.)

ANTIONUM. A Nephite general who commanded a division of 10,000 men at the battle of

Arpad.   85   **Benjamin.**

ARPAD. A city or district in Syria, apparently dependent on Damascus. It is mentioned but once in the Book of Mormon (Nephi, 20: 9) in a quotation from the prophecies of Isaiah.

ASSYRIA. A great and powerful country in western Asia, whose capital was Nineveh. It derived its name apparently from Asshur, the son of Shem. It is mentioned by Nephi eight times, but always in quotations from Isaiah.

ASSYRIANS. The people of Assyria. The name is used by Nephi in three quotations from the prophet Isaiah.

BABYLON. The land into which the people of Judah were carried captive. This coming captivity, together with the destruction of Jerusalem, was revealed by the Lord to Lehi (B. C. 600), and his proclamation of its near approach was one of the causes that led to his maltreatment by the Jews. Nephi also received manifestations of this approaching calamity and so told his brethren, but Laman and Lemuel would receive neither his words nor those of his father. Nephi also prophesied of the destruction of Babylon (II Nephi, 25: 15). Babylon is mentioned several times in the Book of Mormon in quotations from the prophet Isaiah.

BASHAN. A district of Canaan on the east of the River Jordan. It is mentioned once in the Book of Mormon (II Nephi, 12: 13) in a quotation from Isaiah.

BENJAMIN. The second of the three prophet-kings of the Nephites who reigned in the land of Zarahemla. He was the son of Mosiah I, and father of Mosiah II, and, like them, was most probably a seer. He undoubtedly held the priesthood, as he received the ministration of angels, was favored with revelations from the Lord, and organized the Church of Jesus Christ among his people. He was also the custodian of the sacred records, etc., having received them from Amaleki, who was childless. The time and place of his birth is not given, though it was probably in the land of Nephi. He lived to a great age and died full of peace and honor in Zarahemla. (B. C. 122.) He is illustrious for the justice and mercy with which he administered the laws, for his great devotion to God and love for his people, and for the frugality and simplicity of his personal life. Three of his sons are mentioned by name, Mosiah, Helorum and Helaman, whom he caused to be educated in all the learning of his fathers, giving especial attention to their religious training and instruction in the history of God's dealings with their forefathers.

The reign of Benjamin was not one of uninterrupted peace. Some time during its continuance the aggressive Lamanites, not content with occupying the land of Nephi, actually followed the Nephites into the land of Zarahemla and invaded that also. The war was a fierce one. King Benjamin led his forces, armed with the historic sword of Laban, and with it slew many of the enemy. Benjamin was ultimately successful in driving the invading hosts out of all the regions occupied by his people, with a loss to the Lamanites of many thousand warriors slain.

The reign of Benjamin was also troubled with various religious impostors, false Christs, pretended prophets, etc., who caused apostasy and dissensions among the people, much to the sorrow of the good king. However, by the aid of some of the many righteous men who dwelt in his dominions, he exposed the heresies, made manifest the falsity of the claims of the self styled Messiahs and prophets, and restored unity of faith and worship among his subjects; and in such cases where these innovators had broken the civil law, they were arraigned, tried, and punished by that law.

We may presume that the original inhabitants

of Zarahemla, just awakening to a newness of religious life, were particularly subject to the influences brought to bear by these impostors. They had but lately learned the mysteries of the plan of salvation and of the coming of the Messiah to dwell among the sons of men. The glory and beauty of this Divine advent filled their new-born souls with joyous hope. Looking forward for the arrival of that happy day, with their first love undiminished and their zeal unslackened, they were especially open to the deceptions of those who cried, Lo, the Christ is come! or, Behold, a great prophet hath arisen!

There was another class who, moved by the spirit of unrest, were a source of perplexity to the king. They were those who, having left the land of Nephi with the righteous, still permitted their thoughts and affections to be drawn towards their former homes and old associations. The natural consequence was that they were constantly agitating the idea of organizing expeditions to visit their old homes. The first of these that actually started, of which we have an account, fought among themselves with such fury that all were slain except fifty men, who, in shame and sorrow, returned to Zarahemla to recount the miserable end of their expedition. Yet some remained unsatisfied, and under the leadership of a man named Zeniff, another company started on the ill-advised journey. Nothing was heard from them while Benjamin reigned.

When king Benjamin was well stricken with years, the Lord directed him to consecrate his son Mosiah to be his successor on the Nephite throne. Feeling that age was impairing his energies he directed his son to gather the people together at the temple that had been erected in Zarahemla, and he would then give them his parting instructions. (B. C. 125.) Agreeable to this call the people gathered at the temple, but so numerous had they

grown that it was too small to hold them. They also brought with them the firstlings of their flocks that they might offer sacrifice and burnt offerings according to the Mosaic law. As the assembled thousands could not get inside the temple, they pitched their tents by families, every one with its door towards the building, and the king had a tower erected near the temple from which he spake.

The teachings of king Benjamin at these meetings were some of the most divine and glorious ever uttered by man. He preached to his hearers the pure principles of the gospel—the duty which men owed to their God and to their fellows. He also told them how he had been visited by an angel, and what wondrous things the angel had shown him concerning the coming of the God of Israel to dwell with men in the flesh.

When Benjamin had made an end of speaking the words which had been delivered to him by the angel, he observed that the power of his testimony had so worked upon the Nephites that they, in the deep sense of their own unworthiness, had fallen to the ground. And their cries out confessing their faith in the coming Messiah, and pleading that through his atoning blood they might receive the forgiveness of their sins, and that their hearts might be purified. After they had lifted their prayerful cry to heaven, the Spirit of the Lord came down upon them, and because of their exceeding faith they received a remission of their sins. When the king had finished his discourse he gave his people a new name, because of the covenant they desired to make, which thing he greatly desired. The name they were to bear for ever after was the name of Christ, which should never be blotted out except through transgression. Thus was established the first Christian church in Zarahemla (B. C. 125), for every soul who heard these teachings (except the very little children who could not understand) entered into this sacred covenant with

---

Bethabary.   89   **Bountiful, City of.**

God, which most of them faithfully observed to the end of their mortal lives.

King Benjamin's truly royal work was now done. He had lived to bring his people into communion with their Creator, his spirit was full of heavenly joy, but his body trembled under the weight of many years. So before he dismissed the multitude he consecrated his son Mosiah to be their king, appointed priests to instruct the people in the ways of the Lord, and, with his patriarchal blessing, dismissed his subjects. Then, according to their respective families, they all departed for their own homes.

Mosiah now reigned in his father's stead, while Benjamin, beloved and honored, remained yet another three years on the earth before he returned to the presence of his Father in heaven.

BETHABARA. Otherwise BETHABARA. The place "beyond Jordan" where John the Baptist baptized. It is mentioned in Lehi's prophecy (1 Nephi, 10: 9) of the baptism of the Savior.

BIRDS. The Birds named in the Book of Mormon are the Bittern, Chicken, Dove, Fowl, Hen, Owl, and Vulture.

BOAZ, CITY OF. A city evidently situated a short distance north of the Isthmus of Panama. In the last war between the Nephites and Lamanites, the Nephites having on one occasion been beaten in a severe battle, in the land of Desolation, fled to Boaz. To this place the Lamanites followed them, but were unsuccessful in their first attack, as the Nephites defended it with great boldness. In their second attack they carried the city, and the defenders suffered great loss. The conquerors took the Nephite women and children whom they had made prisoners and sacrificed them to their idols. (About A. C. 375.)

BOUNTIFUL, CITY OF. The chief city of the Nephites, in the land Bountiful, situated, apparently, not far from the shore of the great eastern

sea, and but a short distance south of the Isthmus of Panama. It was the key to the Northern continent, and previous to the birth of the Savior none of the invading armies of the Lamanites appear to have been able to pass by it. It was strongly fortified by Moroni and his associate commanders and successors, the Lamanite prisoners of war being used by him on, at least, one occasion in this work (B. C. 64), until the city was encircled with a deep ditch and a high wall of earth and timbers. "And it became an exceeding strong place ever afterward." The Lamanite prisoners were held within an enclosure, the walls of which they were, themselves, compelled to build; and their numbers were constantly added to as the fortunes of war went against them. When the city (Gid was retaken (B. C. 63), a large number of Lamanite prisoners captured therein were sent to Bountiful.

In the great mission performed by Nephi and Lehi, the sons of Helaman, they commenced their labors at the city Bountiful and thence continued southward. (B. C. 31.)

It seems probable that, in the great convulsions that attended the crucifixion of the Redeemer, Bountiful did not suffer as severely as did many other cities; for Jesus appeared to the Nephites who were assembled near the temple that stood in that land; apparently it had not been destroyed, though possibly it was greatly injured.

BOUNTIFUL, LAND OF, (in Arabia.) This must not be confounded with the Bountiful in the northern part of South America, where the Savior appeared and taught the Nephites. It was a portion of Arabia Felix, or Arabia the happy, so called in contradistinction to Arabia the stony, and Arabia the desert, on account of its abundant productiveness and great fertility. It was in this blessed region, on the shore of the Arabian sea, that Nephi built the ship that carried Lehi's colony to the promised land. To the sea itself

they gave the name of Irreantum, which word means many waters.

BOUNTIFUL, LAND OF. The most northerly Nephite division of the South American Continent. It extended in the north to the Isthmus of Panama, where it was bounded by the land Desolation. Its other boundaries are indefinite, and undoubtedly varied greatly at different eras of Nephite history, diminishing in extent as the wilderness was settled, cities were founded and the neighboring regions made tributary to them. Jershon appears to have been south and east of it. Its chief city bore the same name. And on its northwest corner Hagoth built his celebrated ship yards (B. C. 55).

Before the land Bountiful was settled by the Nephites, it was a wilderness filled with wild animals of every kind; some of which had come from the land northward for food (Alma, 22: 31). But the Nephites, to prevent the Lamanites creeping up through the wilderness along the coast, east and west, and in this way gaining a foothold in the land northward, as early a date as possible inhabited the land Bountiful, from the east to the west sea (Alma, 22: 33), thus retaining possession of the whole of the northern continent.

In this land (B. C. 68), a severe battle took place between the Nephite army, commanded by Teancum, and the people of Morianton, in which the latter were defeated and their leader slain.

The next year (B. C. 67), the victorious Lamanites, under Amalickiah, reached the borders of Bountiful from the southeast, driving the Nephites before them, but their advance northward was checked by the forces of Teancum, by whom Amalickiah, their king, was slain.

In B. C. 66, Teancum, under instruction from Moroni, greatly strengthened the fortifications in the land Bountiful, giving special attention to making the Isthmus secure from capture.

In the year B. C. 64, a sanguinary battle was fought in the district between the cities of Bountiful and Mulek, which resulted in Mulek being re-captured from the Lamanites. In this battle the Nephites were commanded by Moroni, Lehi and Teancum; and the Lamanites by Jacob, who was slain. The Lamanite prisoners were so numerous that, as a precautionary step, they were set at the task of intrenching and fortifying the land and city of Bountiful.

In the year B. C. 51 the Lamanites invaded Zarahemla, captured the capital and advanced northward towards Bountiful, but their triumphal march was arrested by an army commanded by Lehi, and they were eventually driven back to their own lands.

In B. C. 35 the Lamanites again invaded the lands of the Nephites, and the latter, owing to their dissensions and wickedness, were everywhere driven before them, until, in B. C. 34, they had overrun and taken possession of all the Nephite possessions as far as the land Bountiful. The Nephites, under Moronihah, then threw up a line of fortifications entirely across the Isthmus, by which means they invaded the northern continent from invasion. In B. C. 32, Moronihah reconquered the most northern portions of South America.

In A. C. 16, Lachoneous, the chief judge, by reason of the perilous condition of the people, from the constant attacks of the Gadianton robbers, decided to mass the Nephites in one region, and chose Bountiful and Zarahemla for that purpose. This bold movement he carried out, and held the people there until after the destruction of the hosts of the robbers. In A. C. 26, the people were permitted to return to their homes throughout the two continents.

It was in the land Bountiful that Jesus appeared and ministered to the Nephites.

CAIN. The son of Adam. He is mentioned

thrice by name in the Book of Mormon; each time in connection with his plottings and convenants with Satan.

CALNO. A place in Palestine, of which little is known. It is mentioned in Nephi's extracts from the prophecies of Isaiah (II Nephi, 20: 9.)

CAMENIHAH. A Nephite general who was slain at the battle of Cumorah (A. C. 385). The army corps of ten thousand men, which he commanded, was entirely destroyed in this battle.

CARCHEMISH. A town near the Euphrates River. It is mentioned in connection with Calno in an extract from the prophecies of Isaiah (II Nephi, 20: 9).

CEZORAM. In the year B. C. 30 Nephi, the servant of the Lord, owing to the rapid increase of iniquity, among the people, resigned the Chief Judgeship in the Nephite Republic, and a man named Cezoram was chosen to fill his place. We infer from the context that Cezoram was the tool of, or a leader among the Gadianton robber bands, and that it was through the widespread corruption of the Nephites, who were rapidly ripening for destruction, that his election was secured. He continued in office, until the year B. C. 26, when he was murdered by an unknown hand as he sat upon the judgment seat. One of his sons succeeded him, but his reign was short, for he also was assassinated, even in the same year as was his father.

When Cezoram was elected chief officer of the Nephite Commonwealth the people were in a pitiable condition. Through their apostasy from God, and disregard of the national law, they had been trampled under foot of the Lamanites, and half their lands, including their great and grand capital Zarahemla, was in the hands of these ruthless foes. But during his judgeship, (though in no way attributable to him, so far as we can gather from the record,) a great change came over the spirit of the Lamanites, and the greater por-

tion of them were converted to the Lord through the preaching of Nephi and his brother Lehi. The Lamanites, in the fulness of their conversion, restored to the Nephites the lands they had taken from them, and the seat of Nephite government was again established at Zarahemla. This conversion and restitution was followed by a most profound and widespread peace, during which commerce was greatly extended, the arts and refinements of life were developed, and both races grew extremely rich. This age marks a new era in ancient American history. Many of the old distinctions between the Nephites and Lamanites were swept away, and the old distinctive names convey somewhat different ideas from this time forth. But, unfortunately, notwithstanding the preachings and example of the now zealous and righteous Lamanites, many of the people of Nephi remained "hardened, impenitent and grossly wicked;" they entirely rejected the word of God and the warning word of prophecy that was so energetically proclaimed in their hearing, by the faithful of both races. To this unhappy state of society may be traced the murder of Cezoram and his son, and the evils that afterwards followed in rapid and desolating succession.

CHALDEANS, CHALDEES. The people of Chaldea, in Asia, of which land Babylon was the capital. These names simply appear in quotations from the writings of Isaiah (I Nephi, 20: 14, 20; II Nephi, 23: 19).

CHEMISH. The son of Omni, a descendant of Jacob, the son of Lehi. He received the sacred records from his father Amaron, in the year 280 B. C. His entire writings only consist of sixty-nine words, and from them we can gather nothing regarding his private life, the history of his times, nor for how long a period he retained the plates. We must, however, suppose that his brother Amaron considered him the most suitable person

on whom to impose this sacred trust, and consequently believe him to have been a good man. He is ranked among the prophets by Mormon. He conferred the custody of the plates upon his son Abinadom.

COHOR. One of the early Jaredites. He was the son of Corihor, the son of Kib, the son of Corihor, the son of Jared. He was associated with his brother Noah, in a rebellion against Shule, the king, who was their uncle, though possibly their junior in years, as he was born when his father, Kib, was very aged. The rebellion of Noah, Cohor and his associates was partly successful, the country was divided into two kingdoms, and Noah reigned in Moron, the land of the Jaredites' first inheritance. Cohor is mentioned but once by name.

COHOR. Nephew of the preceding. He was the son of Noah, the son of Corihor. He succeeded his father as king of the land of Moron. Making war with Shule, the king of the other portion of the country, Cohor was defeated and slain. He was succeeded on the throne by his son Nimrod, who, apparently deeming Shule the rightful monarch of the whole country, gave up the whole kingdom to him; thus once again uniting the entire Jaredite people in one nation, under one king.

COHOR. A Jaredite of the last generation, evidently as wicked and impenitent as the rest of his race. No particulars whatever are given of him. It is simply said that his fair sons and daughters did not repent.

COINS. The following is the table of the coins of the Nephites, given in Alma, chap. 11:

GOLD.		SILVER.	
1 Senine	equal to	1 Senum.	
1 Seon,	2 Senines,	"	1 Amnor.
1 Shum,	4 "	"	1 Ezrom.
1 Limnah,	7 "	"	1 Onti.

Of smaller coins—
1 Shiblon was equal to half a Senine, or Senum.
1 Shiblum " " a quarter of a Senine or Senum.
1 Leah " " an eighth of a Senine or Senum.
An Antion of gold was equal to three Shublons.

Though not directly so stated, we judge from the context that the Shiblon, the Shiblum and the Leah were silver coins.

The names of these coins seem to be indentical with, or derived from those of familiar persons or places. Thus we have a Leah, a Shiblon, and an Amnor, all names of persons. Also an Antion, which word is found in Antionah and Antionum; a Shiblum, which differs from Shiblom only one letter, and a Shublon from Shiblon, and a Limnah from Limnah, to the same extent.

COM. A king of the Jaredites, the son of Coriantum. Com was born when his father was very aged, evidently considerably over one hundred years old, for Coriantum's first wife died at the age of 102 years, after which he married a young mind, who became the mother of several children, among whom was Com. In Com's reign the Jaredites increased greatly in numbers, they also spread widely over the face of the land; but they also grew in iniquity, and the secret associations (see Akish) that a few generations before had caused the almost entire destruction of the race were revived. One of the leaders in these crimes was a son of Com's, named Heth, who was born when Com had reigned 49 years. This young man conspired against his father, slew him with his own sword and reigned in his stead.

COM. A righteous king of the Jaredites, who reigned in the later days of that nation. Like the preceding, his father's name was Coriantum, though they appear to have lived nearly a thousand years apart. Com's father was one of the dynasty of monarchs who were deposed and held in captivity by the successful house. In that cap-

tivity Com was born; but when he attained manhood he rebelled and gained possession of half the kingdom. When he had thus reigned 42 years he made war with Amgid, the ruler of the other half, and after a desolating conflict of many years he gained power over the whole realm. While he was king, robber bands, like unto the Gadiantons, began to appear, who administered secret and damnable oaths, after the manner of the ancients, and sought again to destroy the kingdom. Com fought these robbers with vigor, but without success, for they had the sympathy of the masses of the people, who were rapidly ripening for destruction. Many prophets came in these days, who foretold the impending destruction of the race, if the people did not repent and turn unto the Lord. But the voice of mercy and warning was rejected, and the sin-sunken Jaredites sought the lives of the heaven-inspired messengers. The prophets fled to Com for preservation, and he appears to have valiantly protected them. While with him they prophesied many things for his comfort and edification, and he was blessed of the Lord all the remainder of his days. He lived to a good old age, and begat Shiblom, who, at his death, reigned in his stead.

COMNOR. A hill near the valley of Shurr, location unknown, but apparently nearer the Atlantic than the Pacific seaboard of North America. In one of the last great wars that took place among the Jaredites, Coriantumr massed his troops upon this hill, and there challenged to battle, by call of trumpet, the armies of Shiz. A series of battles then ensued which, in the end, resulted disastrously to Coriantumr.

CORIANTON, SON OF ALMA. Of Corianton's birth and death we have no record. With his brothers, he is first mentioned in the Book of Mormon at the time of the Zarahemla apostasy, when, though young and inexperienced, into the sea. In the year A. C. 363, the Lamanites attacked Desolation, but were repulsed and driven back to their own lands. During the next year they made another ineffectual attack, in which they sustained great loss. So great was the exultation of the Nephites at this last victory that their excesses knew no bounds, and they gave way so grossly to impiety, that Mormon refused to lead them any longer to battle. Strong in their own vain strength, in A. C. 363 the Nephites invaded the lands of the Lamanites, but were disastrously repulsed and pursued, and the city of Desolation was wrested from them; they, however, recaptured it shortly after. In A. C. 366, the Lamanites once more became the masters of the city, but lost it again the following year. The Nephites retained possession of this stronghold until A. C. 375, when the Lamanites drove them out of all that region, and apparently held it until the end of the war, and the extinction of the Nephites at Cumorah.

DESOLATION, LAND OF. Before the time of the Nephites this region was thickly inhabited by the Jaredites. In the days of the latter people *Bountiful* formed its southern border. The two lands apparently joined at the isthmus of Panama. At first, like most frontier districts, it extended indefinitely into the uninhabited regions. When other lands were colonized its boundaries became more definitely fixed. It is generally supposed to have embraced within its borders the region known to moderns as Central America. Its capital was a city of the same name, probably built in later years, as it is never mentioned but by Mormon in the account of the long series of wars in which he took so prominent a part.

DESOLATION OF NEHORS. The name given by the Nephites to the spot where the unstained city of *Ammonihah* once stood. It received that name because it remained a wilderness and a desolation for a number of years after the destruction of the city, the stench from the rotting bodies of its former citizens making it uninhabitable. The name of *Nehors* was added because those who had been slain were followers of that false teacher.

DISCIPLES, THE TWELVE. When the risen Redeemer appeared to the Nephites in the land Bountiful (A. C. 34), he chose twelve men as his disciples, to whom he gave authority to perform the rite of baptism and administer in the other ordinances of the Gospel. On these twelve, who are always called Disciples in the Book of Mormon, and never Apostles, was conferred the power to judge the descendants of Lehi at the final judgment day, as they themselves were to be judged by the Twelve Apostles chosen by the Lord from among the Jews. The names of the twelve Nephite disciples were: Nephi, his brother Timothy and his son Jonas, Mathoni, Mathonihah, Kumen, Kumenonhi, Jeremiah, Shemnon, Jonas, Zedekiah and Isaiah. To these twelve our Savior gave many instructions, which he withheld from the multitude.

On one occasion, toward the close of His ministrations, He asked them, one by one: What is it that you desire of me, after I am gone to the Father? Then nine of them said, We desire, after we have lived unto the age of man, that our ministry, wherein thou hast called us, may have an end, that we may speedily come unto thee in the kingdom. And he said unto them, Blessed are ye, because ye desire this thing of me; therefore, after that ye are seventy and two years old, ye shall come unto me in my kingdom, and with me ye shall find rest.

Then He turned to the three who had not answered, and again asked them what they would have Him do for them. But they faltered in their reply; their wish was such a peculiar one, that they were afraid to express it. Then He told them that He knew their thoughts, that they had desired that they might bring souls unto Him, while the world stood. And because of the purity and disinterestedness of this desire He promised the three Disciples that they should never taste of death, but when He should come in His glory, they should be changed in the twinkling of an eye from mortality to immortality, and should sit down in the kingdom of the Father, and their joy should be full. And further, that while they dwelt in the flesh, they should not suffer pain, nor experience sorrow, save it were for the sins of the world. Then Jesus with His finger touched the nine who were to die, but the three who were to live He did not touch, and then He departed. Afterwards the heavens were opened, and the three were caught up into heaven, and a change was there wrought upon their mortal natures. But, Mormon says (III Nephi, 28: 39, 40):

"This change was not equal to that which should take place at the last day; but there was a change wrought upon them, insomuch that Satan could have no power over them, that he could not tempt them, and they were sanctified in the flesh, that they were holy, and that the powers of the earth could not hold them; and in this state they were to remain until the judgment day of Christ; and at that day they were to receive a greater change, and to be received into the kingdom of the Father to go no more out, but to dwell with God eternally in the heavens." They also saw unspeakable things, which they were forbidden to utter; in fact, the power to tell these mysteries was withheld from them.

The sacred record gives no information as to who the three were who were not to taste of death. Mormon was about to write their names, but the Lord forbade him.

After the final ascension of the Savior the twelve

labored zealously in proclaiming His word. Theirs was a most happy task, for all the people heeded their sayings; and in a short time every soul on both continents had accepted the message they bore. It was now their joy to lead the people upward in all the laws of the everlasting Gospel, bringing them nearer to heaven and to God, each succeeding day. In this glorious ministry, and with these delightful and most peaceful surroundings, nine continued to labor until they passed away to the realms of the blessed. The other three continued their Godlike labors, year after year, until a change began to come over the spirit of the people. Little by little they lost their first love; little by little, but ever at increasing rate, iniquity grew in their midst. By and by, schismatic churches arose, dissenting sects multiplied, infidels abounded. As the decades rolled by, the people waxed greatly in iniquity and in impurity of life. After a time they began to persecute the more faithful and humble, even the three Disciples were not spared from their malignant hate. They were shut up in prison, but the prisons were rent in twain by the power of God; they were cast into fiery furnaces, but the flames burned them not; they were thrown into dens of wild beasts, but they played with the savage inmates as a child does with a lamb, and received no harm. Death had no power over them; swords would not slay them; fire would not burn them; prisons could not hold them; chains could not bind them; the grave could not entomb them; the earth would not conceal them, for they had passed through a glorious change which freed them from earthly pain, suffering and death. The age in which they ministered was a peculiar one. Under ordinary circumstances, the superhuman powers shown by them would have brought the wicked to repentance. But the happy age of peace and innocence that had followed the Savior's

ministry was fast passing away; the people were hardening their hearts; they were relapsing into iniquity with their eyes open, and they were sinning knowingly and understandingly. Angels from heaven would not have converted them; they had given themselves up to Satan, and every manifestation of the power of God in behalf of his servants only made them more angry, and more determined upon the destruction of those who sounded in their ears the unwelcome message of Divine wrath. The hurricane might demolish the dungeon; the earthquake overthrow the walls of the prison; the earth refuse to close when the Disciples were cast into it; these protests of nature simply caused their hardened hearts to conjure up fresh methods of torture and devise new means to destroy those whom they so intensely, and yet so unwarrantably hated. But they ever failed; the three Nephites still live. Encountering thus the rage and cruelty of the wicked they gradually withdrew; their ministrations grew more frequent; until at last they ceased to visit the haunts of men altogether. Moroni states that he and his father Mormon had seen them and been ministered to by them; and these, the last two prophets of their race, were, in all probability, the last of that dispensation who were favored with a visit from these three Nephites. They have also been seen by numbers of the faithful in this dispensation.

EDEN, THE GARDEN OF. Mentioned six times in the Book of Mormon; always, except in one case, in connection with the expulsion of our first parents therefrom.

EDOM. The land east of Canaan, inhabited by the descendants of Esau. It is mentioned but once in the Book of Mormon, in a quotation from the prophecies of Isaiah (II Nephi, 21:14).

EGYPT. The land of that name in Africa. It is mentioned frequently in the Book of Mormon, generally in connection with the life of

they were afraid to express it. Joseph, the son of Jacob; or with the bondage of the Israelites therein.

EGYPTIAN, REFORMED. The name given to the style of characters in use in the days of Mormon, in which the records were engraven on the sacred plates. These characters were greatly modified from those used by Nephi and the other earlier recorders.

EGYPTIANS. The people of Egypt. They are referred to in connection with their language (I Nephi, 1:3), and the deliverance of the Israelites from bondage under Moses.

EGYPTIAN SEA. A name given by Isaiah to the Red Sea, and so spoken of in a quotation from that prophet. (II Nephi, 21:15).

ELAM. The land of the Elamites, a country lying south of Assyria. It is only mentioned in the Book of Mormon in a quotation from Isaiah (II Nephi, 21:11).

ELIJAH. The prophet of Israel. His name only appears in the Book of Mormon in the Savior's quotation from Malachi, "Behold I will send you Elijah, the prophet," (III Nephi, 25: 5).

ELEM. One of the early kings of the Jaredites. Two years before his death, Omer, his father, anointed him to reign in his stead. Emer was the third of the line of kings of his race. He executed judgment in righteousness all his days. In his reign the people greatly increased in numbers and in wealth, becoming the owners of large herds of useful animals, and rich in agricultural and mineral products, in gems and fine manufactured goods. The curse, also, which had come upon the land during the days of Akish because of the iniquity of the people, began to be removed, as there was now living more righteously. Emer's was a lengthy reign; sixty-two years are mentioned; but it is not evident whether this period covers the whole of his reign or not. When he died, full of years and honor, he was succeeded by one of his

Emron. 116 Ephraim, Hill.

numerous sons, named *Corianton*, whom he had anointed king four years before his death. It is recorded of Emer that he saw the Son of Righteousness, and did rejoice and glorify in his day.

EMRON. A Nephite officer, mentioned in Mormon's second epistle to his son as having been slain in a severe battle with the Lamanites. From the context we judge he was held in high regard by Mormon.

ENOS. A Nephite prophet, the grandson of Lehi and Sariah. Enos, if not the leading spirit of the age among his people, was undoubtedly one of the most conspicuous and zealous servants of the Lord who ministered and prophesied to the early Nephites. The son of *Jacob*, the priest and historian of the colony, he succeeded his father in these sacred offices, and appears to have inherited his faith, gentleness and devotion. Of his personal life we have no particulars, but it is evident that he was a very aged man at the time of his departure from the scenes of mortality. His father, Jacob, was the elder of the two sons born to Lehi in the Asiatic wilderness, between the year 600 and 590 before Christ. We have no direct statement either of Enos' birth or the exact time of his death; all we know is that when he left this earth he gave the records and the sacred things associated therewith into the hands of his son *Jarom*, 180 years after Lehi left Jerusalem, or B. C. 421.

EPHRAIM. The name used by Isaiah for the Kingdom of Israel, and used in the same sense in Nephi's quotations from the writings of that prophet.

EPHRAIM, HILL. A hill mentioned in the Book of Ether (Ether 7:9), from which *Shule* obtained iron ore with which to make swords to arm his followers, in their effort to replace his father *Kib* on the throne. We judge this hill to have been situated in Central America, as it

was evidently at no very great distance from the land *Moron*, afterwards Desolation.

ESROM. A son of the unfortunate Jaredite king *Omer*, born to him while he was held in captivity by his son *Jared*. Esrom and his brother Corianton, growing exceedingly angry at the treatment received by their father, raised an army and made a night attack upon the forces of the usurper, in which they gained a complete victory, Jared's army being destroyed and he himself taken prisoner. Esrom and his associates then replaced their father on the throne. In the rebellion of Akish it is said that the Lord was merciful to Omer and also to his sons and daughters who did not seek his destruction. It is, therefore, altogether probable that if Esrom still lived he accompanied his father in his exile to the distant land of *Ablom*.

ETHEM. A wicked king of the later Jaredites, living, most probably, in the eighth century before Christ. He was the son and successor of *Ahah*. In Ethem's days, many prophets came and prophesied that unless the Jaredites repented the Lord would utterly destroy them from the earth. But the people hardened their hearts and repented not; and the prophets mourned over their depravity and withdrew from among them. Ethem was as his people, and did wickedly all his days; and when he died he was succeeded by his son *Moron*, who was like unto his father.

ETHER. The last great prophet of the Jaredites, to whom we are indebted for the history of that race, for it is an abridgment of Ether's writings, made by Moroni, that we have in the Book of Mormon, under the title of the Book of Ether. Ether was of the royal race, his father being *Coriantor*, one of those unfortunate monarchs who lived in captivity all his days. In the reign of *Coriantumr*, the last king of the Jaredites, Ether came forth and proclaimed the near destruction of

the entire people, a prophecy which many of his predecessors had also uttered; but he also prophesied that the king should survive all his subjects and live to see another race occupy the land. Great and marvelous were the prophecies of Ether. He saw the days of Christ, and the great work of the last dispensation, even to the coming of the New Jerusalem. Indeed, he appears to have had revealed to him a complete history of the dealings of the Lord with the inhabitants of this earth, from his own day to the end of time. But the people heeded not his words, and ultimately grew weary of his threatenings, and drove him from their midst. He hid himself in a cavity of a rock, coming forth in the night time to view the course of events, and occasionally appearing and repeating his warnings. While thus hidden, he wrote the history of contemporaneous events, and, year by year, watched the fulfilment of the word of the Lord, as the people gradually destroyed each other in unrelenting warfare. He lived to record the utter destruction of his people at Ramah, (Cumorah,) with the sole exception of Coriantumr, who survived as a witness to the unfailing word of God. We are not told whether Ether died or was translated. We incline, from his own words (Ether, 15:33), to the latter opinion. When he had finished his record, he hid the twenty-four golden plates on which it was engraven, in the place in which they were afterwards found by the people of king *Limhi*, (B. C. 123).

EVE. The mother of all living. Her name is mentioned three times in the Book of Mormon. (I Nephi, 5:11; II Nephi, 2:18, 19), in connection with the Creation and Fall.

EZIAS. An ancient Hebrew prophet, referred to by Nephi. Elder Orson Pratt suggests in a footnote that "Ezias may have been identical with Esaias, who lived contemporary with Abraham." See Doc. and Cov. 84: 11—13.

Flowers. 119 Gadianton.

FLOWERS. The only flowers mentioned by name in the Book of Mormon are lilies.

FRUIT. The fruits mentioned in the Book of Mormon are grapes and olives. Figs

GAD. A city burned with its inhabitants, at the time of the great convulsions that attended the crucifixion of the Savior. These people were extremely wicked, casting out and stoning and slaying the prophets who reproved them for their abominations. Indeed, there were none righteous left among them, so the Lord sent down fire from heaven and destroyed them, that their crimes might be hid from His face; and that the blood of the saints might no longer cry to Him from the ground against them. God is nowhere mentioned except in connection with its destruction, (III Nephi, 9: 10, 11).

GADIANDE. A city which, with all its vile inhabitants, who had persecuted and slain the prophets and people of God, was sunken deep in the earth at the time of the Messiah's crucifixion, and the surface of the land so changed that valleys and hills took its place. This calamity befell them, to use the words of the Savior "to hide their wickedness and abominations from before my face, that the blood of the prophets and the saints should not come up any more unto me against them." (III Nephi, 9: 8.) This is the only mention that is made of Gadiandi in the Book of Mormon; and consequently nothing is known of its situation.

GADIANTON. A Nephite apostate; the founder and first leader of the robber bands that bore his name. He is first mentioned in connection with the attempt by Kishkumen to kill *Helaman*, the Nephite chief judge, (B. C. 50). At that time Gadianton had organized his band, and bound its members together by the most horrible and blasphemous oaths and covenants, to stand by and protect each other in all their treasons, villainies and

crimes. These oaths and secret compacts had not been searched out of the old records by Gadianton, but that same being who had revealed them to Cain, the first murderer, had whispered them to him. Gadianton was a crafty, capable man, full of strategy and cunning; a flatterer, and expert in the use of many words; and at this time he desired to be elected chief judge of the Nephite commonwealth. To this ambition his followers gave full consent, as he promised them that, when elected, they should fill the offices of honor and profit at his disposal. It was decided in their secret meetings that Helaman should be slain to make way for Gadianton, and *Kishkumen*, one of his lieutenants, was chosen to do the murderous work. He made the attempt, but failed; Kishkumen himself being slain. Finding their envoy did not return, and learning that the officers of the law were searching for them, the band, under Gadianton's direction, fled into the hills and the wilderness, which became their places of retreat ever afterwards when they were threatened by the more righteous part of the community. (See Lamanites. (See Gadianton Robbers.) Of Gadianton's personal life we have no further record.

GADIANTON ROBBERS. Of all the factions that separated themselves from the Nephites, none worked so much injury to the people as did the bands of the Gadianton robbers. The very fact of their organization shows the deplorable condition of Nephite society; while their continuance and growth proclaims yet more loudly and emphatically how debased the community had become. The Gadiantons were at first (B. C. 52), apparently, a band of robbers and murderers, bound together by the most horrible oaths of secrecy and satanic covenants, to aid and shield each other in whatever sins and iniquities they might commit.

These covenants did not originate with Gadianton or any of his crew. They were as old as the days of Cain, into whose ear the Son of Perdition whispered these bloodthirsty and infernal suggestions. These same secret societies flourished among the Antediluvians, and had place with the Jaredites and other peoples of antiquity. In the end they invariably wrought ruin and destruction wherever they found a foothold. To their abominations can be traced the fall and extinction of both the Jaredite and Nephite races.

As time went on, the Gadiantons among the Nephites aspired to rule the republic. When, by their combinations, they could not carry their point at the elections, they would murder, or attempt to murder, any judge or other officer who was distasteful to them, and place a more acceptable man in his seat. So fell more than one of the Nephite chief judges. But they frequently had no need to do this, for as the people increased in iniquity they could easily carry the majority or the voice of the people with them. In this way several of their members were elected to the chief judgeship.

After the time of the conversion of the Lamanites by Lehi and Nephi, (B. C. 30), the Gadianton robbers took their place in the history of ancient America. The previous century had seen the righteous Nephites and Lamanites on one side, and the Gadiantons on the other. And, strange as it may appear, these robber bands received greater encouragement and attained to greater power among the Nephites than among the Lamanites; but the fact is, that in that era the Lamanites were a growing race, while the Nephites were a decaying one. Many wars ensued between these two divisions, ending sometimes in the temporary suppression of the robbers, as in the year B. C. 17. But they soon reappeared, as they did five years after the instance here mentioned (B. C.

12. The most assumptions of all these wars was the one that was waged during the earthly life of our Savior. It certainly commenced in the second year of His mortal existence, and continued with slight intermissions until the twenty-first. So powerful and arrogant had the robbers grown in that age that Giddianhi, their leader, in A. C. 16, wrote an epistle to Lachoneus the chief judge, calling upon the Nephites to submit themselves to the robbers and their ways; to accept their oaths and covenants; and in all things become like unto them. The presumption of the robber chief does not appear to have been without foundation, for so desperate had the condition of the people become that Lachoneus devised and carried out the stupendous movement of gathering them all, both Nephites and Lamanites, to one land, where they would be safe by consolidation, and be able to wear out the robbers by masterly inactivity. In this he succeeded, and the robber bands were destroyed by privation, famine, and the sword.

After the days of Jesus, the Gadiantons again appeared, when iniquity began to prevail; and by the year A. Q. 260 they had special over all the land. To their baneful influence may be attributed many of the atrocities and abominations that disgraced the last wars between the Nephites and Lamanites.

GADIONNAH. A wicked city, sunk in the earth in the dire convulsions that occurred on this continent at the time the Redeemer was crucified. In its place hills and valleys appeared, while deep in the bosom of the earth were buried its iniquitous inhabitants, that they might be hidden from the sight of Heaven, and that the blood of the prophets and saints whom they had slain might no more come up before the Lord (III Nephi, 9:8). This city is only mentioned in the Book of Mormon in connection with its destruction.

GALILEE. The northern division of Palestine; mentioned only in the Book of Mormon in a quotation from Isaiah (II Nephi, 19: 1).

GALLIM. A place mentioned twice in the Bible and once in the Book of Mormon, the latter in a quotation from the prophecies of Isaiah (II Nephi, 20: 30). Its situation is unknown.

GAZELEM. The name given to a servant of God, (Alma, 37: 23). The word Gazelem appears to have its roots in Gaz—a stone, and Aleim, a name of God as a revelator or interposer in the affairs of men. If this suggestion be correct, its roots admirably agree with its apparent meaning—a seer. The text reads: And the Lord said, I will prepare unto my servant Gazelem, a stone, which shall shine forth in darkness unto light, that I may discover unto them the works of their brethren; yea, their secret works, their works of darkness, and their wickedness and abominations.

GEBA. A city of Palestine, in the district apportioned to the tribe of Benjamin. It is only mentioned once in the Book of Mormon (II Nephi, 20: 29), in a quotation from the prophecies of Isaiah.

GEBIM. A village in Palestine, north of Jerusalem. It is mentioned but once in the Book of Mormon (II Nephi, 20: 31), in a quotation from Isaiah.

GIBEAH. The early home of Saul, king of Israel. It was situated within the limits of the tribe of Benjamin, and not far from Jerusalem. It is mentioned once in the Book of Mormon (II Nephi, 20: 29), in a quotation from Isaiah.

GID. During the campaign on the Pacific coast, in the year B. C. 63, Helaman, the son of Alma, commanded the armies of the Nephites, and king Ammoron those of the Lamanites. After the recapture of the city of Cumeni, the number of prisoners of war in the hands of the Nephites was so great, and so given were they to break

out, assault their guards and attempt to escape, that their disposal became a matter of serious consideration with the Nephite commanders. It was finally decided to send a large number of them to Zarahemla, under a strong escort, commanded by an officer named Gid.

On the second day of their march, the Nephite scouts brought word to Gid that a large Lamanite force was approaching, on their way to relieve Cumeni. The Lamanite prisoners heard of the proximity of their fellow countrymen, and in the hope which it inspired, they took courage and determined to make a desperate effort for liberty. They made a united break, rushing upon their guards and endeavoring by the greatness of their numbers to overthrow them. The attempt proved very disastrous, for most of the prisoners were slain, while a few managed to escape to the armies of their countrymen. The prisoners having all escaped or been killed, there was no further reason for Gid and his company to continue their march to the Nephite capital, they therefore retraced their steps to the main body of the army.

Their return was most fortunate. For in their absence the Lamanites had been greatly strengthened, most probably by the same force that passed by near to the place where the prisoners held by Gid had revolted. Emboldened by this reinforcement, the Lamanite commander made a sudden and furious attack upon Helaman, which he was illy prepared to resist. A portion of his troops were already wavering, when Gid appeared. His arrival changed the fortunes of the day, the Nephites were victorious, they continued to hold possession of Cumeni, but their loss was very great. This is one of the battles in which Helaman's youthful Ammonite warriors made themselves conspicuous by their unfaltering faith and unflinching courage.

Later in the year, Gid commanded a small division of the Nephite army in the battle in which the city of Manti was recaptured. Helaman, being anxious to obtain possession of this city, sat down before it with his army, which was but a small one. The Lamanites, fearing the presence of this force would cut off their line of communication, attempted to drive them away, and so confident were they, that they did not take proper precautions to preserve the city. The main body of Helaman's army retreated before their rapid advance, while two small divisions, commanded by Gid and Teomer, secreted themselves in the adjoining wilderness; and when the impetuous Lamanite commander had led his troops the necessary distance, they surprised the city, overpowered the guards, and obtained permanent possession at a small cost of life. Gid is no more mentioned after this in the Book of Mormon.

GID, A Nephite city, situated on the east borders by the seashore, that is, on the Atlantic coast; apparently not far from the cities of Mulek and Bountiful. In Amalekiah's great raid, in B. C. 67, through the eastern portions of the Nephite possessions, he captured, garrisoned, and fortified Gid. He also made it the depot for the detention of the Nephite prisoners of war. In B. C. 63, Moroni, by stratagem, placed arms in the hands of these prisoners, women and larger children, as well as men, and they, in connection with the Nephite forces without, overpowered the Lamanites, and took possession of the city. The Lamanite prisoners were used by Moroni in increasing the strength of the fortifications at Gid, which being done, they were removed, for like service, to the city of Bountiful. The only other time that Gid is mentioned is in connection with the missionary labors of Nephi and Lehi, the sons of Helaman. They first ministered in Bountiful, and from there proceeded to Gid, (B. C. 31).

GIDDONAH. A Nephite of the first and second century B. C. He was the son of Ishmael and the father of the prophet Amulek. Nothing more than this is known of him, unless he was the Giddonah, who was the High Priest in the land of Gideon, which is not improbable.

GIDDONAH. The presiding High Priest of the Nephite Church in the Land of Gideon (B. C. 75). The only time that his name is mentioned is on the occasion when Korihor, the notorious anti-Christ, was brought before him and the Chief Judge in that land. On this occasion Giddonah appears to have acted with great wisdom and prudence. Finding that Korihor would revile against God, the atonement, the coming of Christ, the acts of the priesthood, etc., and in the hardness of his heart would lie, traduce, and blaspheme in a breath, Giddonah refused to be drawn into a controversy, and simply heard Korihor's outrageous plea in silence, as did also the Chief Justice. Then, considering the matter was one that should be submitted to the highest officers in the whole land, they delivered the impostor into the hands of the proper officers, with instructions to convey him to the city of Zarahemla, and bring him before the presiding civil and ecclesiastical authorities, which was done. It is not improbable that he was the father of the Prophet Amulek (Alma, 10: 2).

GIDDIANHI. A Gadianton robber chief and general, who lived contemporaneously with the Savior. He was a leader of great boldness and ability, and in his days the robbers gained many advantages over the Nephites. So much so, that the existence of the Nephite race was imperiled. In A. C. 16, Giddianhi had the effrontery to write to Lachoneus, the chief governor of the Nephites, threatening to utterly destroy the people if they did not surrender to the robbers, accept their secret oaths and become like them in all things.

This epistle, which gives an interesting insight into the condition of the times, is found in III Nephi, chapter 4. Lachoneus did not hearken to the epistle of Giddianhi, but perceiving the desperate straits in which his people were placed, issued a proclamation directing them to leave their various homes throughout the two continents, and all gather in one vast host, in a place selected in the lands of Zarahemla and Bountiful, bringing with them everything that would help to sustain the besieging forces of the robbers. The people obeyed, and in the trust of the Lord awaited the coming of the foe. In the latter end of A. C. 18, the armies of the robbers were prepared for the war, and they began to sally forth from the wilderness and the mountains, and from their other strongholds, and to occupy and revel in the deserted homes and lands of the Nephites. But difficulties soon stared them in the face, the greatest of which was the want of food. As the Nephites had removed everything edible, the robbers' only source of supply was the game in the wilderness, when soon proved insufficient. Thus pressed, in the year A. C. 19, Giddianhi gave command to his armies to attack the Nephites. It was in the sixth month of the year (September, we presume), that this command was carried out. Terrible, we are told, was the appearance of the robber hosts. They wore a lamb skin, dyed in blood, about their loins; their heads were shaven, but covered with armor—headplates, as they are called. When the Nephites perceived them coming they bowed before the Lord in prayer. The robbers, seeing their action, counted it as a sign of fear, and set up a horrible shout and rushed upon them. The slaughter was terrible; never had there been so much blood shed in a single fight since the day that Lehi's children first inhabited the land. At last the Nephites were victorious, and pursued their foes to the borders of the wilderness, giving no quarter. Giddianhi himself fought with great courage, but being weary through his exertions, was overtaken in the retreat and slain. Zemnarihah succeeded him as commander of the robbers.

GIDEON. A Nephite patriot, slain by Nehor in B. C. 91. Gideon was evidently born in the land of Lehi-Nephi, and in the rebellion that occurred in that land against the iniquitous king Noah, Gideon, being a strong and zealous man, took a leading part. We judge from the course he then pursued, and the whole tenor of his after life, that he had no hand in the martyrdom of Abinadi, or in Noah's other crimes. When the minority of the people revolted, Gideon, being exceedingly angry, drew his sword and sought to kill the king. Noah, realizing he was about to be overpowered, fled to the tower near the temple. Thither Gideon quickly followed. The king mounted to the top, and there his eye accidentally caught sight of an army of Lamanites in the land of Shemlon. In the terror caused by this unexpected sight, he appealed to Gideon's patriotism and besought him to spare him. Gideon consented, and Noah, in mortal terror, ordered his people to flee into the wilderness from before the advancing hosts of the Lamanites.

The people obeyed their king's command, and with their wives and children fled into the wilderness. But the forces of the Lamanites, unencumbered with women and children, soon overtook them. Then the coward king commanded the men to continue their flight and leave their wives and children to the mercy of the enemy. Some obeyed and fled, others would not, but preferred to stay and perish with those of whom they were the natural protectors. Gideon was among the latter. Those who stayed, in their terror, when the Lamanites drew near, sent their fair daughters to plead with their enemies for their lives. This act saved them. For the dark warriors of Laman

131　Gideon, Land of.

chief, with a large force of volunteers, which he had gathered on his march from Bountiful. The united forces gave battle to Pachus, recaptured Zarahemla, and replaced Pahoran on the judgment seat

In B. C. 6, Samuel, the Lamanite, pronounced a woe against the city of Gideon for the wickedness and abominations that were in her (Helaman 13: 15), but we have no account of the manner of her destruction at the time of the crucifixion of the Redeemer.

GIDEON, LAND OF. In a valley on the east of the Sidon was built, during the early days of the republic, an important city, which was named after the martyr Gideon. The valley itself was also known by the same name, and is frequently called the land of Gideon, for we find no evidence to lead to the conclusion that the land extended beyond the valley. Nearly all that we know of this region is contained in a single passage (Alma 7: 7), which states that Alma left Zarahemla and went over upon the east of the river Sidon, into the valley of Gideon, there having been a city built which was called the city of Gideon, which was in the valley that was called Gideon, being called after the man who was slain by the hand of Nehor with the sword.

From the references in the historical narrative we incline to the opinion that this valley lay either directly east, or somewhat to the south of the city of Zarahemla. Travelers coming from the north are never mentioned as passing through it on their way to Zarahemla, unless they had a purpose in so doing, as in the case where Moroni marched from the northeast to the relief of Chief Judge Pahoran (Alma, 62). In the same chapter it is stated that Moroni and Pahoran " went down " from Gideon to Zarahemla, which, following the course of the Sidon, would be northward.

After the battle with the Amlicites, in the

were so charmed with the beauty of the women that they spared all their lives. Yet they took them captives, carried them back to Lehi-Nephi, and gave them permission to retain that land, but under the conditions that they should surrender king Noah, and deliver up one-half of everything they possessed, and continue this tribute of one-half of their property year by year.

Gideon now sent men to search for Noah, that he might be delivered up to the Lamanites. They found that the men who were with Noah, being ashamed of their cowardly flight, swore that they would return; and if their wives and children, and the men who remained with them, had been killed, they would have revenge. The king commanded that they should not return, at which they became very angry with him, and burned him to death, as he had done Abinadi. When the men who put Noah to death were about to return to the land of Nephi, they met Gideon and his party, and informed him of the end of Noah and the escape of the priests; and when they heard the news that Gideon brought, they also rejoiced much that their wives and children had been spared by the Lamanites.

Noah was succeeded by his son Limhi. Gideon appears in his day to have been an officer of high standing in the Nephite forces, and a man of much wisdom and intelligence. In the war that resulted from the seizure of a number of Lamanite maidens by the priests of Noah, Gideon took a prominent part in bringing about a cessation of hostilities. It was he who suggested who the men really were that committed this vile act. (See Amulon.) In later years, when the people of Limhi escaped from the Lamanites, and returned to Zarahemla under the guidance of Ammon, Gideon took a leading part, by his advice and example, in effecting their deliverance, and directing that march. We next read of Gideon when he had become exceedingly

i

Gideon, Valley of.　132　　Gidgiddoni.

fifth year of the judges, the Nephites, under Alma, pursued them until they reached the valley of Gideon, and there the Nephites pitched their tents. Learning of the approach of an army of Lamanites, Alma moved his troops towards Zarahemla, in order to protect the capital city.

GIDEON, VALLEY OF. See land of Gideon.

GIDGIDDONAH. A Nephite general, who commanded a corps of ten thousand men in the last great struggle between the Nephites and the Lamanites. He, with all his command, was slain in the final series of battles in the land Cumorah (A. C. 385), when the Nephite nation was annihilated.

GIDGIDDONI. A prophet-general of the Nephites, of the time of Christ; he was commander-in-chief of the armies of the commonwealth, in the days when Lachoneus, the elder, was chief judge and governor, and appears to a certain extent to have shared with that illustrious man the powers of the government. Besides being one of the ablest military commanders that ever led the Nephites to victory, he was also a great prophet, and his inspired teachings, wise counsels and timely reproofs were as valuable in preserving that people from destruction as was his skill, strategy, resolution and courage as a general. Gidgiddoni was chosen commander of the Nephite forces the same year that Lachoneus decided, because of the imperiled condition of the Nephites from the ever-recurring attacks of the robbers, to gather all the people in one region (A C. 16). In this gigantic, almost unparalleled labor, Lachoneus was zealously supported by Gidgiddoni, under whose direction the assembled hosts fortified their land of refuge. It was not until the next year that all the people had assembled together, for it proved a slow and tedious work to bring millions of people, many for thousands of miles, with all

old. He was still actively engaged in the service of the Lord. He was a teacher in the Church, yet we cannot help thinking that, like many in these days, though acting as a teacher, he held a higher priesthood. One day he met, in the streets of the city of Zarahemla, an apostate named Nehor, who had grown very popular, and, with his popularity, very conceited, headstrong, and ambitious. He having built up a church composed of persons who accepted his pernicious doctrines. On this occasion Gideon plead with him to desist from his evil ways, and strongly remonstrated against the course he was taking. Nehor, ill-used to such opposition, drew his sword and slew the aged teacher. For this crime he was arrested, tried, convicted and executed. (B. C. 91.) Gideon's memory was held in great respect among the Nephites, and one of their most important cities was named after him.

GIDEON, CITY OF. An important city of the Nephites, situated in a valley of the same name on the eastern side of the river Sidon, and not far from the city of Zarahemla. (See land of Gideon.) It was named in memory of the aged patriarch, slain by Nehor. In B. C. 82, Alma, the High Priest, made this city a missionary visit, and set the Church therein in order, after which he returned to his home in Zarahemla. In B. C. 75, Korihor, the anti-Christ, visited Gideon, and for a short time taught his pernicious doctrines, but he was taken before the High Priest and Chief Judge of that land, examined, and sent over to Zarahemla, to be judged by Alma, the Chief Judge of all the Nephite lands. In B. C. 62, the king-men, under Pachus, drove Pahoran, the Chief Judge, out of Zarahemla, who established himself in Gideon, and issued a proclamation calling the people of the surrounding regions to arms. The patriots assembled at Gideon, where they were, ere long, joined by Moroni, the Nephite commander-in-

133　　Gidgiddoni.

their movable substance, and with a supply of seven years' provisions. In the latter part of the following year (A. C. 18), the robbers sallied out of their hiding places in the deserts and mountains and occupied the cities and lands temporarily deserted by the citizens. But they found no means of subsistence there, and game soon grew scarce in the wilderness. Active warfare was their only resort, so Giddianhi, their leader, determined, if possible, to force his way into the country held by the Nephites. A desperate battle followed, Gidgiddoni acting on the defensive; the slaughter was more terrible than in any previous battle between the descendants of Lehi. Ultimately Gidgiddoni was slain, the robbers repulsed and pursued to the borders of the wilderness (A. C. 19.) The robbers made no further attack the next year, but having chosen one Zemnarihah as their chief, in A. C. 21, he so disposed of his bands as to surround the Nephites. His attempt was ineffectual. The region occupied by the Nephites was far too extended to admit of a siege being successful. The robbers also were short of food. Gidgiddoni perceived that this was his opportunity, time and again he made successful sorties, slaying tens of thousands of the enemy and harassing by continual movements those who remained. At last, the robbers determined to flee to the north and there concentrate in one region. Gidgiddoni, learning of their intentions, and knowing their feeble bodily condition through lack of food, determined to intercept them. This he successfully accomplished, thousands of the marauders were slain, among the prisoners was Zemnarihah, who was afterwards hanged. The people continued in their gathered condition in Zarahemla and Bountiful until A. C. 26. Then, taking with them the provisions they had not consumed, and their gold, silver and precious things, they returned to their old homes. A short period of prosperity followed, the great roads were repaired, old cities were rebuilt, and new ones founded, and many other improvements made for the benefit of the people, in all of which Gidgiddoni and Lachoneus were the leaders. His connection with these labors (A. C. 28), is the last reference made to Gidgiddoni in the Book of Mormon. The soldiers of Gidgiddoni succeeded in taking as prisoners all the robbers that were not killed. The word of God was preached to them, and those who repented of their sins, and covenanted to cease their evil practices, were set at liberty. The remainder were condemned for their crimes and punished according to law. This entirely broke up these bands of murderers and robbers, and peace and righteousness again prevailed.

GILEAH. A Jaredite military commander who contended with Coriantumr for the throne. He succeeded his brother Shared in the command of the armies opposed to Coriantumr. Their first battle occurred in the wilderness of Akish, when many thousands were slain. Gilead remained for a time in the wilderness, watched by Coriantumr; but eventually he made a night attack on the enemy, and the latter, being drunken, suffered great loss. Gilead then placed himself on the throne of Coriantumr, and both commanders buoyed themselves in gathering men to strengthen their respective armies. Gilead, who had the sympathy of some of the secret combinations, received great strength during the two years they were thus engaged, but he was slain by his own high priest as he sat on the throne; an evidence of the intensely corrupt state of society among the Jaredites of that time (towards the close of the seventh century B. C).

GILGAH. One of the four sons (his name is given the second place) of Jared. He was in all probability born in Asia before his father and associates commenced their wonderful journey to America. All we know of him is that when the

day. From this time the Nephites paid considerable attention to ship-building, and the sea became the highway between the two continents.

HAMATH. The principal city of Upper Syria (now Hamah). It is mentioned twice in the Book of Mormon, in Nephi's quotations from the prophecies of Isaiah (II Nephi, 20: 9; 21: 11).

HEARTHOM. A king of the Jaredites; he was the son of Lib, whom he succeeded. When he had reigned twenty-four years the kingdom was wrested from him, and he was held in captivity by the successful party all the remainder of his life. Only one of his sons is mentioned, whose name was Heth. Of Hearthom's private character the record is silent.

HEBREW. This word only appears in one verse of the Book of Mormon (Mormon, 9: 33), where it occurs three times; always referring to a language used in connection with the engravings on the Nephite records. The language to which this name was applied in the days of Mormon and Moroni was greatly changed from the Hebrew spoken by the Israelites at the time Lehi left Jerusalem, nearly a thousand years before.

HELAM. A Nephite of the land of Lehi-Nephi, in the days of king Noah. He accepted the teachings of Alma, the elder, and was the first man baptized by him in the waters of Mormon. One thing remarkable about his baptism is that both he and Alma were together buried in the water; and they arose and came forth out of the water rejoicing, being filled with the Spirit of God. We have no further mention of Helam; but from the fact that the land (eight days' journey from Mormon) to which Alma and the saints soon fled, received the name of Helam from them, it is highly probable that Helam was one of the leading officers of the church established by Alma, and greatly respected by the people.

HELAM, CITY OF. The city built by the

Jaredites desired a king, he was one of those to whom this honor was offered, and who refused. From the general summary given us of the character of the people at that generation, we have every reason to believe he was a righteous man.

GILGAL. A Nephite general who commanded a corps of ten thousand men in the last great struggle between the Nephites and the Lamanites. He, with all his command, was slain in the final series of battles in the land Cumorah. (A. C. 385), when the Nephite nation was annihilated.

GILGAL, CITY OF. A wicked city of the Nephites, which is only mentioned in connection with its destruction in the awful convulsions of nature that took place on this continent when the Savior was crucified. By the power of God it sunk and its corrupt inhabitants were buried in the depths of the earth. No clue is given to its locality. (III Nephi, 9: 6.)

GILGAL, VALLEY OF. A valley mentioned as the locality of several desperate battles in the last Jaredite war. The first of these battles was between the armies of Shared and those of Coriantumr; it lasted three days. The losses on both sides were exceedingly heavy, and ended in a victory for Coriantumr, who pursued the enemy as far as the plains of Heshlon. There, another hotly contested fight took place, in which the tide of fortune turned, and Coriantumr was driven back to the valley of Gilgal. Here, a third conflict ensued, in which Shared was killed and Coriantumr wounded. Nothing is said in the Book of Ether that gives any clue to the locality in which Gilgal was situated.

GIMGIMNO, CITY OF. One of the iniquitous cities of the Nephites, whose inhabitants had persecuted, cast out and slain the prophets and saints of the Lord, and for that cause was destroyed by being sunk, with all its sin-stained

people of Alma, the elder, in the land of Helam, eight days' journey from the waters of Mormon, in the direction of Zarahemla, when that people fled from the murderous persecutions of king Noah. After a few years of peaceful occupancy it was discovered and taken possession of by the Lamanites, and placed by the king under the rule of Amulon, one of the former priests of Noah. By him and his associates the Christian people of Helam were outrageously abused, until the Lord, in His mercy, opened up the way for their escape. These events took place, as near as can be told, between the years B. C. 147 and B. C. 122. Nothing is recorded of the history of this city after it was deserted by the people of Helam.

HELAM, LAND OF. The country immediately surrounding the city of Helam. It lay somewhere between the cities of Lehi-Nephi and Zarahemla; eight days' journey, for emigrants, from the former city, and fourteen from the latter. It is only mentioned in the Book of Mormon in connection with its occupancy for a few years by the persecuted people of Alma. After they left, it fell into the hands of the Lamanites and became a subdivision of the land of Nephi.

HELAMAN. One of the sons of the Nephite king, Benjamin. He is only mentioned once, and then in connection with his brothers, Mosiah and Helorum. Nothing is said with regard to his private character.

HELAMAN, THE SON OF ALMA. We have no account of the date or place or birth of this prophet and general of the Nephites; but as his father's permanent residence was in the city of Zarahemla, it is not unreasonable to suppose that it was there that he first saw the light of day. He is not introduced to the reader of the Book of Mormon until he had arrived at the age of manhood (B. C. 75), when it is stated that Alma took his two younger sons with him on his mission to

citizens, in the great earthquakes, etc., that convulsed this continent when Jesus was crucified. Hills and valleys occupied the place where Gimgimno had before stood. (III Nephi, 9: 8).

GOMORRAH. Sister city to Sodom. Its name is mentioned once (II Nephi, 23: 19) in a quotation from the prophecies of Isaiah.

GRAINS. The grains mentioned in the Book of Mormon are wheat, barley, corn and peas. Chaff is also named.

HAGOTH. A Nephite ship-builder and promoter of emigration. He was a very ingenious mechanic, and in the thirty-seventh year of the Judges (B. C. 55), he settled on the Pacific side of the Isthmus of Panama, where the lands Desolation and Bountiful ran parallel. There he built an exceedingly large ship, and launched it on the Pacific Ocean. This ship he filled with men, women, and children, after which it set sail northward; and having delivered its living freight, it returned the next year, again to start northward loaded with passengers and provisions. He also built other ships, which engaged in the same trade. Some of these never reached their destination, they were either lost in the depths of the sea or were carried by storms and adverse winds to some of the many groups of islands that dot the Pacific Ocean. In this manner it is more than probable the Sandwich Islands were peopled with the ancestors of the present inhabitants. The loss of these vessels did not stop the outflow by sea northward. The voyage obviated the tedious land journey through the regions now known as Central America and Mexico. At what point these emigrants disembarked is solely a matter of conjecture, and it is highly probable that the configuration of the western coast, northward from the Isthmus, was very different, previous to the immense convulsions and upheavals that occurred at the death of Christ, to what it is to-

the Zoramites, while Helaman was left in Zarahemla, most probably to take charge of the interests of the Church in that land during the absence of the presiding high priest, his father.

When Alma returned home from this mission, he called his three sons to him, and gave to each his blessing and instructions. His admonitions to Helaman are recorded at great length in the inspired pages. Alma therein reviews his own life and the history of the Nephites, prophesying many things with regard to the future of that people. He also exhorts Helaman to be diligent as a preacher of God's holy word, and to lead an individual life of righteousness as an example to the Church. At this time he likewise gave him strict charge with regard to the keeping of the records, to continue the annals of the nation thereon, to preserve them sacred, and to prevent certain portions (containing the secret oaths, covenants and other works of darkness of the Jaredites,) being published to the world, lest others be ensnared by the same abominations.

After receiving their separate instructions, Helaman, as also his two brothers and their father, went forth among the Nephites declaring the word according to the spirit of prophecy and revelation; and they preached after the holy order of God, by which they were called.

In the year following, the Lord took Alma, as he had previously taken Moses. The prophet, being doubtless aware of his speedy departure from this dwelling-place of humanity, took his son Helaman, and having received the latter's confession of faith in the coming of the Christ, he blessed him, and prophesied of things that should occur even until the people of Nephi should become extinct. Having done this, he blessed the Church and its faithful members, and departed out of the land, never by mortal eyes to be seen again. His son Helaman and others then went through the cities of the Nephites and regulated the affairs of the Church; but owing to the pride of many who would not give heed to the instructions given them, nor walk uprightly, dissension arose, which in after years led to numerous evils, among the greatest of which was a long-continued war, or series of wars, between the faithful Nephites on one side, and the apostates, and afterwards the Lamanites, on the other. Still, for four years, Helaman and his associate priesthood were enabled to maintain order in the Church, and many died in full faith of the Gospel, and the joyous hope of its never-ending rewards; indeed, during that period there was much peace and great prosperity enjoyed by those who remained faithful.

The leader of those who apostatized from the true faith and commenced to wage war against their former brethren, was named Amalickiah. Being defeated by Moroni, the Nephite commander, and his army crushed (B. C. 73), he went over to the Lamanites, and stirred them up to anger against the race to which he belonged. For some time he was unsuccessful in this attempt, as the Lamanites had too lately received severe defeats to be anxious again to try the fortunes of war. By his craft, however, he removed every obstacle, until he was acknowledged the king of the descendants of Laman. Towards the end of the year his armies advanced into the land of Ammonihah, and from that time the war was carried on with slight intermissions and with varying success, for about thirteen years (to B. C. 60), when the Lamanites had been driven out of the possessions of the Nephites and peace was restored. Owing to the utter prostration of the Lamanites, hostilities were not resumed until the year B. C. 53, when they again made an incursion into the Nephite territory, but were speedily driven back to their own lands, suffering great loss. It

was during this thirteen years' war that Helaman appears most prominently in the record of his nation, and in the annals of his life is contained one of the sublimest and sweetest episodes in Nephite history.

The war (B. C. 66) had been working disastrously to the Nephites, when the people of Ammon, feeling that they were a burden rather than a help to their benefactors, though indeed they were not, desired to be released from their oath and covenant "never again to take up deadly weapons against their fellows." They desired in this hour of extreme peril to take up arms in defense of the liberties of their adopted country. From this rash step Helaman and his brethren dissuaded them, lest by so doing they should imperil their eternal salvation. But they had sons that had grown far towards manhood, who had not entered into this covenant, and consequently were not shut off from participating in the dangers and glories of the war. So with their fathers' and mothers' consent, faith, prayers and words of encouragement, two thousand of these youths were mustered into the Nephite army. These striplings were all men of truth, faith, soberness and integrity, and were conspicuous for their courage, strength and activity, Being organized, they desired that Helaman, for whom they had great love and respect, should be their leader. He consented, and at their head marched to the relief of the forces of the republic that were struggling against considerable odds on the southern borders of the Nephite dominions, from the shores of the Pacific Ocean eastward.

Helaman found the Nephite forces, numbering about six thousand warriors, in a somewhat deplorable condition. The Lamanites, in the strength of greatly superior numbers, had captured the cities of Manti, Cumeni, Zeezrom and Antiparah, and held possession of the country round about.

These cities had not been taken without much bloodshed on both sides. The Nephites had especially lost large numbers in prisoners, who were generally put to death by their captors, except the superior officers, who were sent to the land of Nephi. Antipus, the Nephite commander, was locked up in the city of Judea, where, dispirited and weakened by excessive toil and fighting, his troops were making a desperate and painful effort to fortify the city. The arrival of Helaman and his corps brought hope and joy again to their hearts, and renewed vigor to their endeavors.

King Ammoron, learning that reinforcements had reached the defenders of Judea, ordered all active operations to be suspended for a season. The suspension was most providential to the soldiers of Antipus, as it gave them time to finish the work of fortifying the beleaguered city, and also to recruit their health and energies. By the commencement of the following year the works of defense were completed, and the Nephites became anxious for the onslaught they had so greatly dreaded a few months previous. But they were disappointed. The Lamanites did not feel sufficiently strong to renew aggressive movements. They contented themselves with occupying the Nephite cities they had already captured. In the second month of this year (B. C. 65), a convoy of two thousand additional warriors arrived from the land of Zarahemla, with abundant provisions. The Nephites in the city of Judea were now ten thousand strong, and they were anxious for a forward movement in order, if possible, to retake some of their cities which were in the hands of the enemy.

Antipus and Helaman resolved on a ruse to entice the Lamanites from behind their fortifications. It was decided that Helaman and his command should march out of Judea with the apparent intention of carrying supplies to one of

the cities in the borders of the Nephites, that was built near the sea shore. In executing this manœuvre, they purposely passed at no great distance from the city of Antiparah, in which was stationed the most numerous of the Lamanite armies, in the hope that the Lamanites would notice that their numbers were few, and thus be led to attack them. The stratagem proved successful. The garrison of Antiparah issued forth in pursuit of Helaman, who, with all haste, retreated into the wilderness northward, his intent being to draw his pursuers as far as possible from Antiparah. When the Lamanites had started in pursuit of Helaman, Antipus, with a considerable portion of his army, marched out of the city of Judea and fell in the Lamanites' rear. The retreat soon became a race. The Lamanites crowded forward with all possible expedition in the endeavor to reach Helaman before Antipus caught them. Helaman, on the other hand, used his utmost energy to keep out of their clutches. Neither of the three bodies turned to the right or to the left, but kept straight on in the effort to outmarch their foes. Night came and went, and on the morrow the double pursuit was still kept up. Another night fell, but not one dare turn from his course.

On the third morning the race for life and victory was again renewed, but before long the Lamanites, concluding they could not overtake Helaman, suddenly stopped, and awaited the coming of Antipus and his weary soldiers, whom they unexpectedly attacked with great fury, slew Antipus and several of his captains, threw the Nephite troops into great confusion and forced them to commence a retreat. In the meantime, Helaman discovered that he was no longer pursued, and not knowing the reason, was in doubt what course to take. He called a hasty council of war, at which it was determined to return at once, and risk the chances of being caught in a trap by the crafty

Lamanites. The statement which Helaman makes regarding the conduct of his young soldiers at this council is very interesting. After he had explained the situation to them, he inquired: What say ye, my sons, will ye go against them in battle? Without hesitancy they answered in the affirmative, saying: Father, behold our God is with us, and He will not suffer that we shall fall; then let us go forth; we would not slay our brethren if they would let us alone; therefore let us go lest they should overpower the army of Antipus. Here Helaman remarks: Now they never had fought, yet they did not fear death; and they did think more of the liberty of their fathers than they did upon their lives; yea, they had been taught by their mothers that if they did not doubt that God would deliver them. And they rehearsed unto me the words of their mothers, saying, we do not doubt our mothers knew it.

Helaman and his sons arrived none too soon on the field of battle. The soldiers of Antipus were already fleeing before their more numerous foes, but the valor and impetuosity of the youthful Ammonites were irresistible. They fell on the Lamanite rear with a daring and miraculous strength, possessed only by men who put their whole trust in God. Thus attacked in the rear, the Lamanites immediately halted, changed front, and threw their whole force against the Ammonites. The surviving officers of Antipus' army, finding that Helaman had come to their rescue, stopped their retreat, reorganized their scattered bands, and renewed the attack. The Lamanites were compelled to succumb; they could not resist the desperate courage of the Nephites that was driving them in at both front and rear. Their legions all surrendered, and, by Helaman's orders, were sent as prisoners of war to Zarahemla.

And what about the young warriors of Ammon? So great was their faith, so great

its workings, that when, after the battle, Helaman called the roll of his youthful heroes, not one was missing. The faith sown by their mothers' words had borne fruit—they were all preserved. To their undaunted prowess, for they fought as if with the strength of God, the Nephites unhesitatingly accorded the glory of the day.

Still the hardly contested war continued Six thousand men, with provisions, reached Helaman from Zarahemla and the regions round about (B. C. 63), besides sixty more young Ammonites, who had grown sufficiently vigorous to assume the hardships of military life. The city of Cumeni shortly afterwards capitulated through the want of provisions, its supplies having been continuously cut off by Helaman's troops. This surrender threw so many prisoners on the hands of the Nephites that they were unable to guard or feed them. An officer named Gid, with a sufficient force, was detailed to convey them to Zarahemla, but on their way, passing near an invading body of Lamanites, the prisoners made a desperate attempt to escape. A few succeeded in getting away, but the greater number were slain by their guards. Gid and the escort having no further occasion to go on to Zarahemla, returned to Helaman.

His arrival was most opportune, for Ammoron, having received large reinforcements, suddenly attacked the Nephites, and was driving all their corps from their positions, except the youthful Ammonites, who stood firm as a rock, when the arrival of Gid and his company turned the tide of battle. The young warriors again received the warm praise of their father and general. They had remained firm and undaunted through all the perils of the fight, obeying and performing every command with the exactness and coolness of veterans. In the hottest of the encounter they never forgot their mothers' words, nor their heavenly Father's protecting blessing. Though in this fierce conflict, wherein they undoubtedly bore the brunt of the enemy's savage onslaughts, every one was wounded, even that two hundred fainted for loss of blood, yet not one was slain, and their preservation was marvelous in the eyes of their fellow-soldiers.

After this battle the Nephites retained the city of Cumeni, while the Lamanites retreated eastward to Manti, which was situated on the upper waters of the Sidon. Nor was it for several months that that city could be taken, as, owing to internal dissensions at the Nephite capital, and the attempt on the part of some of the people to overthrow the republic and establish a monarchy. Pahoran, the chief judge, was unable to supply the necessary provisions and reinforcements.

In this strait, Helaman and his fellow-officers called on the Lord in fervent prayer, which was not unanswered. They received assurances of deliverance and victory. These blessed assurances inspired fresh faith and infused renewed courage in the war-weary hearts of those not given over to the love of carnage. Fired with the determination, by God's grace, to conquer, they entered on a campaign against the city of Manti, which by strategy they captured before the end of the year (B. C. 63). The moral effect of this victory was so great, that the Lamanites retreated into the wilderness, evacuating the whole of the Nephite territory on the west, but unfortunately taking with them, as prisoners, many women and children. Such was the condition of affairs when Helaman wrote to Moroni, the Nephite commander-in-chief, who was directing the campaign on the eastern side of the continent, and it is from this letter that the above details of the war on the Pacific slope are condensed.

For more than a year Moroni could not send the needed help to Helaman. The rebels in Zarahemla had driven the chief judge out of the city,

and he had taken refuge in Gideon. From there he wrote to Moroni to come to his assistance, which that officer did at the earliest possible moment, leaving the armies in the northeast under the command of Lehi and Teancum. As he advanced he rallied the people on his line of march to the defense of the liberties of the republic, and was so successful that, after having joined the chief judge, Pahoran, he succeeded in overthrowing the "king men," killing their leader, Pachus, and completely crushing the rebellion. This being accomplished, he sent 6,000 men with the necessary provisions to reinforce Helaman (B. C. 61).

The campaign during this year, along the Atlantic coast, was a decisive one. The Lamanites, in many stubborn battles, were driven from city to city, until they were forced out of every one that they had captured, during the progress of the war, from the Nephites. On the west coast they do not appear to have renewed hostilities. The consequence was, that in the next year peace was established in all the land, not a Lamanite warrior remaining on Nephite soil. Then Pahoran returned to his judgment seat, and Helaman recommenced his labors in the ministry (B. C. 61).

The long continued and savage war just closed had brought various evils to the Church, in many parts of the land it may be said to have been disorganized. The occupancy of so many of the Nephite cities by the unbelieving Lamauites had produced numerous demoralizing effects; murders, contentions, dissensions, and all manner of iniquity had become rife, and the hearts of the people became hardened, yet not altogether so, for there were some who acknowledged the hand of the Lord in all their afflictions, and these humbled themselves in the depths of humility; and because of the prayers of these righteous ones, the people were spared

Such was the state of affairs when Helaman

went forth to call the people to repentance and set the Church in order. In this blessed work he had much success, and with the help of his brethren he again established the Church of God throughout all the land. These labors he continued until the time of his death, and his joy therein was greatly increased by the continued faithfulness of the people, who, notwithstanding their repentance, they remained humble, fervent in prayer and diligent in works of righteousness. Such was the happy condition of the people of Nephi when Helaman died (B. C. 57), he having survived his illustrious father sixteen years. And Shiblon, his brother, took possession of the sacred things that had been delivered unto Helaman by Alma."

HELAMAN, THE SON OF HELAMAN. The life of this patriarch is not given with the same details in the inspired record, as are those of his father, and his illustrious son Nephi. In the year B. C. 53, he was entrusted with the care of the sacred plates by his uncle Shiblon, and three years later (B. C. 50) he was elected by the Nephite people to be their chief judge, in which office he administered the law with justice and equity until the year B. C. 39, when he died. He had two sons, whom he named after the first fathers of his people—Nephi and Lehi. It was his eldest son, the righteous and faithful Nephi, who succeeded him on the judgment seat, and who also took charge of the sacred plates and the other holy things that accompanied them.

The few years that preceded the elevation of Helaman to the judgment seat, were among the most important in Nephite history, for at that time arose that terrible and devilish organization, the Gadianton robbers, who for so long cursed the inhabitants of ancient America.

Helaman being a God-fearing, just man, his election was very distasteful to the Gadianton

band and his sympathizers. They resolved to slay him, as they had before slain the younger Pahoran, and place Gadianton on the judgment seat in his stead. To accomplish this, the same vile instrument was chosen—Kishkumen. But the protecting hand of the great Jehovah was over and round about Helaman, and He preserved him from the assassin's knife. A servant of Helaman (possibly a detective commissioned in such times of peril to watch the movements of the dangerous classes,) by disguise became acquainted with the doings of the robber band, and of their intentions towards his master. As Kishkumen was on his way to fulfil his bloody work, this servant, whose name is not recorded, met him, and gave him one of their secret signs. This admitted him into the confidence of the assassin, who explained his errand, and asked to be conducted privately into the judgment hall where Helaman was then sitting in the performance of his duties. This was agreed upon; the two proceeded to where the murderer expected to find his victim. The strategy of the servant had disarmed suspicion—Kishkumen was off his guard. At the opportune moment the servant stabbed him, and so adroitly did he perform his work, that the robber fell dead without a groan. The servant immediately ran to the judgment hall, and informed Helaman all that he had heard, seen and done. Without delay orders were issued for the arrest of the band, but its members, finding that Kishkumen did not return, and fearing that he had miscarried in his unholy work, under the guidance of their leader, fled precipitately into the wilderness by a secret way, and in the depths of its luxuriant vegetation, hid in a place where they could not be found.

The succeeding years were of peculiar prosperity, though not of great righteousness, among the Nephite people. They spread out and colonized in every direction. Many thousands emi-

grated to the northern continent, among them great numbers of the Ammonites, who were originally Lamanites. Numerous new cities were built, and the old ones repaired; ship-building was largely carried on, and the arts and manufactures encouraged. Temples, tabernacles and sanctuaries were erected in great numbers; in fact, the people spread out and covered both continents, north and south, east and west. The sacred historian states that he has not recorded one-hundredth part of the doings of the people—their wickedness and righteousness, their wars and contentions, their peace and prosperity; but many records were kept upon which the history of these things were engraved, all of which that are necessary for the world's good will be brought to light in Heaven's own time.

The annals of the remainder of Helaman's rule are very short. In the years B. C. 45 and 44, there were many contentions in the land, but in the latter portion of the succeeding year they measurably ceased, and tens of thousands were baptized unto repentance. So great was the prosperity of the Church at this time, that even the priesthood were surprised thereat, and at the multiplicity of the blessings that were poured out upon the people. This happy state of affairs continued until the death of Helaman, though somewhat marred by the increasing pride and vanity that long-continued prosperity had begotten in the hearts of many of the Christians.

HELEM. A brother of Ammon, the leader of the party that went from Zarahemla to Lehi-Nephi to discover the people of Zeniff (B. C. 122). He accompanied his brethren on this expedition, and was one of the four cast into prison by king Limhi, under the supposition that they were some of the priests of his father, Noah, who had carried off the daughters of the Lamanites. Helem is only mentioned by name in connection

with this incident; but it is evident that if he was a brother of Ammon, according to the flesh, he was a descendant of Zarahemla, and doubtless was born in the land of that name and returned to it with the rest of the party when they led the people of Limhi out of the land of Lehi-Nephi.

HELORUM. A Nephite prince, one of the sons of king Benjamin. He was instructed by his father in all the learning of his people, both sacred and secular, and in the history of the Nephites, with especial reference to God's dealings with, and preserving care over them. His name is only mentioned once, and then in connection with his two brothers.

HEM. A brother of Ammon, who accompanied him on his expedition to Lehi-Nephi. What is said of Helem, can be said of Hem, and no more.

HERMOUNTS. A wilderness, north and west of Zarahemla, which was infested with wild and ravenous beasts. Into this wilderness the victorious Nephites drove the remnants of the Lamanites and Amlicites (B. C. 87), where great numbers were devoured by wild beasts and vultures.

HESHLON, PLAINS OF. After the defeat of Shared by Coriantumr, in the valley of Gilgal, the first named fled to the plains of Heshlon, (Ether 13: 28), thither Coriantumr pursued him, and another battle was fought, in which Shared was victorious, and Coriantumr again retreated to the valley of Gilgal. It is only in connection with this war that these plains are mentioned, and there is nothing in the record of the inspired historian to point out their location.

HETH. A cruel and vicious king of the Jaredites. He was the son of Com. His grandfather, Coriantum, was a righteous ruler, and the people prospered greatly during his reign; but in the days of Com the increase of wealth and prosperity was accompanied by an increase of wickedness, and the old secret plans and associations were revived. Heth became a leader in these things and rose in rebellion against his father, slew him with his own sword, and became king in his stead. The Lord then sent many prophets, who called upon the people to repent, declaring that if they did not, a terrible famine should come upon the land. The people, led and inspired by Heth, rejected the words of the prophets and cruelly persecuted them; some they cast out, some they threw into pits and left them to perish. Before long the rains from heaven ceased, and there was a great dearth over all the land; and poisonous serpents made their appearance and killed many people. These serpents also attacked the flocks of the Jaredites and drove them in vast bodies towards the southern continent. Many perished by the way, but some reached the land known to the Nephites as Zarahemla. Restrained by the power of God, the serpents stopped at the Isthmus of Panama, where they formed a cordon, preventing the Jaredites from further following their scattered flocks. The carcasses of the beasts which fell by the way were ravenously eaten by the famished people, until they had devoured them all. We can scarcely imagine the horrors that must have attended this famine, when the people consumed the poisoned flesh of the creatures thus killed. Disease in its most terrible form must have followed famine. Before long even this loathsome food was all consumed and the people rapidly perished. Then those who remained began to repent of their sins and call on the Lord; and when they had humbled themselves sufficiently, the Lord sent the long-needed rain and the remnants of the race began to revive. Soon there began to be fruit in the north country and the regions around about, and Shiz, the only survivor of the royal house, reigned over the few that were left; for Heth and all his household, except Shiz, had perished in the famine.

Ishmael. 155 **Ishmael, Land of.**

meaning of the passage is entirely altered; for instance: Thou hast multiplied the nation and not increased the joy (Isaiah, 9: 3,) appears, Thou hast multiplied the nation and increased the joy. (II Nephi, 19: 3.)

ISHMAEL. A righteous Israelite of the tribe of Ephraim, who, with his family, which was large, lived in Jerusalem, B. C. 600. At this time Ishmael must have been advanced in years, for he had five marriageable daughters, besides several grown up sons. By the commandment of the Lord, the sons of Lehi returned from their encampment on the border of the Red Sea to Jerusalem, and invited Ishmael and his family to join them in their journey to a promised land. The Lord softened their hearts and they accepted the invitation, left their home, and went down with the young men into the wilderness; though from the oft-repeated rebellious conduct of some of Ishmael's sons, it appears that they never had much faith. If any at all, in the prophetic mission of Lehi, or in the woes pronounced upon Jerusalem by the servants of the Most High. Soon after the arrival of the party at the tents of Lehi, the eldest daughter of Ishmael was married to Zoram, and four others wedded the sons of Lehi. In the vicissitudes of the toilsome journey in the Arabian desert, Ishmael appears to have been faithful to the Lord, but when the company reached a place to which was given the name of Nahom, Ishmael died, and was there buried. His demise was the cause of much sorrow to his family, and was made the pretext, by his rebellious portion, for renewed murmuring and fresh outbreaks. (See Nephi.)

ISHMAEL. A descendant of Nephi living in the second century before Christ. He was the grandfather of the prophet Amulek. No particulars are given of his life or death.

ISHMAEL, LAND OF. The first land of the Lamanites visited (B C. 91) by Ammon, the

HETH. A Jaredite prince, who was, by the usurping dynasty, held in captivity all his days. He was the son of king Hearthom, who was deposed and kept a prisoner all his life. Heth's son, Aaron, was also held captive from the day of his birth to his death.

HETH, LAND OF. A land of the Jaredites, apparently not far from Moron, the land they first occupied. When Jared, the son of king Omer, rebelled against his father, it is said that he came and dwelt in the land of Heth. This is the only time that this country is mentioned. (Ether 8: 2.)

HIMNI. One of the four sons of king Mosiah, and apparently the youngest, who went up to the land of Lehi-Nephi to minister among the Lamanites. (B. C. 91.) With the rest of his brothers, he was faithful in the performance of the labors of this great mission, and with them he returned at its close to his home in Zarahemla. Of his individual labors, or in what particular lands he ministered, we have no account. After his return he still continued a zealous and devoted servant of the Lord; and in B. C. 75, when Alma, the high priest, took his brothers to the land of Antionum to preach to the Zoramites, we are told he left Himni with the church at Zarahemla. This is the last notice we have in the Book of Mormon of this God-fearing and virtuous prince.

HOREB. This name is only used once in the Book of Mormon (III Nephi, 25: 4) in our Savior's quotation from the prophecies of Malachi. It is generally understood to be another name for Mount Sinai, which idea this quotation confirms.

IMMANUEL. This name appears twice in the Book of Mormon (II Nephi, 17: 14; 18: 8) in quotations from the writings of Isaiah.

INSECTS AND REPTILES. There are mentioned in the Book of Mormon the asp, bee, hat, honey-bee, cockatrice, fly, moth, serpent, and worms; largely in quotations from the Bible.

Ishmaelites. 156 **Jacob.**

missionary prince. It was then ruled over by a king named Lamoni. Its situation is not clearly stated; it was drawn from the land of Nephi (Lehi-Nephi). This leads to the thought that it was situated in the alluvial plains to the east of the Andes. It does not seem consistent with the narrative of Ammon's mission to believe it was situated in the strip of wilderness that lay between the mountains and the Pacific Ocean. Its relative position to other lands forbids this idea. Near the highway that connected Ishmael and Nephi, lay the land of Middoni. This is shown by the fact that when King Lamoni and Ammon were traveling from Ishmael towards Middoni they met Lamoni's father coming from Nephi. This leads to the conclusion that the same road from Ishmael led to both Nephi and Middoni. Nephi is called up from both the other lands. The land was named after the sons of Ishmael, from whom the then reigning dynasty were descended.

ISHMAELITES. The descendants of that Ishmael who, with his family, left his home in Jerusalem and accompanied Lehi on his journey to the promised land. After the death of Lehi they became absorbed in the Lamanite race and formed a part of that people. When corruption and dissension had entered into the true church (A. C. 231,) some reassumed the name of Ishmaelites. We are told (IV Nephi, 1: 38), they who rejected the gospel were called Lamanites, and Lemuelites, and Ishmaelites; and they did not dwindle in unbelief, but they did wilfully rebel against the gospel of Christ; and they did teach their children that they should not believe, even as their fathers, from the beginning, did dwindle in unbelief.

ISRAELITES. The people of Israel; called by that name once in the Book of Mormon. (Helaman, 8: 11.)

JACOB. The elder of the two sons born to Lehi and Sariah (say between B. C. 599 and 595)

IRREANTUM. The name given by Lehi's colony to an arm of the Indian Ocean, on the eastern coast of Arabia. On its shore Nephi and his brethren built the ship that carried them to this continent. It was either the Persian Gulf or Gulf of Oman, the which does not clearly appear from the records Nephi informs us that the meaning of the word Irreantum is many waters.

ISAAC. The son of Abraham. The Lord is several times called in the Book of Mormon, "the God of Abraham, the God of Isaac, and the God of Jacob," and it is in this connection that the name of this patriarch most frequently occurs.

ISABEL. A harlot of the land of Siron, who stole away the hearts of many. Among those seduced by her mercuricious charms was Corianton, the son of Alma, the younger, who forsook the ministry among the Zoramites, on purpose to enjoy her company, greatly to the injury and scandal of the work of God among that people, and to the great grief of his father (B. C. 75).

ISAIAH. One of the Twelve Disciples called and chosen by Jesus to minister to the Nephites at the time of his visit to that people (A. C. 34). Isaiah was present near the temple in the land bountiful when Jesus appeared, and was baptized by Nephi on the day following. He is not again mentioned by name in the sacred record.

ISAIAH. The Hebrew prophet. His prophecies were engraven on the plates obtained from Laban, and were greatly valued by Nephi and his righteous descendants. The following chapters from the Book of Isaiah are quoted in full in the Book of Mormon: chapters 2, 3, 4, 5, 6, 7, 8, 9, 10, 11, 12, 13, 14, 48, 49, 50, 51, 53, 54. They are given to us very much as they appear in the Bible, with here and there an important addition, which had evidently been left out of the manuscripts from which the Bible, as we have it to-day, were originally taken. In a few instances the

Jacob. 157

while they were traveling in the Arabian wilderness He was a mighty man of God, and, apparently, next to Nephi, the greatest and most devoted of all the sons of Lehi. When the little colony divided after the death of their patriarch, Jacob, who was yet young, followed Nephi, and was ordained by him a priest to the people. Undoubtedly he received the higher priesthood, or he could not have acted in the rites of the lesser priesthood, he being of the tribe of Manasseh, and not of Levi. He magnified this calling with much zeal and prudence, and Nephi records, at considerable length, extracts from his teachings. When Nephi died, Jacob appears to have taken charge of the spiritual concerns of the people, and to have presided over the church; he also became the custodian of the sacred treasures. He received many revelations, and was blessed with the spirit of prophecy. So great was his faith that he could command, in the name of Jesus, and the trees, the mountains, and the waves of the sea obeyed his word. For all this, some of the Nephites of his day were not strong in the Lord, they gave way to the spirit of greed and lust, and had to be sharply reproved by the word of the Lord through Jacob. In his day also the first anti-Christ, Sherem, appeared, a type of many who came after. But this presumptuous impostor was stricken by the power of God, and paid the penalty of his folly with his life, and Jacob had reason to rejoice in the eradication of his heresies, and the return of the Nephites to sound doctrine. Jacob lived to a good old age. We have no account of the time or circumstances of his death, but before he passed away he gave the sacred records into the keeping of his son Enos

JACOB. A Nephite apostate of the Zoramite sect. He joined the Lamanites in the war inaugurated by Amalickiah, and was placed in command of the city of Mulek, the most northern of the

Nephite cities, on the Atlantic coast, captured by the Lamanites. It was a key to the surrounding country. While it remained in Lamanite possession, it was very little use for Moroni, the Nephite commander-in-chief, to attempt to recover the cities that lay along the shores of the east sea, yet farther south. The Nephite generals did not consider themselves justified in making an attempt to carry the place by assault. Such an effort would have cost too many noble lives, and probably have proven unsuccessful. Moroni had with him at this time two of his most trusted lieutenants, Lehi and Teancum, both of whom were little inferior to the chief captain in wisdom and valor. At a council of war it was determined to attempt the capture of Mulek by strategy. They had already sent embassies to Jacob, desiring him to bring his armies into the open plain to meet the Nephites in battle, but the Lamanite commanders were too well acquainted with the discipline and courage of the Nephite forces to take such a risk. There was, therefore, but one plan left, other than to patiently sit down before the city and reduce it by a regular siege, and that was to decoy a portion of its defenders beyond the protection of its walls, and when it was thus weakened, to carry it by storm. Moroni determined on this course. (B. C. 64.)

By command of Moroni, the gallant Teancum, with a small force, marched along the sea shore to the neighborhood of Mulek; while Moroni, with the main body of the army, unperceived by the enemy, made a forced march by night into the wilderness which lay on the west of the city. There he rested. Lehi, with a third corps, remained in the city of Bountiful.

On the morrow, Teancum's small division was discovered by the Lamanite outposts, and from the fewness of its numbers they judged it would fall an easy prey. Jacob at once sallied forth at

the head of his warriors to attack the presumptuous Nephites. On their approach Teancum cautiously retreated along the sea shore towards the city of Bountiful. Jacob followed in vigorous pursuit. Moroni, in the meanwhile, divided his army into two corps, one of which he dispatched to capture the city, and with the other he closed in between Jacob's army and Mulek. The first corps accomplished its work without difficulty, for Jacob had left but a small force behind him, and all who would not surrender were slain.

The Lamanites crowded after Teancum in hot pursuit until they came nigh unto Bountiful, when they were met by Lehi and the small force under his command. At his appearance the Lamanite captains fled in confusion, lest they should be outgeneraled and cut off from their fortifications. Jacob's warriors were weary by reason of their long and hasty advance, while Lehi's soldiers were fresh and unfatigued. But Lehi refrained from pressing too vigorously on his retreating foes, as his object was not to exhaust his men until the hour of battle came, and he was anxious to avoid a conflict till he and Moroni could, at the same moment, attack the Lamanites in front and rear.

When Jacob drew near the city he found himself confronted by the soldiers of Moroni, who closed in around his warriors and barred their further progress southward; while Lehi, putting forth his pent-up energies, fell with fury on their rear. Weary and worn though his troops were, Jacob would not surrender. He determined, if possible, to cut his way through to Mulek. With this intent he made a desperate, though ineffectual, charge on Moroni's lines. The Nephites being fresh and unwearied, never wavered. The battle here raged with indescribable fierceness, and with heavy losses to both sides. The wild Lamanites, in the frenzy of desperation, dashed with all their

strength and prowess against the well-ordered ranks of the Nephites in the one-absorbing endeavor to force their way through. While the Nephites, in the heroic courage which religion and patriotism inspire, stood cool and undismayed. In this desperate encounter Moroni was wounded and Jacob slain.

While Jacob was thus impetuously charging on Moroni's corps, Lehi with his "strong men" was as furiously driving in the Lamanite rear. At last the soldiers of Jacob in that part of the field surrendered. Their leader being slain, the remainder of the troops hesitated between throwing down their arms and continuing the hopeless strife. Moroni, with his intense hatred of unnecessary bloodshed, when he noticed that they wavered, cried out that if they would lay down their weapons and deliver themselves up he would spare their lives. His offer was accepted. The chief captains, who remained, came forward and placed their weapons at his feet and commanded their men to do the same. Most of the warriors obeyed, yet numbers would not. They preferred death to surrender, and force had to be used to wrest their weapons from them. The Lamanite prisoners were then sent under an escort to the city of Bountiful, and when counted were found to exceed in numbers the slain on both sides in the late battle.

JACOB. In the years just previous to the fall of the Nephite commonwealth, (A. C. 30) a relentless persecution was waged against the followers of Christ, when many of the believers, under the color of the law, were unjustly put to death. But though executed by order of the corrupt courts, the proceedings were in the highest degree illegal, as it was contrary to the Nephite law for any prisoner to be put to death unless the warrant therefor had first been signed by the chief governor of all the land. Contrary to the provision of this statute,

---

the persecutors of the saints, feeling strong in their numbers and influence, set the law at open defiance, and continued to condemn and execute the Christians. Among these conspicuous for this revengeful and illegal course, was a man of much influence among the corrupt and degraded majority, whose name was Jacob.

The very of these infamies reached the chief judge, but when he expostulated the offenders treated his requirements with contempt, and broke out in open rebellion, associating themselves together by the same unholy oaths and covenants that had heretofore done so much towards destroying the nation. In these traitorous movements Jacob made himself conspicuous.

The leaders in these conspiracies determined to overthrow the republic and establish a monarchy. To this end the chief judge was assassinated and Jacob proclaimed king.

The result was not as successful as the royalists anticipated. The majority of the people would not be ruled by a king. They preferred rather to break up into numerous tribes, each with its own chieftain and internal regulations; but all these tribes of the people united in their objections to the proclamation of a monarchy.

Jacob, who had with him the majority of the most vile and corrupt of the nation, those who had been most officious and relentless in persecuting the servants of God, did not despair. He imagined that in course of time he would be so greatly strengthened by dissatisfied members of the tribes that he would eventually be able to conquer them and establish his supremacy. For the present he determined to remove, with those who recognized his authority, to the northernmost part of the land, there consolidate his power and found his kingdom. So ably did he carry his intentions into effect that the tribes were unable to arrest his movements.

Arrived at the chosen land, Jacob and his people laid the foundation of a magnificent city, to which was given the name of Jacobugath (A. C. 311). His subjects were mostly rich, and their material progress was remarkable, but they exceeded in vice, in depravity, in corruption, all the inhabitants of the continent. Their history is a short one. In the terrible convulsions of nature that marked the sacrifice of the Lord of Life and Glory, Jacobugath, with many other Nephite cities, was entirely consumed by fire. (A. C. 34.) Its population of traitors and murderers was destroyed, that the blood of the prophets and the saints should not come up unto God any more against them. If Jacob was yet alive he undoubtedly perished at this time with his people.

JACOB. The Bible patriarch of that name. Individually he is seldom referred to in the Book of Mormon, but the Israelites are frequently spoken of as the seed or the house of Jacob, and the Lord as the God of Jacob; while the promise is made on several occasions to the righteous that they shall sit down with Abraham, Isaac and Jacob in the kingdom of heaven.

JACOB, CITY OF. One of the cities sunk in the depths of the earth at the time of the great convulsions that attended the crucifixion of the Savior. Its iniquitous citizens had persecuted and slain the saints of God, and the Lord destroyed them from before His face, that the blood of the righteous might not come up unto Him any more against them.

JACOBITES. One of the divisions of the Nephite people. They were the descendants of Jacob, the son of Lehi.

JACOBUGATH. The city of the followers of king Jacob. Its history was short, but its people were pre-eminent in iniquity. When the Nephite republic was broken in fragments (A. C. 30), and the people divided into tribes, the royalists, who

embraced the vilest of the race, endeavored to gain control and establish a monarchy. Among them were very many office-holders, lawyers and judges, who thirsted for extended power. They had been the foremost in persecuting and slaving the servants of God, and, more than any others, contributed to the overthrow of the government. But the confederate tribes were stronger than the monarchists and opposed the establishment of a kingdom. Jacob therefore determined to take his followers to the northernmost part of the land and there establish that form of government. So speedily and unexpected were his movements that the tribes were unable to intercept him. He accomplished his purpose, built a large city and reigned over that region as king. We can well imagine the condition of society composed as it was entirely of the vilest class of men; for everything abominable, and turbulent. Jacob, however, flattered himself that dissenters from the tribes would flock to his standard and soon make him powerful enough to extend his authority over the whole land. In this he was disappointed, for in the horrors of the upheavals of nature that came with the death of the Savior, Jacobugath and its people disappeared forever. Of their destruction Jesus himself says: "That great city Jacobugath, which was inhabited by the people of the king of Jacob, have I caused to be burned with fire, because of their sins and their wickedness, which was above all the wickedness of the whole earth, because of their secret murders and combinations; for it was they that did destroy the peace of my people and the government of the land: therefore I did cause their destruction Jesus himself; or there destroy them from before my face, that the blood of the prophets and the saints should not come up unto me any more against them."

JACOM. The eldest son of Jared, the father

of the Jaredite race. He, with others, was offered the kingly authority by the people, but refused that honor. His name is only once mentioned in the Book of Mormon (Ether, 6: 14).

JARED. The founder of the Jaredite race. He was apparently, one of those engaged in the building of the Tower of Babel. It is presumable that he was a descendant of Shem, as he, and most certainly his brother, held the holy priesthood. We are inclined to believe, from the brief narrative in the Book of Ether, that Jared's brother was the leading spirit of the colony that accompanied these brothers on their toilsome journey to this continent. Of Jared's private character we are told but little, but he appears to have been more conservative, more pliable and less energetic than his brother. The race was named after him, we presume, because one of his sons, Orihah, became its first king, and Jared's thus became the royal family. Jared had four sons and eight daughters: the names of his sons were Jacom, Gilgah, Mahah, and Orihah. Jared lived to a great age. He died and was buried in the land of Moron. (For particulars of the journey of Jared and his people see Jared, Brother of.)

JARED. One of the most unscrupulous and bloodthirsty of the ancient Jaredites. In early life he rose in rebellion against Omer, his father, eventually dethroned him, and held him a captive for many years, while he (Jared) occupied the throne. Some of Omer's younger sons, incensed at the treatment to which their father was subjected, raised an army and totally routed the forces of the usurper. Jared was taken prisoner and only saved his life by humble submission to his father. At first he kept his promise, but his ambition would not remain dormant. He sighed and wearied for the kingly authority, until his unrest became marked by all. He had a daughter

who shared her father's feelings, and at her instigation he sent for a friend of Omer's named Akish, through whom he hoped to regain the throne. An entertainment of some kind, by which Jared's daughter could be introduced, was given. By prearrangement with her father, she danced before Akish, and so exhibited the beauties of her person and the graces of her movements that he became desperately enamored of her. As she anticipated, Akish asked Jared to give her to him as a wife. The latter consented, but on most revolting conditions. The father and daughter had planned that the price of her hand was to be the head of her grandfather, the king. Did ever ambition conceive a more unnatural crime? Akish, though a friend of Omer, consented to the proposed terms, and to help him in his treason Jared suggested to him, again at the instance of his daughter, the plans and oaths common among the antediluvians, originally used by Cain, by which the wicked accomplished their vile and bloody purposes. He consented, Omer was driven from the throne, though by God's mercy his life was spared; Jared was again proclaimed king, and Akish became his son-in-law. Soon the latter coveted the royal dignity; possibly the woman who plotted the death of her grandfather was willing to sacrifice her father also that she might be queen; such a supposition is not improbable. At any rate, Jared was slain on his throne while giving audience to his people, by some of the members of the secret society of assassins that he had been the means of calling into existence; and Akish reigned in his stead.

JARED, BROTHER OF. The prophet and leader of the founders of the Jaredite race. His name is not given in the Book of Mormon, but we learn through modern revelation, that it was Mahonri Moriancumer. He was in all probability a descendant of Shem, and was present at the

building of the Tower of Babel, if not actually engaged in that work; though he and his brother had not fallen into idolatry, as had so many of the builders of that notorious edifice. When God scattered these presumptuous builders, Jared and his brother pleaded with the Lord that their language and that of their friends, might not be confounded. Their prayer was heard, their mother tongue was preserved. In answer to their further entreaties, the Lord promised to lead them into a land whereof he would make of them a great people; and He Himself would go before them, as their guide. In obedience to the heavenly command, Jared, his brother, and their friends, with their respective families, gathered their flocks, and seeds of various kinds, and started to follow as the Lord should lead. The valley into which the Lord first led them was called Nimrod, after that mighty hunter of the early post-diluvian age. Here the people of Jared tarried for a time, while they prepared for the long journey which was before them. Their flocks and herds they had with them; they now went to work and snared fowls; they carried with them hives of honey bees (known to them by the name of deseret); and prepared a vessel in which they transported the fish of the waters. They appear to have collected everything that could possibly be of use to them. They were going to a land that had been swept clean by the waters of the Deluge; it had been bereft of all its animal life; the seeds of grains and fruits no longer germinated in its soil; and the colony had to replenish the continent with the animal and vegetable life necessary for their comfort and sustenance, as though it was a new earth. When in the valley of Nimrod, the Lord came down and talked with the brother of Jared. But the brother of Jared saw Him not, for the Lord remained concealed in a cloud. And God directed that the company

should go forth into the wilderness, into that quarter where man had never yet been. As they journeyed the Heavenly Presence went before them in the cloud, instructed them and gave directions which way they should travel. In the course of their journey they had many waters—seas, rivers, and lakes, to cross, on which occasions they built barges, as directed by the Lord. It must have been an arduous labor, requiring much time and great patience to transport their flocks and herds, with all the rest of their cumbrous freight, across these many waters. As they advanced to a great distance from the centre of population in western Asia, it is possible they traveled beyond the limits to which the larger animals had by that time scattered; and if so, they were entirely without the aid of the food obtained by the chase; on the other hand, it is probable that the fish in the lakes and rivers formed a valuable source of food supply, yet it must also be remembered they carried fish in a vessel with them.

Led by the Lord personally, instructed by His own mouth, protected by His presence, the colony, of which Jared's brother appears to have been the prophet and leader, at last reached the borders of the great sea which divides the continents. To the place where they tarried they gave the name of Moriancumer. Here they remained for a period of four years, in the end of which time the Lord again visited the brother of Jared in a cloud, and chastened him and his brethren, because of their neglect to call upon His name. Repentance followed this reproof, and because of their repentance their sins were forgiven them.

The brother of Jared was then commanded by the Lord to build eight barges, after the same pattern as those he had previously constructed. This command he obeyed with the assistance of the company. The vessels were small, light in construction and water tight. As they were dark

in the interior, by reason of being without windows, the Lord, at the entreaty of the brother of Jared, touched sixteen small white stones, which the latter had molten out of a high mountain called Shelem; and after the Lord touched them they shone forth and gave light to the vessels in which they were placed. When the Lord put forth His finger to touch these stones, the veil was taken from before the eyes of the brother of Jared and he saw the finger of the Lord; and it was as the finger of a man, like unto flesh and blood.

And because of the brother of Jared's great faith the Lord showed Himself unto him, and declared Himself to be Jesus Christ, who should come into the world to redeem His people.

All things being prepared, Jared and his people, with their animals, fishes, bees, seeds and multitudinous other things, went on board; a favorable wind wafted them from shore, and they gradually crossed to the American coast. At the end of a somewhat stormy voyage of three hundred and forty-four days the colony reached this continent. It is generally understood that the place where they landed was south of the Gulf of California and north of the land Desolation, which was north of the Isthmus of Panama.

No sooner had the people of Jared landed than they humbled themselves before the Lord, many of them shedding tears of joy because of the multitude of His tender mercies in bringing them so safely to this new land of promise. Their next duty was to prepare for the future. They commenced to till the soil and perform the other labors incidental to founding a new home. In these efforts they prospered greatly. They began to grow and increase in numbers and in wealth; and even better than this, they were a righteous people, being taught directly from on high. In process of time Jared and his brother grew old, and perceiving that their course on earth was

nearly finished, the latter proposed that they gather the people, number them, give them necessary teachings, and learn their wishes. This was done; but to the grief of the brother of Jared, the people desired that a king be anointed to rule over them. He saw, by the spirit of prophecy, that this action would lend to many evils, and he was inclined to refuse their request, but Jared pleaded that the wishes of the people be granted, and his brother finally consented. It was the first step in the wrong direction, and led to much sin, misery, contention and captivity. The people having the privilege granted them, chose Pagag, the eldest son of their prophet. He declined, as did all of his brothers, and then all the sons of Jared except Orihah. The last named accepted the royal dignity and was anointed king. Soon after this the brother of Jared died, full of years and honor. Like Enoch, he had been privileged to enter the presence of the Lord, and to have revealed to him the history of the world in all its generations. He was also a man, having received the priceless gift of a Urim and Thummim. His faith was never exceeded by the sons of men; he laid hold of the promises of the Almighty with unshaken confidence. By that faith he performed miracles. Moroni tells us that by its power he "said unto the mountain Zerin, remove, and it was removed." (Ether, 12: 30); but of the circumstances that attended this manifestation of Divine power, we have not the slightest details. The brother of Jared is also said to have been "mighty in writing;" the uncorrupted language which he used being unquestionably, most favorable for expressing niceties of thought in written characters. He was a "large and mighty man" in personal appearance, and undoubtedly as strong in his integrity to God, and in his moral courage, as he was in physical characteristics. Altogether, we deem him one of the greatest prophets and leaders of God's people that ever graced this earth. When he died he left behind him twenty-two sons and daughters.

JAREDITES, THE. The descendants of Jared and his associates, who were led by the power of God from the Tower of Babel to this continent. Here they became one of the mightiest of nations, and flourished in a manner unsurpassed in the history of the post-deluvian races, until they fell into decay through corruption and iniquity and were ultimately destroyed in a desolating internecine war, at the end of which but one man, Coriantumr, remained as the representative of this once mighty people. The destruction of the Jaredites took place, as nearly as can be gleaned from the record, about the same time as the Nephites reached this land. (say B. C. 590.)

JAROM. A Nephite prophet who lived in the fourth and fifth centuries before Christ. He was the son of Enos, the son of Jacob, the brother of Nephi, and was intrusted with the care of the plates of Nephi, which he appears to have retained 59 years, or from the 180th to the 239th year of the Nephite annals. From his record we learn that during his days many of the Nephites were a stiff-necked and hard-hearted people, among whom the prophets and priesthood labored diligently, warning them of the great evils that must ultimately result to the nation if they did not repent. Their labors were blessed with measurable success. It is pleasing to learn from Jarom's writings that the Nephite kings and leaders were mighty men in the faith of the Lord, who not only led them to victory over their earthly enemies, but instructed them in the ways of eternal salvation. The laws of the land were exceedingly strict, the law of Moses was rigorously observed, the Sabbath day was kept holy unto the Lord, and profanity and blasphemy were unknown. Under the wise and righteous administration of these kings, the Nephites spread widely over the land of Nephi.

Jerusalem. 173 **Jerusalem, City of.**

No sooner had the Ammonites taken possession of the land Jershon than a church was established there, with Ammon, the son of king Mosiah, as the high priest. The first attempt on the integrity of its members was made by the anti-Christ Korihor (B. C. 75), but by Ammon's orders he was escorted beyond the borders of Jershon. When division arose among the Zoramites, in the land of Antionum, regarding the preaching of Alma and his associates, and the gospel believers were driven from their homes by their intolerant fellow citizens, Jershon became their place of refuge. The Ammonites having in like manner suffered persecution received the fugitives gladly, and, indifferent alike to the threats and appeals of the Zoramite leaders, found them homes and afforded them the needed succor and helpful guidance (B. C. 75). In the war that followed, Jershon was dispossessed of its citizens and occupied by an army of the Nephites. No battles, however, appear to have been fought here, as the Lamanite commanders transferred the scene of hostilities to other regions (B. C. 74.) After this, Jershon is not mentioned by name in the Book of Mormon.

JERUSALEM, CITY OF. A Lamanite city within the borders of the land of Nephi. (See land of Jerusalem.)

JERUSALEM, CITY OF. The chief city of the Jews. It was the home of Lehi (B. C. 600); there he prophesied and thence he was led by the hand of the Lord. It is often spoken of by the writers in the Book of Mormon, more especially in connection with its destruction by the Babylonians, and is mentioned in frequent quotations from Isaiah. The year of the departure of Lehi from Jerusalem was made the initial date in Nephite chronology; that people counting their years as so many "after Lehi left Jerusalem." With the establishment of the republic, the Nephites added "year

which was then their home, and increased greatly in numbers, though they were nothing like so numerous as the Lamanites, with whom they had several wars during the time embraced in Jarom's record. The Lamanites invaded the Nephite possessions "many times," but were driven out as often as they came. During this period the arts of peace were also encouraged, and the Nephites grew exceedingly rich; it also appears to have been an epoch in which manufactures took a decided step in advance. Reference is made to progress in the working of the precious metals, in the manufacture of machinery and tools, as well as of weapons of war; greater attention was paid to fine workmanship in wood and to improvements in building; altogether we may consider it a very prosperous portion of this people's existence. If Jarom died in the year he delivered the plates to his son Omni, that event took place 362 years before the advent of the Messiah.

JASHON, CITY OF. The chief city of the land of Jashon. We are told that it was situated near the land where Ammaron had deposited the records unto the Lord. That land (Mormon, 1: 3) was called Antum.

JASHON, LAND OF. During the last great war between the Nephites and Lamanites in A. C. 345, the former were driven to the land of Jashon, and hence northward to the land of Shem. This is the only time that this land is mentioned in the Book of Mormon (Mormon, 2: 16). It is supposed to have been situated on the northern continent.

JEHERECHIAH. The father of a certain Zechariah mentioned in Isaiah, 8: 2, and appearing in the Book of Mormon in the quotation of that passage (II Nephi, 18: 2). Some suppose it to be a corruption of the name Berechiah.

JEHOVAH. This name appears but twice in the Book of Mormon. Once (II Nephi, 22: 2)

Jerusalem, Land of. 174 **Jesus Christ.**

of the Judges" to their former system, and their annals sometimes refer to a date in both methods of computation.

JERUSALEM, LAND OF. A land or the Lamanites. It was in the immediate vicinity of the waters of Mormon, probably east or north from Lehi-Nephi. There (about B C. 100) the Lamanites, Amulonites and various Nephite apostates built a large and thriving city, and named it after their fathers' ancient home in Judea. In this city Aaron, the son of king Mosiah, unavailingly preached the gospel. Its apostate citizens were too sin-hardened to accept the glorious message which he bore. They continued in their career of crime and iniquity until it was engulfed in the bowels of the earth in the dire calamities that attended the crucifixion of the Lord of Life and Glory. Waters came up in the place of this proud city, and a stagnant sea, akin to that which hides Sodom and Gomorrah, occupied the place where its grand palaces and rich synagogues previously stood.

JERUSALEM, LAND OF. The name given by the Nephites to that country which we call Judea. (I Nephi, 2: 11; 16: 35.)

JERUSALEM, NEW. The city spoken of by John, in the Book of Revelations; but ages before his time, prophesied of by Ether, the last seer of the Jaredite race. (Ether, 13: 3-10.) Among other things Ether foretells that this blessed city shall be built upon the American continent. Jesus, in his teachings to the Nephites, confirms the truth of this prophecy (III Nephi, 20: 22, 21: 23, 24)

JESSE, ROOT OF. The prophecy of Isaiah regarding the root of Jesse is quoted by Nephi (II Nephi, 21: 1-10).

JESUS CHRIST. PROPHECIES REGARDING HIS ADVENT, LIFE, MINISTRY AND DEATH. One of the most remarkable things connected with the history of the Nephites is the great plainness and

in a quotation from the writings of Isaiah; and (Mormon, 10: 34) in Moroni's closing remarks, before finally bidding up the records of the Nephites.

JEREMIAH. One of the Twelve Disciples, called and chosen by Jesus to minister to the Nephites at the time of His visit to that people (A. C. 34.) Jeremiah was present near the temple in the land Bountiful when Jesus appeared and was baptized by Nephi on the day following. He is not again mentioned by name in the sacred record.

JEREMIAH. The Jewish prophet. He lived and prophesied at the same time as Lehi, and appears to have been personally acquainted with him. Many of his prophecies were recorded on the plates of brass obtained by Nephi from Laban (I Nephi, 5: 13.) His prophecies regarding the destruction of Jerusalem and the advent of the Messiah are referred to by Nephi, the son of Helaman. (Helaman, 8: 20.)

JERSHON. This was the name given to the regions set apart by the Nephites (A. C. 78) as the home of the Ammonites, or Christian Lamanites. It was situated to the north of Zarahemla and was evidently chosen for the reason that the strength of the Nephite nation would lie between the fugitives and their former countrymen, the Lamanites, who then thirsted for their blood. It was bounded by the Caribbean Sea and the land Bountiful on the north and east, and by the land of Antionum on the south. Its western boundary is not defined, but we are inclined to believe, from the context, that it was the river Sidon. Its geographical situation is partly described in Alma, 27: 22, thus: We [the Nephites] will give up the land of Jershon, which is on the east by the sea, which joins the land Bountiful, which is on the south of the land Bountiful. With regard to its southern boundary, Alma, 31: 3, states that Antionum lay to the south of it.

Jesus Christ. 175

detail with which the coming of the Redeemer and the events of His life in Judea were revealed to their prophets, who lived before the time of His advent. Among other things connected with His mortal existence it was declared of Him that:

God Himself should come down from heaven among the children of men and should redeem His people

He should take upon Him flesh and blood

He should be born in the land of Jerusalem, the name given by the Nephites to the land of their forefathers, whence they came.

His mother's name should be Mary.

She should be a virgin of the city of Nazareth; very fair and beautiful, a precious and chosen vessel.

She should be overshadowed and conceive by the power of the Holy Ghost.

He should be called Jesus Christ, the Son of God.

At His birth a new star should appear in the heavens.

He should be baptized by John at Bethabara, beyond Jordan.

John should testify that he had baptized the Lamb of God, who should take away the sins of the world.

After His baptism, the Holy Ghost should come down upon Him out of heaven, and abide upon Him in the form of a dove.

He should call twelve men as His special witnesses, to minister in His name.

He should go forth among the people, ministering in power and great glory, casting out devils, healing the sick, raising the dead, and performing many mighty miracles.

He should take upon Him the infirmities of His people.

He should suffer temptation, pain of body, hunger, thirst and fatigue; blood should come from every pore of His body by reason of His anguish because of the abominations of His people.

He should because out and receded by the Jews be taken and scourged, and be judged of the world.

He should be lifted upon the cross and slain for the sins of the world.

He should be buried in a sepulchre, where He should remain three days.

After He was slain He should rise from the dead and should make Himself manifest by the Holy Ghost unto the Gentiles.

He should lay down His life according to the flesh and take it up again by the power of the Spirit, that he might bring to pass the resurrection of the dead, being the first that should rise.

At His resurrection many graves should be opened and should yield up their dead; and many of the saints, who had heretofore passed away, should appear unto the living.

He should redeem all mankind who would believe on His name.

In the above we have not mentioned the sayings of Isaiah and other Jewish prophets, which are inserted in the Book of Mormon, but which also appear in the Bible.

UNITS OF JESUS BEFORE HIS ADVENT. On this continent, as on the eastern, Jesus manifested Himself from time to time to His faithful servants, before His coming in the flesh. He was the guide of His people, the guardian of the church, and the revealer of the mind and will of the Godhead. He went before the people of Jared in their journey, instructing them and covenanting with them. Few events recorded in the Book of Mormon are more widely known than His appearance in the body of His spirit to the brother of Jared. His statements with regard to Himself then were: "I am he who was prepared from the foundation of the world to redeem my

Salvation had entered its most glorious phase; but the wicked quaked with awful dread, they realized the extent of their iniquity, they knew that they were murderers at heart, for they had plotted to take the lives of the righteous, and in the terror that this overwhelming sense of their piteous condition wrought, they sank to the earth as though they were dead.

Many now believed who, previously, had scorned the divine messages that the prophets bore; but others, inspired of Satan, as soon as they recovered from the fright which the appearance of the promised signs had produced, began to explain them away, and, by various lying rumors, endeavored to nullify the good that had been done in the hearts of many. Others again commenced to teach that it was no longer expedient to observe the law of Moses, or to offer sacrifices, not comprehending that the infinite sacrifice had not yet been made.

SIGNS OF THE DEATH OF CHRIST. On the fourth day of the thirty-fourth Nephite year after Christ's birth, the promised signs of the Savior's crucifixion began. A terrible and devastating tempest burst upon the land. The earth quivered and groaned and opened in wide, unfathomable chasms. Mountains were riven and swallowed up in yawning gulfs, or were scattered into fragments and dispersed like hail before the tearing wind. Towers, temples, houses, were torn up, scattered in fragments or crushed by falling rocks, and, together with their inmates, were ground to dust in the convulsion. Blue and yellow flames burst from the edges of sinking rocks, blazed for a moment and then all was the deepest darkness. Rain poured down in torrents; cloud-bursts, like floods, washed away all with which they came in contact, and pillars of steaming vapor seemed to unite the earth and sky. This unparalleled storm rage dthroughout the land for

people. Behold, I am Jesus Christ. * * and even as I appear unto thee to be in the spirit, will I appear unto my people in the flesh."

In later centuries, when making known the Divine will to the elder Alma regarding the discipline of His church, He declares: "It is I that taketh upon me the sins of the world; nor it is I that hath created them; and it is I that granteth unto him that believeth unto the end, a place at my right hand."

Not only were the Nephites very familiar with the details of the earthly life of the Redeemer, but they also were made acquainted by their prophets, from Lehi to Samuel the Lamanite, with the fact that after his resurrection He would visit them. This was shown in a vision to Nephi (I Nephi, 12: 6), and he taught it to his people; (III Nephi, 26: 1, 9). And it so continued to be taught by the priesthood throughout all their generations. (Alma, 16: 20.)

The time of his birth at Bethlehem was also declared by the prophets with great exactness. Nephi states that it should be 600 years from the time his father, Lehi, left Jerusalem, and this prophecy was known to all his descendants See I Nephi, 10: 4; 19: 8; II Nephi, 25: 19. We quote the last: For according to the words of the prophets, the Messiah cometh in six hundred years from the time that my father left Jerusalem, and according to the words of the prophets, and also the word of the angel of God His name shall be Jesus Christ, the Son of God.

In the year B. C. 6, Samuel, the Lamanite, prophesied that on this continent, at the time of the Savior's birth, there should appear great lights in the heavens, so that there should be a day, a night and another day without darkness; a new star should arise, and many signs and wonders should be seen in the heavens. Again, at the time of the Redeemer's death, the sun should be

three hours only, but during its short continuance the whole face of Nature was changed. Mountains sank, valleys rose, the sea swept over the plains, large stagnant lakes usurped the place of flourishing cities, great chasms, rents and precipices disfigured the face of the earth.

Three days of unnatural and impenetrable darkness followed the horrors of the tempest, and from the heavens the voice of the Lord was heard by the afflicted people, proclaiming in their terrified ears the destruction that had taken place

Terrible was the catalogue of woes which that heavenly voice rehearsed. Nearly all their cities, great and small, were destroyed by flood or fire, by earthquake or hurricane. The desolation was complete; the face of the land was changed, tens of thousands, probably millions, of souls had been suddenly called to meet the reward of their sinful lives; for this destruction came upon them that their wickedness and abominations might be hid from the face of heaven, and that the blood of the prophets and saints might not come up any more in appeal unto God against them.

When the heavenly voice had finished the recital of the calamities that had befallen the land and its inhabitants, the Speaker appealed to those who yet lived to repent of their sins and return unto Him, and they should have eternal life, and revealed to them who He was. He declared unto them:

I am Jesus Christ, the Son of God. I created the heavens and the earth, and all things that in them are. I was with the Father from the beginning. I am in the Father, and the Father in me; and in me hath the Father glorified His name.

I came unto my own, and my own received me not. And the Scriptures concerning my coming are fulfilled

And as many as have received me, to them have I given to become the sons of God, and even

darkened and refuse to give his light and also the moon and stars; and there should be no light upon the face of this land, from the time He died to the time that he arose again from the dead. At His death there should be mighty thunderings and lightnings for many hours, and the earth should shake and tremble, and the rocks which are upon its face should be broken up, and there should be great tempests, and many mountains should be laid low, and valleys should become mountains of great height, and many cities should become desolate. And many graves should yield up their dead; and many saints should appear unto the living

SIGNS OF HIS BIRTH. When six hundred years had passed from the time Lehi left Jerusalem, the time arrived of which Samuel, the Lamanite, and other prophets had borne testimony, when the phenomena should appear to bear witness of the birth of the Son of God. As the day drew near, signs and miracles increased among the people. But the hardened in heart began to circulate the idea that the time had passed and the prophecies had failed. They even went so far as to appoint a day when all who believed in the coming of the Savior should be slain, except the sign be first given.

This gross wickedness caused Nephi, the high priest, great sorrow. Before God, in mighty prayer, he bowed all the day long. At last the comforting word of the Anointed One came unto him, saying: On this night shall the sign be given, and on the morrow come I into the world, to show unto the world that I will fulfil all that which I have caused to be spoken by the mouths of my holy prophets. As was declared, so was it fulfilled. At the going down of the sun it was as light as day, and so continued until the morning, when the sun again rose in its usual course. A new star had also appeared in the heavens. Then the faithful rejoiced. They knew that their Redeemer was born, and that the great plan of

so will I to as many as shall believe on my name, for behold, by me redemption cometh, and in me is the law of Moses fulfilled.

I am the light and the life of the world. I am Alpha and Omega, the beginning and the end.

After the people had heard this glad message they ceased their mourning for their dead relatives, and there was silence in the land for the space of many hours. Then again the voice of Jesus heard, recounting how often He had sought to gather His Israel, but they would not, and promising in the future that He would again gather them, if they would listen unto Him. But they would not heed Him, the places of their dwellings should become desolate until the time of the fulfilling of God's covenant with their fathers. When the people heard this awful prophecy they began to weep and howl again, because of the loss of their kindred and friends.

As on the eastern continent, so on this; at the time of Christ's resurrection, numbers of their saints who were dead arose from their graves and were seen and known by many of the living.

Three days had passed in darkness, in terror and in woe, when the thick mist rolled off the face of the land, revealing to the astonished eyes of the survivors how great had been the convulsions that had shaken the earth. As the darkness passed away the earth ceased to tremble, the rocks were no longer rent, and the tumultuous noises ended. Nature was again at peace, and peace filled the hearts of the living; their mourning was turned to praise, and their joy was in Christ their deliverer.

CHRIST MINISTERS TO THE NEPHITES. Some time after these terrible events, exactly how long we know not, a multitude assembled near the temple, which was in the land Bountiful. Possibly many of the high priesthood had assembled there to call upon the Lord, and to officiate in the

duties of their calling. The multitude spake one
to another with regard to the Savior, of whose
death the three days of unexampled, impenetrable
darkness had been a sign.

While thus engaged, a strange, sweet voice tell
upon their ears, yet it pierced them to the centre,
so that their whole frames trembled. At first they
knew not what it said or whence it came; nor even
when the words were again repeated did they
understand. But when they came a third time
they understood their glorious import, and knew
that it was the voice of God. He said unto them:
Behold, my beloved Son, in whom I am well
pleased, in whom I have glorified my name: hear
ye Him. Obedient to this heavenly voice they cast
their eyes upward, and to their joyous astonishment beheld the Messiah, clothed in a white robe,
coming out of heaven.

Even yet they did not comprehend who He
was, but thought Him an angel. As He descended
to the earth and stood in their midst, their won-
dering eyes were all turned towards Him, but for
awe not a mouth was opened or a limb moved.
Then the Redeemer stretched forth His hand and
said unto the multitude: Behold, I am Jesus Christ,
whom the prophets testified should come into the
world; and behold, I am the life and light of the
world; and I have drunk out of the bitter cup
which the Father hath given to me, and have
glorified the Father in taking upon me the sins of
the world, in the which I have suffered the will of
the Father in all things from the beginning.

Then the whole multitude fell to the earth,
they remembered the sayings of the prophets; they
realized that their God stood in the midst of them.

Again the risen Redeemer spake: Arise, said
He, and come forth unto me, that you may thrust
your hands into my side, and also that ye may
feel the prints of the nails in my hands and in my
feet, that ye may know that I am the God of

Israel, and the God of the whole earth, and have
been slain for the sins of the world.

Now they who heard Him from the first to the
last went forth and assured themselves that it
was He of whom the prophets had spoken. Then
with shouts of praise they cried: Hosanna! blessed
be the name of the Most High God. And they fell
down at His feet and worshiped Him.

Jesus next called Nephi to Him, then eleven
others, and gave them authority to baptize the
people, at the same time strictly charging them as
to the manner in which they should perform this
ordinance, that all disputes on this point might
cease among the believers. (See Twelve Disciples.)

After Jesus had chosen the Twelve, he commenced to teach the people the principles of the
fulness of the Gospel. Step by step He led them
over the same precious ground of universal truth
as He had done his followers in Galilee, Judea and
Samaria. Sometimes, through the difference of the
inspired translation of the Book of Mormon and
the worldly-wise one of the Bible, a slight difference is noticeable in the wording of the instructions, but as a rule these differences are trivial, the
advantage being with the Nephites, whose greater
faith drew from the Savior deeper truths than
Judah had received, or caused Him to display
greater manifestations of His omnipotence and
boundless love. From the believers He would turn
to the Twelve, and give them special instructions
as His ministers; then again He would shed forth
upon the multitude; and by and by again address
the disciples. So He continued day by day until
all was revealed, either to the multitude or to the
Twelve, that was necessary for the eternal salvation of the obedient. Then He left them to the care
and ministry of the chosen Disciples.

Some have wondered why Jesus should have
given so many of the same teachings to the Ne-

phites as He did to the Jews. The reason is that
those teachings were perfect, and could not be improved. They were universal, that is, they were
adapted to the wants of all peoples, whether of
Israel or of the Gentiles, whether of Judah or Joseph. Among the teachings that He gave the
Nephites which do not appear in the Bible account
of His ministrations to the Jews, are His references
to the "Lost Ten Tribes." His explanations of the
prophecies of Isaiah and Malachi. His statements
regarding the then future history of the peoples on
this continent, particularly drawing attention to
those events that would concern and be connected
with the remnants of the house of Lehi; and His
declarations regarding the name by which His
Church should be known.

The miracles that attended His ministry on
this land were, many of them, of the same character as the wondrous works He performed among
the Jews; only frequently more marvelous and
more glorious, on account of the greater faith of
the Nephites. He healed the sick, cast out devils,
raised the dead in Bountiful as he did in Judea and
Galilee. But there were other manifestations that
were somewhat different. In the land of Jerusalem Jesus miraculously fed five thousand by increasing the store of loaves and fishes that had
been provided; in Bountiful he administered the
emblems of His body and blood when neither the
disciples nor the multitude had brought either
bread or wine. Angels ministered to men during
His labors among the Jews; they did so more
abundantly during his visits to the Nephites.
Again, though we are told in the Bible of the Holy
Redeemer blessing little children, we nowhere read
therein of the glorious manifestations, the out-
pourings of the Spirit, the ministry of the angels,
the baptism of fire that took place when the risen
Redeemer condescended to bless the little ones of
the Nephites.

John.   185

NAMES AND TITLES GIVEN TO JESUS CHRIST.
Among the names and titles given to Christ
in the Book of Mormon are: Mediator, Messiah,
Redeemer, Shepherd, Great and True Shepherd,
Lamb, Lamb of God, Son of Righteousness, Son
of the Eternal Father, Only Begotten of the
Father, Creator, The Eternal Father of Heaven
and Earth, King, King of Heaven, Heavenly King,
King of all the Earth, God of Israel, God of the
whole Earth, Most High God, Lord Omnipotent,
Lord God Omnipotent, Mighty God, Holy One,
Holy One of Israel, Mighty One of Jacob, Won-
derful Counsellor, Prince of Peace, and several
others.

JOHN. The Apostle, usually called John the
Revelator. He is mentioned by name three times
in the Book of Mormon. Twice regarding the
things revealed to him (I Nephi, 14: 27; Ether, 4:
16); and once regarding his request, similar to
that of the three Nephites, that he might live and
minister on the earth until Jesus returned (III
Nephi, 28:6).

JOHN. The Baptist. This prophet is not
mentioned by name in the Book of Mormon, but
that he would baptize the Savior is foretold by
Lehi and Nephi (I Nephi, 10: 7-10; 11; 27; II
Nephi, 31: 4)

JONAS. The name of Jonas, the son of Nephi the Disciple, and himself a member of the
Quorum of the Twelve, is but once mentioned
in the Book of Mormon, and then only in the list
of those chosen by the Messiah to form that
august body, where it occupies the third place,
coming next after Nephi his father, and Timothy
his uncle, consequently all we can say of him is
inferential. It is altogether probable that by following the virtuous examples of his eminent forefathers, he had rendered himself worthy of the
glorious position to which the Savior called him,
as among a generation who were all righteous,

Jonas.   186

we cannot imagine that Jesus would select any
but the most worthy and illustrious to be the
teachers of the whole people and the heads of the
Church. He was one of those of whom it was directly said by the angel to Nephi (the son of
Lehi): "Behold they are righteous forever, for because of their faith in the Lamb of God, their
garments are made white in His blood."

JONAS. One of the twelve disciples, called
and chosen by the risen Redeemer to minister among
the Nephites. He is the second of that name found
in that quorum, the other being the son of Nephi.
He is not again mentioned by name in the Book of
Mormon. (See Twelve Disciples.)

JONEAM. A Nephite general, who commanded a corps of ten thousand men in the last
great struggle between the Nephites and the
Lamanites. He, with all his command, was slain
in the final series of battles in the land Cumorah
(A. C. 385), when the Nephite nation was annihilated.

JORDAN. The Bible river of that name. It
is mentioned thrice in the Book of Mormon; once
in connection with the occupation of Canaan by
the Israelites (I Nephi, 17: 32); once in Lehi's
prophecy concerning the labors of John the Baptist (I Nephi, 10: 9); and in an extract from the
writings of Isaiah. (II Nephi, 19: 1).

JORDON, CITY OF. A city mentioned only
in connection with the final war between the
Nephites and Lamanites; of its situation we can
tell nothing, except that it was in the northern
continent. Here the Nephites, under Mormon,
made a brave stand (A. C. 370), and twice defeated the attacking hosts of the Lamanites. In
the third attack, however, the Nephites, by reason
of the overwhelming number of their assailants,
after desperate resistance were driven from the
city with great loss (A. C. 380). Jordon appears
to have been a key to the surrounding country,

Joseph.   187   Josh.

and was consequently stubbornly held by Mormon. The war at this time was carried on with
ruthless cruelty on both sides, and the conquering
army ravaged and utterly desolated the country
through which it passed.

JOSEPH. The younger son of Lehi and
Sariah, born to them during the difficulties and
sorrows of their journey across the Arabian Peninsula (about 595 B. C). We are told very little of
his life or character, but he appears to have been
an upright man and a faithful servant of the Lord.
At the time of his father's death he was still small,
but was blessed by that patriarch with the rest of
the family, shortly before Lehi's departure from
this earth. Joseph with his elder brother Jacob,
was ordained by Nephi, a priest, to minister to the
Nephites, after the separation of that people from
the adherents of Laman. Of his private history
or death we are told nothing. Jacob, speaking
of himself and Joseph, says: We did magnify our
office [of priests] unto the Lord, taking upon us the
responsibility, answering the sins of the people
upon our own heads, if we did not teach them the
word of God with all diligence.

JOSEPH. The son of the patriarch Jacob,
and the ancestor of the Nephites and Lamanites.
Lehi was descended from his son Manasseh, and
Ishmael from Ephraim. He is referred to with
great affection by a number of the Nephite worthies. Lehi quotes (II Nephi, 3.) some very important prophecies of Joseph, which do not appear
in the Bible. These are frequently called,
by their teachers, the seed or house of Joseph.

JOSEPHITES. A portion of the Nephite
race, presumably the descendants of Joseph, the
younger son of Lehi. This name is only used four
times in the Book of Mormon.

JOSH. A Nephite general, who commanded a
corps of ten thousand men in the last great
struggle between the Nephites and the Lamanites.

He, with all his command, was slain in the final series of battles in the land Cumorah. (A. C. 385), when the Nephite nation was destroyed.

JOSH. One of the iniquitous cities destroyed by fire from heaven at the time of the crucifixion of Christ, because of the wickedness of its people in casting out the prophets and stoning those whom the Lord had sent to declare to them their sins and abominations. The Savior announced the terrible fact that there was not one righteous person to be found in it, therefore He had destroyed it, that the blood of the martyrs might not cry from the ground to Him any more against those who had slain them. (III Nephi, 9: 10, 11.) Josh is only mentioned in the Book of Mormon in connection with its destruction.

JOSHUA. A city mentioned only in the account of the great closing war between the Nephites and Lamanites. It was situated near the Pacific Ocean, either in the extreme northern portion of South America or in Central America. Here Mormon endeavored to gather his forces in one vast host to stay the advance of the victorious Lamanites; and we are of the opinion that it was in the vicinity of this city that the great last battle between Mormon and king Aaron was fought in A. C. 330, when the former turned the tide of victory against the Lamanites. (Mormon, 2: 9.) The city of David appears to have been situated near Joshua, to the south.

JOTHAM. The tenth king of Judah. He was a contemporary of Isaiah, and his name is mentioned in the Book of Mormon only in a quotation from the writings of that prophet. (II Nephi.17: 1.)

JUDAH. This name is found principally in the Book of Mormon in quotations from the prophet Isaiah; and in the statement of the fact that Lehi left Jerusalem in the reign of Zedekiah, king of Judah. In two places it refers to the Jews, as the descendants of the patriarch Judah.

dom," or he put to death. But few refused to make this covenant. (B. C. 73.) When the elder Paboran died (B. C. 68), great contentions arose between the king-men and the "free-men." The former thought this an opportune time to re-establish the royal power. They desired the new chief judge, Pahoran, the younger, to amend the laws, so that this end might be accomplished. Pahoran declined, considering he had no authority to so change the national constitution. At the demand of the royalists, the question was put to the popular vote, or "to the voice of the people." The majority voted in favor of the continuance of the existing form of government. The king-men, greatly angered at the result, broke out in open rebellion.

At this critical juncture, Amalickiah invaded the Nephite territory. The monarchists refused to assist in the defense of the fatherland. At his own request, full power was granted to Moroni, the Nephite commander-in-chief, to deal with them. He was made, for the time being, military dictator; he occupied a position nearly analagous to the Pendragon of the ancient Britons. Moroni attacked the malcontents in their cities and forts, slew about 4,000 of them, and cast into prison those who would not take up arms in defense of their country. This outbreak, which was led by those claiming to be of noble birth, resulted disastrously for the Nephites; for while Moroni was engaged in putting it down, the Lamanites made rapid advances northward, capturing many cities on their route. (B. C. 67.) Four years later, another royalist uprising took place. As usual, it commenced at the capital, and for a time was quite successful. Pahoran was driven from the judgment seat and fled to the land of Gideon, while a man named Pachus was made king. He opened a treasonable correspondence with the Lamanites, in which he made a treaty with them,

JUDEA, CITY OF. A city of the Nephites, situated in the southwestern portion of their dominions, somewhere between the Pacific Ocean and the land of Manti. It is only mentioned in Helaman's letter to Moroni, giving an account of the military operations in that region (B. C. 66 to 63). In the first-named year it was garrisoned by a Nephite force of about 6,000 men under Antipus; who, by reason of their reverses and the severe labors of the campaign, were depressed in mind and body. At this time they were strengthened by the arrival of Helaman with 2,000 young Ammonites, who found the soldiers of Antipus working night and day in the effort to strengthen the fortifications of the city. United they accomplished this purpose. In the second month of the next year (B. C. 65), 2,000 more men arrived from Zarahemla, and a supply of provisions from the fathers of the young Ammonites. In this year the campaign occurred in which Antipus was slain, and the young Ammonites showed such exceeding great valor. After this campaign, the troops which took part in it returned to Judea, and Helaman appears to have taken the chief command. In B. C. 63, reinforcements, to the number of 6060 men arrived, with provisions, and the Nephites felt strong enough to carry on offensive operations. They apparently still made Judea their headquarters, and the point from which they made their attacks. After this war Judea is not again mentioned in the Book of Mormon.

KIB. The second king of the Jaredites. He was the son of Orihah, and grandson of Jared. He was born in his father's old age, and succeeded him on the throne. Among Kib's sons was one named Corihor, who, when he was thirty-two years old rebelled against his father and drew many people after him. He first established himself in the land of Nehor, and when strong enough came against Kib in the land of Moron, which

and agreed to hold the city of Zarahemla in their mutual interest, which he supposed would so weaken the Nephites as to enable the Lamanites to conquer the remainder of the land. This being accomplished, he would be made king of the Nephites. The success of the royalist cause was of short duration. Moroni and Pahoran united their forces, and being joined by thousands of volunteers, they attacked the city of Zarahemla and defeated the revolutionists. In this battle Pachus was slain, and his followers, who were captured, were speedily tried for treason, as were also the king-men of the previous abortive revolt, who, for about five years, had been lying in prison awaiting trial. Those of both periods, who would not take up arms in defense of their country, but would fight against it, were executed according to law. (B. C. 62.)

In later years, the Gadianton robbers, when it suited their purposes to obtain power and plunder, declared in favor of a kingly form of government, but they had to satisfy themselves by electing to or otherwise placing on the judgment seat men of their own order, which amounted to much the same thing, as it placed the reins of government in their hands. In A. C. 30, the final attempt to restore the monarchy was made. As usual, petty place-men, and those claiming to be of higher birth, were the instigators and leaders of this disastrous uprising. The chief spirit of the revolution was a demagogue named Jacob. He was the one they chose for king. The outbreak resulted in the assassination of the last chief judge, Lachoneus the younger, and the breaking up of the nation. A kingdom was not established, but the people separated into numerous tribes, each with its independent ruler or chief. Disorganization, degradation and partial anarchy followed, crime and sin abounded, and bloody and wide-extended wars would doubtless have fol-

Moron was near the land called Desolation, by the Nephites. Having taken his father prisoner, Corihor held him in captivity for many years. In his old age Kib begat Shule, who, when grown to manhood, overthrew Corihor and replaced his father on the throne. His father having then arrived at an exceedingly great age, resigned the kingdom to Shule, who reigned in his stead.

KIM. A king of the Jaredites. He was the son of Morianton, born to him when he (Morianton) was very aged.

The days of Morianton were among the most prosperous that the Jaredites saw; they grew exceedingly rich during his reign. But when he became very aged he abdicated in favor of Kim, who reigned in his father's place for eight years before the latter died. Kim, however, did not reign in righteousness, and by his wickedness he displeased the Lord, so that He permitted the brother of Kim to rebel against him, dethrone him and hold him in captivity all the remainder of his life. During his captivity he begat sons and daughters, the only one whose name is mentioned is Levi, who was born to him in his old age.

KIMNOR. One of the early Jaredites. He is simply known to us as the father of Akish, the friend of king Omer.

KING-MEN. The name given by the Nephites to those who, in the days of the republic, desired to re-establish the monarchy. The first royalist outbreak was led by one Amlici, in the fifth year of the commonwealth, and cost much blood and sorrow; Amalickiah was another prominent leader of those who wished to overturn the government, but being defeated by Moroni, he fled to the Lamanites, and by treason and murder worked himself on to the throne of that people. His followers who remained within the borders of the Nephites were compelled to enter into a covenant to support the republic, or "the cause of free-

Kish.   193   Kishkumen.

lowed, had not the greater portion of the more wicked been slain in the convulsions that attended the crucifixion of the Redeemer. King Jacob, finding his plots had miscarried, hurried his followers to the far north, where they built a city, called Jacob-ugrath. During its short existence it became a head centre of depravity and cruel licentiousness, and was destroyed with its sister cities in the general upheaval at Christ's death.

KISH. A king of the Jaredites. He was the son of Corum, and succeeded his father on the throne. Nothing is said in the Book of Ether about his character, the events of his reign, or the length of his life. All we are told of him is that he reigned in the place of his father and that, when he died, he was succeeded by his son Lib.

KISHKUMEN. An assassin, and a leading man among the Gadianton robbers at the time of the organization of their marauding bands. In the year B. C. 52, Pahoran, the chief judge of the Nephite commonwealth, died, which event gave rise to serious contentions among the Nephite people. Three of his sons, named Pahoran, Pacumeni and Paanchi, were ambitious to fill the exalted position left vacant by their father's death. Each had his subcrites and following, but, according to the national law, the matter was decided by the voice of the people, and Pahoran was chosen.

Pacumeni assented to the decision of the citizens, but Paanchi attempted to raise a rebellion, for which crime he was arrested, tried by the law and condemned to death. Still, the more wicked part of the community supported his unlawful claims. These determined to kill Pahoran, which resolve they carried into effect, and the chief judge was slain by Kishkumen. This foul murder was brought about by the secret magistrate was sitting in the judgment seat administering the law, but, through the connivance of the murderer's associates in iniquity, he escaped. Pacumeni, Pahoran's

brother, was next elected chief judge, but he was
slain in war with the Lamanites the following
year. In B. C. 50, Helaman, the son of Helaman,
was chosen to fill the judgment seat. Being a
righteous man, his election was very distasteful to
the Gadianton robbers. They determined to slay
him, as they had slain Pahoran, and the same vile
instrument was chosen to do the murderous work.

As Kishkumen was on his way to fulfil his
bloody errand, a servant of Helaman, whose
name is not recorded, met him and gave him one
of the secret signs of the Gadiantons. This admitted him into the confidence of the assassin,
who explained his purpose, and asked to be conducted into the judgment hall, where Helaman
was then sitting in the performance of his duties.
This was agreed upon; the two proceeded to
where the murderer expected to find his victim.
The strategy of the attendant disarmed Kishkumen's suspicions. At an opportune moment the
servant stabbed him, and so adroitly did he perform his work, that the robber fell dead without a
groan. The servant immediately ran to the judgment hall, and informed Helaman of all that he
had heard, seen and done. Without delay, orders
were issued for the arrest of the band, but its
members, finding that Kishkumen did not return,
fled precipitately into the wilderness, beyond the
reach of the officers.

KISHKUMEN, CITY OF. One of the iniquitous cities which the Lord, at the time of His
crucifixion, caused to be buried with fire from
heaven, with its inhabitants, because of their
wickedness in casting out the prophets and stoning those whom He sent to proclaim their sinful-
ness and abominations. So depraved were its
people that the Lord declares that there were
none righteous among them, and that He destroyed them that the blood of the prophets and
saints whom He had sent, and they had slain,

might no longer cry unto Him from the ground
against them. Kishkumen is mentioned only in
connection with its destruction.

KORIHOR. An anti-Christ, who appeared
among the Nephites B. C. 75. He taught many
of the heresies of Nehor, prominent among which
were the denial of the coming of the Redeemer
and of the efficacy of His atonement. [His doctrine was that every man fared in this life according to his management, prospered according to
his shrewdness, and conquered according to his
strength.] He proclaimed that whatsoever a man
did was no crime, for when a man was dead there
was an end thereof.

As a missionary Korihor was, for a short
time, a success. We first hear of him preaching
his satanic doctrines in the land of Zarahemla,
and, as he claimed to fully believe all he taught,
the law could not touch him, as full religious
liberty was guaranteed under the constitution
and laws of the Nephite commonwealth. From
Zarahemla he went to the land of Jershon, to
inoculate the Ammonites with his soul-destroying
vagaries. But they were a wiser and more zealous
people for the gospel than were many of the
Nephites. They took him, bound him, and
carried him before Ammon, their high priest. He
directed that Korihor should be removed beyond
the border of their land, which command having
been obeyed, we next find the unabashed impostor
laboring among the people of the land of Gideon.
There he also met with rebuff. He was arrested
by the people and taken before the chief officers in
that land. They found they could do nothing
that would lie satisfactory with him, so they remanded him into the custody of the proper
officers with instructions to carry him before
Alma and Nephihah, in Zarahemla. When brought
before these worthies—the highest dignitaries of
the church and state—Korihor continued in his

course of loud-mouthed blasphemy, defiant as-
sumption, and wilful falsehood. He argued
against the existence of the Father, and the coming of His only Begotten. Alma accused him of
arguing against his convictions, but this he stoutly
denied, and clamored for a sign to be given, as he
pretended, that he might be convinced. Alma, at
length, wearied by his impious importunities, told
him that God, as a sign, would smite him dumb.
This terrible warning, though it carried the pre-
tender some uneasiness, only resulted in an attempt at prevarication. He said: I do not deny
the existence of a God, but I do not believe there
is a God; and I say also, that ye do not know
that there is a God; and except ye show me a sign
I will not believe. Then Alma answered: This
will I give unto thee for a sign, that thou shalt be
struck dumb, according to my words; and I say
that, in the name of God, ye shall be struck dumb,
that ye shall no more have utterance.

Korihor received his sign: Alma's words were
fulfilled; the sign-seeker never more spoke on
earth. When the hand of the Lord fell on him he
recanted. By writing, as he could not speak, he
confessed the power of God, and acknowledged
that he had been led astray by Satan, who had
come to him in the form of an angel of light. He
begged that the curse might be removed, but
Alma, well knowing the baseness of his heart,
refused to intercede before heaven in his behalf, lest
when restored to speech he would again strive to
deceive the people.

A proclamation was next sent throughout all
the land. In it the chief judge recited what had
happened to Korihor, and called upon those who
had believed in his words to speedily repent, lest
the same judgments should come upon them.
This proclamation put an end to the iniquity of
Korihor, for his followers were all brought back
again to the truth, but Korihor, deserted by the

---

devil, a vagabond and a beggar, still continued to
beg his way from town to town, from house to
house, until one day, in a city of the Zoramites,
he was run over and trodden down. The injuries
that he received at this time were so great that he
soon after died.

KUMEN. One of the twelve Disciples called
and chosen by Jesus to minister to the Nephites,
at the time of his visit to that people (A. C. 34).
Kumen was present near the temple in the land
Bountiful when Jesus appeared, and was baptized
by Nephi on the day following. He is not again
mentioned by name in the sacred record.

KUMENONHI. One of the twelve Disciples
called and chosen by Jesus to minister to the
Nephites, at the time of his visit to that people
(A. C. 34). Kumenonhi was present near the
temple in the land Bountiful, when Jesus appeared,
and was baptized by Nephi on the day following.
He is not again mentioned by name in the sacred
record.

LABAN. A rich, unscrupulous and powerful Israelite of the tribe of Joseph, though a
dweller in Jerusalem (B. C. 600). While Lehi
and his little company were resting in the valley
of Lemuel, that patriarch was commanded of the
Lord to send his sons back to Jerusalem to obtain
certain records that were in the possession of
Laban. The records, which were engraven on
plates of brass, being intimately associated with
Lehi's ancestors, were highly necessary for the
welfare of his descendants when they established
themselves in a new home, far from communication with any other people.

When the elder sons of Lehi were informed of
the Lord's wishes, there entered many objections
to returning to Jerusalem. They claimed to be
afraid of Laban, who was a man of considerable
influence, having much wealth and many servants
at his command. It was not until Nephi had plead

with them that they would consent to go.
Though young, he had learned an exceedingly
valuable lesson, that the Lord does not require
His children to do impossible things, but that
when He gives them a command He opens up the
way for them to accomplish His requirements.
Nephi felt at this time that if the Lord desired
that they should have the records, then in the possession of Laban, He would control circumstances
in such a way that they could obtain them.

The young men accordingly returned to Jerusalem. When they reached the holy city, it was
decided that Laman, being the eldest, should
first go to Laban and endeavor to obtain the
records. Laman had no faith in his mission
and, consequently, was unsuccessful. He was
much abused by Laban for asking for the records,
and returned to his brothers feeling very down-
hearted. The young men then decided that they
would endeavor to purchase the records from
Laban, so they went to their father's house, and
gathered up some of the valuables that they
had left therein when they deserted their home
for the journey into the wilderness. Taking these
precious things to Laban, they offered them to
him in exchange for the plates. He, seeing how
great was the value of the property offered him,
desired to obtain it without giving up the
records in return. He, therefore, with the aid
of his servants, drove the young men from his
house and sent his retainers to slay them, but
he did not permit them to carry back the valuables they had brought. These he kept for
himself.

After this second unsuccessful effort, Laman
and Lemuel were very angry, and they went so
far as to beat their younger brothers, Sam and
Nephi, with a rod. While doing so, an angel
appeared before them and upbraided them for
their evil conduct. This rebuke for a time quieted

them, but the effects of this heavenly visitation
were short lived.

Laman and Lemuel were now very anxious
to return to the wilderness, but Nephi would
not consent. He was determined that, by the
help of the Lord, he would not go back without the records. Accordingly, he resolved to make
the next attempt himself; so when night came,
he walked towards the city, being followed at
some distance by his brothers. They do not
appear to have had the courage to enter the
gates, but stood without the walls, while Nephi
entered the city, not knowing exactly where
he should go, or what he should do, being led
by the Spirit of the Lord within him. As he
approached the house of Laban, he perceived
a man lying on the ground in a drunken stupor.
A brief examination showed him that the man
was Laban. The Spirit of the Lord directed
Nephi to slay Laban, for he was a robber and,
at heart, a murderer. He had robbed the sons
of Lehi of the property they had taken to him
in their effort to exchange it for the records, and
had afterwards sought their lives. But, though
fully justified, Nephi shrank from taking the life
of a fellow being. Never before had he shed
human blood. But the Spirit of the Lord whispered to him it was better that one man should
be slain than that a whole people should perish
in ignorance. If Lehi's company and their descendants should go to the new land, which
would afterwards be their home, without any
account of the dealings of God with their forefathers, the mighty works He had done for their
preservation, and the laws which He had given
them, they might please Him, they would gradually
grow in darkness in all these respects, and by
and by lose sight of their Creator, and become a
wicked, degraded and unbelieving people.

Served by this monition, Nephi drew Laban's

sword from its scabbard, and cut off his head. He then quickly disrobed the body and placed the dead man's armor on his own person. Thus attired, he entered the house of Laban, and, it being dark, it was not easy to recognize him. Assuming the voice of Laban, he called to a servant named Zoram, who had the keys of the treasury, and told him to bring the plates which he needed. Zoram, deceived by the voice and the armor of his master, at once obeyed.

LACHONEUS, THE ELDER. One of the greatest prophets and judges of the Nephites. We are not informed when he was elected to the judgment seat, but we are told that he occupied it at the time of the Redeemer's birth in Bethlehem. His reign was a long and troublous one; it was one of continued warfare with the Gadianton bands, who, year by year, grew in numbers and increased in audacity. The forces of both Nephites and Lamanites were unable to cope with them, and their leader, Gidhianhi, had the effrontery to write an epistle to Lachoneus (A.C. 16), asserting the powers of the robbers, their undoubted ability to conquer all opposed to them, and suggesting that the people whom Lachoneus judged should surrender and affiliate with them, and become like them. This arrogant proposition was indignantly rejected. (See III Nephi, chap. 3.)

So great was the misery entailed by the invasions of the robbers, that Lachoneus at last determined to gather all the people into one place, and by a policy of masterly inactivity wear out or starve out the invaders. We can scarcely understand how terrible must have been the misery endured by the nation at this time, to cause the conception and execution of such a measure. Can we picture to ourselves the scenes that must have occurred as the people of two continents converged into one gathering-place? From the shores of the great lakes in the north, from the stormy

Atlantic seaboard, from the coast where the mild Pacific ebbs and flows, from the regions of the southern Andes, the migrating hosts flowed together to Zarahemla and Bountiful, the lands selected as the temporary gathering place. They came with their flocks and herds, their grain and provisions, leaving nothing that would help to sustain the robber bands while they continued to wage their uninallowed war. (A.C. 17.)

When the people reached the gathering place they fortified it so strongly that it became impregnable to their enemies. Under the instructions of Gidgiddoni, the Nephite commander-in-chief, they also made themselves strong armor and shields, as well as all kinds of weapons, so that they might be fully prepared for the day of battle. Lachoneus, in the meantime, preached to them in great power, so much so that they feared his denunciations, forsook all their sins, and turned to the Lord in great humility and devotion. The result was that when the robbers came against them, the attacking force was driven back with great slaughter.

Game soon became so scarce in the wilderness that the Gadiantons began to suffer for food while besieging the Nephite stronghold. In addition to this, the Nephites made frequent attacks upon them. Seeing his armies wasting away through famine and the sword, Zemnarihah, their commander, gave up all hope of success, withdrew from the siege, and formed the design of marching his followers to the most distant parts of the land northward.

To permit the Gadianton robbers to escape would have increased the difficulties under which the Nephites had so long suffered. Gidgiddoni, having learned of their purpose, and knowing their weakness for want of food and because of the great slaughter made among them through the successful attacks of his own troops, sent his

armies to cut off their retreat. During the night they got beyond the robbers, who, when they began their march on the morrow, found themselves between the armies of the Nephites. Many thousands surrendered, and the remainder were slain. Zemnarihah was taken and hanged to the top of a tree; which, when he was dead, the Nephites cut down. They then greatly rejoiced and praised God for His mercies and blessings in delivering them; but it was not until five years later (A.C. 26), that the Nephites returned to and possessed their old homes.

The next year (A.C. 27), the laws were revised according to justice and equity. They had, doubtless, been greatly tampered with during the times that the Gadianton robbers held control of the administration and elected the officers. Good order now prevailed throughout the whole land. Soon new cities were founded and built, and many improvements made. Yet for all this, the peace was short lived. Iniquity and dissension soon began to again raise their hideous heads, and the prophets and servants of God were persecuted and illegally condemned to death.

We are not informed when Lachoneus died, but in A.C. 30, another Lachoneus, probably his son, filled the judgment seat.

LACHONEUS, THE YOUNGER. The last of the Nephite judges, probably the son of the preceding judge who bore the same name. He was assassinated in the year 30 A.C.

It is not entirely certain from the sacred record when Lachoneus, the younger, assumed the reins of government, but the idea seems to be conveyed that it was in the year 30 A.C. His dominion fell in perilous times. The people had ripened in iniquity and were ready for destruction. The prophets of God who raised their warning voices were slain by unjust judges and unscrupulous officers, and the laws were perverted and trampled under

foot. When these corrupt rulers were called to account by the supreme authority at the capital, they set the laws at defiance, refused to answer, broke out in open rebellion, endeavored to establish a monarchy, and assassinated the chief judge.

LAISH. A place in Palestine, probably the small village, Luishah, lying between Gallini and Anathoth. It is only mentioned once in the Book of Mormon (II Nephi, 20:30), in a quotation from the prophecies of Isaiah.

LAMAH. A Nephite general who commanded a corps of ten thousand men in the last great struggle between the Nephites and the Lamanites. He, with all his command, was slain in the final series of battles in the land Cumorah. (A.C. 385), when the Nephite nation was annihilated.

LAMAN. The eldest son of Lehi and Sariah. From the fact that his father dwelt in Jerusalem all his days, it is presumable that Laman was born in that famed city and during the reign of king Josiah. Laman was a stubborn, wilful, unbelieving and desperate man. He had no faith in the revelations given to his father, and was the leader in all the troubles and contentions in the wilderness, going so far as to propose the murder of his brother Nephi, and also of his father. Placing no credence in the prophecies that Jerusalem would be destroyed, he unwillingly left that city, and as unwillingly journeyed in the wilderness, every difficulty, every hardship encountered by the party being a fresh pretext for murmurs against God and his father. For renewed assaults upon Nephi. Giving way to this spirit of rebellion and cruelty, he grew more hardened as he advanced in years. One of his great complaints was that Nephi had usurped the position properly belonging to his elder brothers, as the active leader of the company, though Lehi was recognised as their

head as long as he lived, and the Lord appears to have so honored him. Laman and Lemuel were not unaware that God had chosen Nephi for the position he occupied. They well knew that the expedition under their guidance would be a failure, as their desires were continually to return to Judea, and that, therefore, they would be most unsuitable to carry the purposes of their father to a successful issue. Laman, with his brothers, returned twice to Jerusalem, the first time to obtain the plates of brass from Laban, the second time to bring Ishmael and his family.

Soon after their return this second time, Laman married one of the daughters of Ishmael, and from this marriage appears to have sprung the royal house of the Lamanites, and the leading spirits of that race, until the times when Nephite apostates gained the supremacy in the Lamanite nation and became the kings, rulers, commanders and teachers of that people. For details of the journey in the Arabian wilderness and across the ocean, see Nephi, Lehi. Laman lived to witness the death of his father, and no sooner had this occurred than he entered into a conspiracy with those who sympathized with him to kill Nephi and take charge of the colony. So embittered was their hate, so determined their purpose, that Nephi's friends deemed it advisable to separate; and this left Laman and his followers to the quiet possession of the first home of the race on the land of promise. Those who remained with Laman were his own family, Lemuel and his sons, If, and the sons of Ishmael and their families. If there were any others they are not mentioned. So sooner had the division taken place than the Lamanites began to sink into barbarism. The nomadic habits which they had acquired in their wanderings in the wilderness remained with them and dominated their lives; they were shut out from the

presence of God, as they were left without the priesthood when Nephi withdrew; the other party had also the possession of the records, which in itself was regarded as a great grievance by the children of Laman. In the next generation, when those who were familiar with the civilization of the Jews had passed away, their descent became more rapid, and we read of them as a cruel, degraded, dark-skinned race, living by the chase, feeding on raw meat, idle and ignorant and exceedingly loathsome in their habits.

LAMAN. The king of the Lamanites, who entered into a treaty with Zeniff and ceded to him the cities of Lehi-Nephi, and Shilom, and the land around about. (About B.C. 200.) King Laman's intention in making this concession was to get Zeniff's small colony into his power and bring them into bondage. After the Nephites had dwelt in the land for about twelve years, Laman grew uneasy at their increase, and began to stir up his people to hostilities. The result of which was that in the thirteenth year the Lamanites made an attack upon the Nephite farmers in the southern part of the land of Shilom, drove them off, captured their flocks and carried off the corn from their fields. Those who escaped fled into the city of Lehi-Nephi for safety. Zeniff armed his people, advanced against the Lamanite marauders, and after a severe battle, lasting a day and a night, forced them back of their own lands. In this battle 3,043 Lamanites and 279 Nephites were slain. After this, by the wise precautions taken by Zeniff to defend his people, there was continual peace in the land for twenty-two years. About this time king Laman died, and was succeeded by his son. (About B.C. 160.)

LAMAN. A king of the Lamanites, apparently the son of the last named, though it is possible he was his grandson. His father's name is said to have been the same as his own. Presuming him to have been the son of the monarch who made the treaty with Zeniff, he came to the throne about B. C. 160, and immediately commenced war with the Nephites in the land of Lehi-Nephi. As long as Zeniff lived the Lamanites were unsuccessful, and were driven back to their own possessions with great slaughter; but when the weak and corrupt Noah reigned in the place of his father, they became more successful. Their first invasion in Noah's reign was, however, unsuccessful, but after his people had slain the prophet Abinadi, the Lord used the Lamanites to scourge them for their iniquities. The hosts of this people came upon Lehi-Nephi from the borders of Shemlon. Noah ordered a precipitate retreat into the wilderness, but being incumbered with women and children, the Lamanites overtook them. The coward king commanded that the women and children should be left to the mercy of the invaders, and that the men continue their flight. Some obeyed but many refused. Those who remained with their families caused their women to plead with the Lamanites for their lives. Then the latter, charmed with the beauty of the Nephite women, had compassion on them, spared their lives, but held the Nephites in tribute—one-half of all they possessed was the amount of the Lamanite exaction. Laman set guards around the land of Nephi, to prevent the escape of any of the Nephites; their tribute was too valuable to the indolent Lamanites to permit of its decrease or stoppage. In this condition things remained for two years.

At this time there was a romantic spot in the land of Shemlon, where the Lamanitish maidens where in the habit of gathering on pleasure bent. Here they sang, danced and made merry with all the gaiety of youthful innocence and overflowing spirits. One day, when a few were thus gathered, they were suddenly surprised, and twenty-four of their number were carried off by strange

---

men, who, from their appearance, were unmistakably Nephites.

On learning of this act of treachery the Lamanites were stirred to uncontrollable anger, and without seeking an explanation they made a sudden incursion into the territory held by king Limhi. This attack, however, was not successful, for their movements, though not understood, had been discovered, and their intended victims poured forth to meet them.

With Limhi and his people it was a war for existence; to be defeated was to be annihilated; his warriors therefore fought with superhuman energy and desperation, and eventually they succeeded in driving the Lamanites back. So speedy did the flight become, that in their confusion the Lamanites left their wounded king lying among the heaps of slain. There he was discovered by the victors. In the interview between him and Limhi that followed, mutual explanations ensued. The Lamanite king complained bitterly of the outrage committed on the daughters of his people, while Limhi protested that he and his subjects were innocent of the base act. Further investigation developed the fact that some of the iniquitous priests of king Noah, who had fled into the wilderness from the dreaded vengeance of their abused countrymen, at the time that monarch was killed, were the guilty parties. Being without wives, and fearing to return home, they had adopted this plan to obtain them.

On hearing this explanation, king Laman consented to make an effort to pacify his angry hosts. At the head of an unarmed body of Nephites he went forth and met his armies who were returning to the attack. He explained what he had learned, and the Lamanites, possibly somewhat ashamed of their rashness, renewed the covenant of peace. This peace, unfortunately, was of short duration. The Lamanites grew arrogant and griev-

---

ously oppressive, and under their exactions and cruelty the condition of Limhi's subjects grew continually worse, until they were little better off than were their ancestors in Egypt before Moses their deliverer arose. Three times they broke out in ineffectual rebellion, and just as often their taskmasters grew more cruel and exacting, until their spirits were entirely broken; they cowered before their oppressors, and bowed "to the yoke of bondage, submitting themselves to be smitten, and to be driven to and fro, and burdened according to the desires of their enemies."

In process of time the Lord softened the hearts of the Lamanites, so that they began to ease the burdens of their slaves, but He did not deliver the Nephites out of bondage at once. They, however, gradually prospered, and raised more grain, flocks and herds, so that they did not suffer with hunger. And in the Lord's due time they escaped from their Lamanite oppressors and in safety reached the land of Zarahemla.

Great was the excitement among the subjects of Laman when they found their Nephite vassals had disappeared. An army was immediately sent in pursuit. It followed the fugitives for some distance, but did not overtake them, and lost itself in the wilderness. In their wanderings the Lamanite troops found the priests of Noah and their Lamanitish wives, and later they came across the people of Alma in the land of Helam. The Lamanites extended their suzerainty over these peoples, and king Laman appointed Amulon, the leader of the priests of Noah, the local ruler.

Amulon and the priests, possibly because of their Lamanitish wives, soon gained great favor with king Laman and were made teachers to his people. Educated in the language of the Nephites, they began to instruct the Lamanites therein. They taught the Lamanites nothing of the

---

religion of their Israelitish fathers, or of the law of Moses, but instructed them how to keep their records, and to write one to another. Laman now ruled over a numerous people, inhabiting distant regions, governed by tributary kings and rulers. Having no written standard, the language of the Lamanites had become greatly corrupted. The coming of the priests of Noah among them gave rise to the introduction of a higher civilization. As a result, they increased in wealth, and trade and commerce extended among them. They became cunning and wise, and therefore powerful, but were still addicted to robbery and plunder, except among themselves.

LAMAN. Originally a servant of the king of the Lamanites, who was slain by the cunning and deceit of Amalickiah (B. C. 73). When the royal cortege issued from the city of Nephi to welcome the supposedly victorious general and his army, Laman accompanied his master. When that master was treacherously slain, and the cry was, adroitly raised that his even retainers had committed the atrocious deed, Laman with the rest of the servants fled. We next find him (B. C. 63) in the service of the Nephites, and engaged in the army of Moroni, most probably as an inferior officer. At the time that Moroni determined to release the Nephite prisoners held by the Lamanites in the city of Gid, Laman, on account of his nationality, was chosen to carry out the details of the stratagem by which Moroni hoped to deliver his fellow countrymen. He was placed in command of a small body of troops, loaded with wine, and sent out at evening towards the place where the Nephites were held captive. When the guards saw the prisoners saw him approaching, they hailed him. He told them that he was a Lamanite, and that he and his companions had just escaped from the Nephites, but luckily they had been able to secrete some

---

wine and bring it with them. The Lamanites at once became exceedingly anxious to get hold of the booty, and enthusiastically welcomed Laman. He, very cunningly, pretended that he wished to preserve the wine until the day of battle, but the more he protested the more anxious the soldiery became to drink it. This was exactly what he wished, and at last, with well feigned reluctance, he handed over the coveted liquor. It had been purposely made very strong and sweet, and when the Lamanites found it was so palatable they drank copiously. Deep sleep followed. Now was the hour of action. Laman returned to Moroni and reported his success. The Nephite general had everything prepared; while the guard were yet in their deep drunken stupor, he hastened to the city, as noiselessly as possible he conveyed over its walls sufficient weapons to arm all the prisoners, even to the women and the children who were old enough to use them. When the guards awoke from their drunken sleep they found themselves surrounded by the armies of Moroni without, and the prisoners armed and marshaled within. Deeming discretion the better part of valor, their officers surrendered and the new prisoners were set to work increasing the strength of the fortifications of Gid, while the released Nephite warriors joined the forces of Moroni, to whom they were a great help.

LAMAN, CITY OF. One of the iniquitous cities destroyed by the Lord, with fire from heaven, at the time of the mighty convulsions which, on this continent, marked the hour of the Savior's death. From the names of the cities destroyed with it—Josh, Gad and Kishkumen—we are led to think that it was a city originally built by the Lamanites or Gadianton Robbers. Of its location and history the record is silent, except we are told that its crime-

---

stained people rejected, cast out and slew the prophets and saints of God who were sent among them.

LAMAN, RIVER. A small Arabian river which emptied into the upper waters of the Red Sea. When Lehi and his little colony had traveled for three days in the wilderness which bordered on the Red Sea, they reached a pleasant valley through which this stream flowed, and Lehi gave to it the name of Laman, in honor of his eldest son. In the valley the company rested for some time; and it was during their sojourn here that Nephi and his brothers twice returned to Jerusalem—once for the plates of brass, and once for Ishmael and his family. When, by the Lord's command, Lehi's party continued their journey, they crossed the river Laman and proceeded southward.

LAMANITES, THE. The people who, in connection with their kindred, the Nephites, occupied the American continent from about B. C. 590 to A. C. 385, in which latter year they destroyed the Nephites and remained possessors of the entire land. The American Indians are their degraded descendants. These people were of Hebrew origin, being members of the half tribe of Manasseh, and are called Lamanites, from Laman, the eldest son of Lehi, who was the leading spirit in the events that led to the separation from the Nephites and their formation as a distinct people. Originally, the Lamanites were the children of Laman, Lemuel, and some of the family of Ishmael; but as the centuries passed there were many defections in both nations, when the dissatisfied would join the opposing race and affiliate and intermarry with them, so that the two names at last became more an indication of religion and civilization than of birth.

LAMONI. The Lamanite king of the land of Ishmael. He was the first of his race converted to Christianity by the sons of Mosiah. At the time of their coming (B. C. 91), he reigned under the supreme authority of his father, who was monarch of all the Lamanites. Lamoni appears to have ruled with severity, if not with cruelty, and his action in executing any of the servants having charge of his herds who permitted the royal cattle to be stolen, undoubtedly excited a spirit of discontent among his subjects. After his conversion his character appears to have entirely changed, and he became gentle, loving, patient and humble. The details of this conversion are given under the head of *Ammon*. After his change of heart he became the protector and chief pillar of the Church, which, through his zealous assistance, was established in the land of *Ishmael*. He accompanied Ammon to the land *Middoni*, and by his influence with *Antiomno*, the king of that region, he succeeded in releasing Aaron and the other Nephite missionaries, who had been held in prison there and so barbarously treated. (B. C. 86?) In later years, when the anger of the Nephite apostates and unconverted Lamanites was raging against the new born disciples, Lamoni was trusted as a wise counselor, and the missionaries and others visited Ishmael to advise with him regarding the best course to pursue to protect the lives of the unoffending people of Anti-Lehi-Nephi. (B. C. 82.) After this, we read no more of Lamoni, and we have no means of telling if he suffered martyrdom when so many of his fellow converts were slain, or whether he lived to accompany the fugitives who forsook their homes, threw themselves on the magnanimity of the Nephites, and found a resting place in Jershon.

LAURAM. A Nephite officer under Mormon, killed in battle with the Lamanites. He is only mentioned in the second epistle of Mormon to his son Moroni, and there simply referred to as having, with many other choice men, been slain in a disastrous battle with the enemy. The fact of his name being mentioned infers that he was an officer of distinction.

LEBANON. The Mount Lebanon of the Bible. It is mentioned four times in the Book of Mormon, always in quotations from the writings of Isaiah.

LEHI. A Hebrew prophet, of the tribe of Manasseh, whom the Lord called to warn the Jews of their coming captivity in Babylon. Lehi was a man of considerable means, and of good repute among the Jews. He had dwelt in Jerusalem all his life, though, from the influence that the language of the Egyptians appears to have had on him, it is not improbable that he was brought, in some way, in intimate contact with that people. In the first year of the reign of Zedekiah, king of Judah (B. C. 600), the Lord gave Lehi a number of prophetic dreams and visions, and, in compliance with the admonitions of those manifestations, he went forth among the Jews proclaiming the sorrows that would inevitably be theirs if they did not repent and return to the Lord. But the Jews treated Lehi just as they were treating all the rest of the prophets who came to them. They paid no heed to the message he bore. When he reproved them for their wickedness and abominations, they grew angry with him; and when he talked of the coming of the Messiah and the redemption of the world, they mocked him. But he did not cease to labor in their midst until their anger grew so intense that they sought his life; and they would have slain him if the Lord had not protected him; for it was not to be that Lehi should fall a victim to their hatred. The Lord had designed him for a greater work—he was to be the father of a multitude of people, and to that end God delivered him from the fury of the Jews. When it became impossible for him to remain longer and minister unto them, he was instructed

to gather up such things as he could carry and take them into the wilderness with his family, where the Lord would reach him what more He required at his hands.

When Lehi received the command to depart, he immediately set about fulfilling it, and taking with him his family and such goods and food as he could carry, he left the doomed city, where he had so long dwelt, leaving behind him his house and property, his gold, his silver and other precious things, all of which he willingly gave up that he might be obedient to the heavenly message.

Lehi's family consisted of his wife, *Sariah*, and his four sons, *Laman, Lemuel, Sam and Nephi*. Lehi had also daughters, but whether they were born at this time is not evident from the record. We have no account in the Book of Mormon of the precise road which Lehi and his family took when they left Jerusalem. Undoubtedly they traveled through the wilderness of Judea southward till they reached the eastern arm of the Red Sea. They journeyed along the Arabian shore of that sea for some little distance, till they came to a valley through which a small stream flowed. To the river Lehi gave the name of Laman, after his eldest son; and the valley he called Lemuel. Here they pitched their tents and rested for some time. While tarrying in this valley, Lehi, by Divine direction, twice sent his sons to Jerusalem; the first time to obtain certain most precious records, the second, to bring a family to join them in their journey. The head of this family was named *Ishmael*. In both undertakings the young men were successful, and the company was strengthened by the addition of Zoram, and Ishmael and his family. Soon after, five marriages took place; Zoram married Ishmael's eldest daughter, and the four sons of Lehi espoused four younger ones.

While Lehi and his party dwelt in the valley of Lemuel, he received many glorious manifestations

from the Lord. Like Enoch, John the Revelator and others, the world's future history was mapped out before him, and he not only saw things that related to his own posterity, but the scene widened until he appears to have been shown all that would happen to the sons and daughters of mankind to the very last generation. (See I Nephi, chap. 8.) Nephi, his son, was favored of the Lord with similar manifestations.

Before long, Lehi was directed to resume his journey; and a wonderful instrument, prepared by Divine condescension, called a *Liahona*, or compass, was given him to guide the wandering feet of the company in their travels.

So particular was the Lord that Lehi's party should not come in contact with the people of Arabia, through which land they passed, that He gave them the command that they should not cook their meat, lest the flame or smoke from their fires should draw attention towards them; but He promised that He would make their meat sweet to them, that they could eat it with pleasure and satisfaction without it being cooked with fire. Probably it was dried after the manner that the people in this region often dry beef and other meats.

To their next tarrying place, which they reached in four days, they gave the name of Shazer. After a short rest, during which time they killed game for food, they again took up their line of march, keeping in the most fertile parts of the wilderness, which were near the borders of the Red Sea. Thus they continued journeying for some time, when, by direction of the Liahona, they changed the course of their travels, and moved almost directly east across the Arabian peninsula, until they reached the waters on its eastern coast. There they found a very fruitful land, which they called Bountiful, because of the abundance of its natural productions. To the sea which washed its shores they

gave the name of Irreantum, which, being interpreted, means many waters. If we understand correctly, these waters were a portion of the gulf of Oman, or Arabian sea. The journey thus far occupied eight years from the time they left Jerusalem.

When the people of Lehi reached the sea shore they rejoiced greatly that their tedious wanderings were over. Nephi, by Divine direction, built a ship to carry them across these great waters. When the vessel was finished, the voice of the Lord came to Lehi, commanding that he and his people should arise and go aboard the ship. The next day they embarked, every one according to his age, taking with them their provisions, seeds, and such other things as it was desirable they should carry across the ocean to their new home, far away on its opposite shores.

During Lehi's travels in the wilderness two sons were born to him, whom he named Jacob and Joseph, respectively. The patriarch and his wife were now advancing in years, and their peace was much disturbed on the ocean by the cruel conduct of Laman and others towards Nephi. In fact the miseries induced by this conduct nearly resulted in the death of the aged couple.

After many days, the vessel with its precious freight reached the shores of this continent, at a place, we are told by the Prophet Joseph Smith, near where the city of Valparaiso, Chili, now stands. Then, with hearts full of rejoicing, they left the vessel that had carried them safely across the wide sea, now advancing in years, and their peace was much disturbed on the ocean by the which God had given to them and to their generations after them. And they pitched their tents and began to make a new home. They put the seeds into the earth, which they had brought from Jerusalem. To their great joy these seeds grew exceedingly, and they were blessed with

abundance. Upon the land they found many beasts of the forest, also cows, asses, horses, goats, and other animals that are for the use of man; and in the earth they found precious ores of gold, silver and copper. Then they erected an altar, and, to show their thankfulness to God, they offered sacrifices and burnt offerings, according to the law of Moses, as was their wont under such circumstances.

The course taken by Lehi and his people has been revealed with some detail. We have it that the Prophet Joseph Smith said that Lehi and his company traveled in nearly a south-southeast direction until they came to the nineteenth degree of north latitude, then, nearly east to the sea of Arabia, then sailed in a southeast direction, and landed on the continent of South America, in Chili, thirty degrees south latitude. This voyage would take them across the Indian and South Pacific Oceans.

Some time, we know not how long, after Lehi's arrival, believing that his end was approaching, he gathered his children together as did his forefathers before him, and being inspired by the spirit of prophecy, he blessed them, foretelling many things that should occur to them to their latest generations.

Soon after Lehi had uttered these blessings, the Lord took him from this earth to dwell with Him in eternity. Of the death of Sariah, his wife, we have no account.

LEHI. One of the greatest of Nephite military commanders and the associate of Moroni and Teancum, both of whom he survived for many years. It is not evident from the record, but we think it highly probable, that Lehi was the same person as Lehi the son of Zoram (Alma, 16:5,) that young man being then (B. C. 81) distinguished officer under his father. Lehi first prominently appears in the Nephite annals in the great battle fought (B. C. 74) with the Lamanites under Zerahemnah on the banks of the Sidon, not far from Manti. Moroni was commander-in-chief of the Nephite forces, while Lehi commanded an army corps. Before the battle commenced, Moroni skilfully concealed his troops on both sides of the river, and permitted the Lamanites to pass between. Lehi's men, who had been massed on the east side of the river, on the south of a hill named Riplah, closed in on the rear of the Lamanites, when the latter faced about and gave battle. The fight soon grew fast and furious. The Lamanites perceiving that Moroni was attacking them on both sides, fought with desperation, but with immense loss; and in a short time they fled before Lehi and were driven by him into the waters of the river. Lehi did not cross in pursuit, but halted his soldiers on the eastern side, while the troops more directly commanded by Moroni drove the enemy before them on the western banks. The day ended in a complete victory for the Nephites. When the devastating wars which Amalickiah inaugurated were begun, we again find Lehi in high command. He was chief captain in the city of Noah, and when the Lamanites attacked it, his name alone added to their discomfiture, for, we are told, "they feared Lehi exceedingly." (Alma, 49:17). Lehi's cautious but resolute defense, combined with the perfection of the fortifications built by Moroni around the city, caused the Lamanites to throw away more than one thousand men, and all their chief captains, in the futile attempt to carry the city by storm (B. C. 73).

Lehi continued to be actively engaged during the next war, and appears to have been second in command to Moroni over the army of the northeast. His next conspicuous recorded exploit was

Lehi, Land of. 221 **Lehi-Nephi, City of.**

spective homes. In B. C. 67 this city, with many others, fell into the hands of the Lamanite armies under Amalickiah, who appear to have retained it until B. C. 61, when it was recaptured by the Nephites. This city is not again mentioned by name in the Book of Mormon.

LEHI, LAND OF. The name by which the whole of South America was known to the Nephites, in contradistinction to North America, which was called Mulek, because the Lord brought Mulek into the land north, and Lehi into the land south. (Helaman, 6: 10.)

LEHI, LAND OF. A small region of South America, on the Atlantic seaboard, immediately surrounding the City of Lehi, and adjoining the land of Morianton. In B. C. 68, a feud arose between these two districts, the people of Morianton unjustly claiming a portion of the land of Lehi. The former determined to assert their claims by force of arms, when the people of Lehi for protection fled to the camp of Moroni, the Nephite commander-in-chief. Morianton, the leader of the people of that name, determined to flee northward with his followers, but was stopped at the land Bountiful by the Nephite armies. A battle ensued in which Morianton was slain and his people were escorted back to their own lands. Upon their making an agreement to keep the peace, a union was effected between them and the people of Lehi, who also returned to their homes.

LEHI-NEPHI, OR NEPHI, CITY OF. The capital city of the land occupied by the Nephites, for a period of uncertain length, immediately preceding the exodus of the righteous portion of the race to Zarahemla, under Mosiah I, rather more than two hundred years before Christ. It is supposed to have been situated in the region known to moderns as Ecuador. When the Nephites evacuated this city, the Laman-

assisting in the defeat of Jacob, between Bountiful and Mulek, and the recapture of the latter city (B. C. 64). Moroni placed Lehi in command of the captured city. When (B. C. 62) the revolt of the king-men under Pachus took place, Moroni, at the suggestion of Pahoran, the chief judge, hastened to the aid of the government at Zarahemla, and left Lehi and Teancum in charge of the armies in the northeast, who were then reduced by years of continued fighting, and sadly in need of provisions. The next year, Moroni sent them a reinforcement of 6,000 men and a sufficient supply of food, which was followed by a brilliant campaign, in which Moroni, Lehi and Teancum, by prearranged tactics and simultaneous movements, drove the Lamanites beyond the Nephite territory and ended the long-continued and exhausting series of wars. (B. C. 61.) When Moroni died (B. C. 56), he was succeeded by his son Moronihah as commander-in-chief of the armies of the Republic, and Lehi, now getting up in years, appears to have stood in the same position to him, as he did to his father.

In the calamitous invasion of the land of Zarahemla by the Lamanites, under Coriantumr (B. C. 51), Lehi was the first to stay their devastating march northward. He met them somewhere between Zarahemla and Bountiful, and drove them back towards the former city. Their retreat was cut off by Moronihah, and the two Nephite generals, one in the front and the other in the rear, signally defeated the invaders and made prisoners of all who were not slain. It is in connection with this campaign that Lehi's name is last mentioned in the Book of Mormon. In character, we are told by the historian, that Lehi "was a man like unto Moroni," God-fearing, wise, prudent and brave. "They were beloved by each other, and also beloved by all the people of Nephi." Alma, 53: 2.)

Lehi-Nephi, Land of. 222

ites took possession of it, and held it, only by treaty between king Laman and Zeniff, it was, with the surrounding district, ceded to the Nephite colony that had returned from Zarahemla. It now became the chief city of this branch of the race, and Zeniff, Noah and Limhi reigned there as kings. The Nephites, finding that the indolent Lamanites had permitted it to fall into decay, went to work to repair its walls and residences, and in the days of king Noah it was greatly beautified and improved. Among its other buildings it contained a temple, near to which king Noah built a high tower. It was in this city that Abinadi was martyred, and on its outskirts, shortly after, Alma, the elder, established a Christian Church at the waters of Mormon. Lehi-Nephi was again evacuated by the Nephites, (B. C. 122; when it was again possessed by the Lamanites, and was made by them the capital of the whole land of Nephi, and the abode of their head king. Aaron, the son of Mosiah, found the chief monarch (the father of Lamoni) residing there when he went up to the land of Nephi to preach the gospel to the Lamanites (about B. C. 85). Lehi and Nephi, the sons of Helaman, were cast into prison in this city, when they ministered among the Lamanites; and it was in this prison that there was such a glorious manifestation of the power of God in their behalf, that resulted in the conversion of so many thousand Lamanites. (B. C. 30.)

LEHI-NEPHI, LAND OF. A small division of the land of Nephi, originally settled by the Nephites, but after their departure it was taken possession of by the Lamanites, and by them made the chief centre of their government. It appears to have been simply the valley in which the city of Lehi-Nephi stood, but because it at one time comprised all the territory occupied by the Nephites,

Lehi, son of Helaman. 220 **Lehi, City of.**

LEHI, THE SON OF HELAMAN. Were we to attempt to sketch the life of Lehi, we should simply have to repeat the most striking features of that of his elder brother, Nephi. In their labors, journeyings, ministrations, etc., they seem to have always been together. Like Samuel of old, in their childhood they "began to grow up unto the Lord," and in riper years they lived to His glory. In speaking of the exalted character of Nephi, the historian adds, "And behold, Lehi, his brother, was not a whit behind him as to things pertaining to righteousness."

The date of Lehi's birth is not recorded. In the year B. C. 44, the fact that Helaman had two sons, named Nephi and Lehi, is mentioned; but at that time they must have grown to manhood, as their public labors begin shortly after. Lehi accompanied his brother in his extended labors throughout the lands of the Nephites; he was with him in prison among the Lamanites, in the city of Lehi-Nephi, at the time of the great manifestation of God's power, and the conversion of the greater part of that people to the service of the true God; he went with Nephi to the northern continent, and labored there several years. Again we hear of them (B. C. 13) all laboring in the might of Jehovah and the powers of the priesthood for the salvation of the souls of men. After this we lose sight of Lehi, the date, the place, or circumstances of his death are not stated.

LEHI, CITY OF. A city on the Atlantic seaboard of South America, apparently near the Caribbean Sea. It is described as lying "in the north, by the borders of the sea shore" (Alma, 50: 15). It was founded in B. C. 72, possibly by Lehi, one of the great Nephite generals of that era. In B. C. 68, its citizens being threatened by their neighbors of the city of Morianton, fled for protection to the camp of Moroni. When the difficulty was settled they both returned to their re-

Lehonti. 223

whence they spread out and colonized, it is more often called the land of Nephi than the land of Lehi-Nephi; but it must not be confounded with the larger land of Nephi which grew out of it. This smaller land of Nephi is supposed to have been situated in the country now called Ecuador.

LEHONTI. A Lamanite officer, chosen by the opponents of the war policy of the reigning sovereign, as their leader in their armed resistance to the royal proclamation (B. C. 73).

When the Nephite traitor, Amalickiah, fled to the Lamanites, the first step he took to accomplish his ambitious, though at present defeated, purposes, was to excite public feeling against the Nephites. The king gave way before his wiles and persuasiveness, but the great mass of the people, not being brought in contact with his brilliant person and shining abilities, were averse to hostilities. They too well remembered the horrors and disasters of the previous campaign. Amalickiah had, however, gained such influence over the king's mind that he was inexorable, and insisted on the invasion of Zarahemla. For this purpose, he issued a proclamation and sent it among all his subjects, commanding them to gather to his standard. The people greatly dreaded the arbitrary power of the throne, but they feared the Nephites more. Consequently, many refused to heed the proclamation, and assembled themselves at Onidah, the place of arms, for protection against an army the king had placed under the command of Amalickiah to bring them to terms, and which was now rapidly advancing towards them. Here they chose Lehonti as their leader and king, for they were strong in their determination not to go to war with the Nephites. Lehonti assembled his forces on a mount called Antipas, and there awaited the arrival of the royal troops.

Lehonti, however, little knew the temper or

craft of the man with whom he was dealing. Amalickiah had no intention to spill Lamanite blood. He wanted their friendship now, that he might use them as his willing tools hereafter. To this end, when night came, he sought an interview with Lehonti, who, fearing treachery, refused to go down near to his camp. Three times did Amalickiah send his message, and as often was the proposal declined. At last, the platter went up the mountain, to near where Lehonti's camp was situated, and there told him to come out and meet him, and if he feared any evil, to bring his guard with him. This time the cautious Lehonti acquiesced. At the interview that followed, Amalickiah agreed to surrender his forces to Lehonti, on condition that he (Amalickiah) should be placed second in command of the united forces. The plot was successfully carried out. Lehonti surrounded the royal troops before morning; they, seeing their predicament, were loth to do battle with their countrymen and pleaded with their commander to surrender. This he did, for it was exactly what he had been working for. Lehonti faithfully carried out the terms of the agreement and placed Amalickiah second in command. The conscienceless traitor soon removed the commander-in-chief; Lehonti was killed by slow poison, administered by a creature of his subordinate, and Amalickiah assumed supreme command.

LEMUEL. The second son of Lehi and Sariah, born in Jerusalem, about B. C. 620 or 625. He appears in history as the shadow of his elder brother, Laman; where the latter led he followed, but lacked, to some extent, the active, aggressive malignity of Laman's turbulent and vindictive character. In all the rebellions in the Arabian wilderness, in all the murmurings against the providences of the Lord, in all the inhuman assaults upon Nephi, Lemuel sided with and

sustained Laman, and when, after the death of Lehi, the colony divided, Lemuel and his family joined their fortunes to that of his elder brother. Of Lemuel's domestic life we only know that he married a daughter of Ishmael. Of the time and place of his death we are told nothing. The descendants of Lemuel appear to have inherited the characteristics of their progenitor — they took a secondary place in the Lamanite nation, and we do not read of one prominent character, either in Nephite or Lamanite history, who was descended from him.

LEMUEL, CITY OF. A city of the Lamanites, whose inhabitants were converted to the Lord by the preaching of the sons of Mosiah, and became a portion of the people of Anti-Lehi-Nephi. They, no doubt, afterwards suffered in the ruthless persecutions inflicted upon the Christian Lamanites, and those who survived migrated to the land of Jershon, with the rest of their brethren. (B. C. 78.)

LEMUEL, VALLEY OF. After three days' journey through the desert bordering the upper waters of the Red Sea, (Gulf of Akaba,) Lehi and his colony reached a small valley wherein they camped and built an altar to the Lord. A river ran through it and emptied into the sea. To the river, Lehi gave the name of Laman, and to the valley, that of Lemuel, after his two eldest sons, remarking to Lemuel "O that thou mightest be like unto this valley, firm and steadfast, and immovable in keeping the commandments of the Lord." After a stay of considerable length, Lehi continued his journey down the shores of the Red Sea. (B. C. 600.)

LEMUELITES. The descendants of Lemuel. They formed a portion of the Lamanite nation, but do not appear to have taken a prominent position in the conduct of its affairs. The descendants of Laman were the controlling ele-

ment in the race, in whose movements the Lemuelites acquiesced.

LEVI. A Jaredite prince, the son of Kim. His father was driven from the throne and held in captivity for the remainder of his days. Levi was born in captivity and so remained until 42 years after the death of his father; when he rose in rebellion against his uncle, who occupied the throne, deposed him, and reigned in his stead. During his reign he did that which was right in the sight of the Lord, and his people were greatly prospered. He lived to a good old age, was blessed with a large family, and when old died his son Corom succeeded him as king.

LEVI. The son of Jacob. His name is only mentioned in a quotation from Malachi (III Nephi, 24:3), "and he shall purify the sons of Levi."

LIAHONA, THE. While Lehi and his little colony were encamped near the river Laman, the voice of the Lord came unto him, and commanded him to resume his journey on the morrow. When Lehi stepped out of his tent door the next morning, he was much surprised to behold lying upon the ground close by, a round ball of curious workmanship. It appeared as though it was made of fine brass, and within it were two spindles; one of which pointed the way which Lehi and his party should travel as they journeyed through the wilderness.

God had prepared this strange instrument or guide for them. In the days of Moses, when He led the children of Israel out of Egypt, a pillar of cloud by day and of fire by night moved in front of them. This the Hebrews followed. But to Lehi He gave this Liahona, or compass, as the ball was called, and it pointed the way they should travel. It had one strange peculiarity, which was that it worked according to their faith and diligence. When they kept God's law it showed them much more clearly the way they should

go than when they were careless or rebellious. Some people have confused this ball, because it is called a compass, with the mariner's compass, that sailors use at sea to direct the course of their ships. But there is a great difference between the two. The Liahona pointed the way that Lehi's company should travel, while the needle in the mariner's compass points to the north. The one showed the way Lehi should go, the other informs the traveler which way he is going. The one was specially prepared by the Lord for Lehi and his companions, and was used through faith only; the other can be used by all men, whether believers in the true God, pagans or infidels. At times, also, writing would miraculously appear on the Liahona, giving directions or reproving for sin, as the company most needed.

LIB. A righteous king of the Jaredites, in whose reign the nation prospered and multiplied greatly. He was the son and successor of Kish. In the reign of a former monarch named Heth, the Lord had deeply afflicted the people, because of their sins; and among other things he had caused numbers of poisonous serpents to occupy the regions in the neighborhood of the Isthmus of Panama, and thus prevented the people from gaining access to the southern continent. In Lib's days these venomous reptiles were destroyed, and the land southward was found to be full of beasts of the forest. That country was preserved as one enormous hunting ground of the race, Lib. himself, becoming a great hunter. He also built a large city at the narrowest portion of the Isthmus, apparently for the purpose of guarding the regions south from settlement, so that it might be the source of their meat supply, for the country northward was covered with inhabitants. In this reign the people greatly developed in the arts of civilization, they prosecuted mining with much vigor, improved in the manufacture of textile

fabrics; agriculture made marked advance through the invention and application of improved machinery in the cultivation of the earth and the harvesting of their crops. They also made all manner of weapons of war, though, as this was a time of profound peace, this can only be regarded as a precautionary measure. In fact, to use the words of the sacred historian: "never could be a people more blessed than were they, and more prospered by the hand of the Lord. And they were in a land that was choice above all lands, for the Lord had spoken it."

Lib lived many years, was blessed with a numerous posterity, and when he died he was succeeded by his son Hearthom.

LIB. A commander opposed to Coriantumr, in the great series of wars that ended in the destruction of the Jaredite race. In size he was a giant, being the largest man in the nation. He was also high in authority among the warriors of the secret associations that at that time held almost unbounded power among that people. He came to the throne through the murder of his predecessor, having himself committed the vile deed. In the first year of his reign, Coriantumr came up against him, and drove his forces to the borders of the sea. In this battle, however, Lib and Coriantumr met in single combat, and the latter was severely wounded by his adversary. A second battle took place on the sea shore, in which Lib was victorious, and the enemy retreated to the wilderness of Akish, and Coriantumr made another stand, and in the battle that ensued Lib was killed. His brother, named Shiz, took command, continued the fight, and obtained a decisive victory.

LIMHAH. A Nephite general, who commanded a corps of ten thousand men in the last great struggle between the Nephites and the Lamanites. He, with all his command, was slain in

the final series of battles in the land Cumorah (A. C. 385), when the Nephite nation was annihilated.

LIMHER. A Nephite military officer of the early days of the Republic. He, with Amnor, Manti and Zeram, and their commands, was sent to watch the retreating Amlicites after their defeat by Alma, (D. C. 87). They returned next day in great haste, and reported that the Amlicites had joined an invading army of Lamanites, and together they were advancing by way of the land of Minon to Zarahemla. Limher is nowhere else mentioned in the Book of Mormon.

LIMHI. The son of Noah, and the third king over the colony in Lehi-Nephi. His reign was little more than a nominal one, as his people were in bondage to the Lamanites, to whom they paid one-half of all they possessed, and one-half of the products of their yearly toil. Out of this wet paid the guards who were set to watch that none of the Nephites escaped. Limhi's reign was marked by several disastrous wars, one brought on by the fugitive priests of king Noah (see Laman, Amulon); the others were the abortive attempts of the people of Limhi to throw off the oppressor's yoke; but in every case the revolt ended in its suppression and the infliction of heavier burdens and more cruel indignities upon the unfortunate Nephites. All of which were in fulfilment of the words of the Prophet Abinadi. Thus the years already and painfully wore away. The Lord, after a time, softened the hearts of the Lamanites, so that they treated their captives with less cruelty, he also prospered them in their labors, that they did not suffer any more from hunger.

In this sad condition of bondage and serfdom, the people of Limhi had one hope. It was to communicate with their Nephite friends in the land of Zarahemla. To this end Limhi secretly fitted out an expedition consisting of a small number of men. This company became lost in the wilderness, and traveled a long distance northward, until they found a land covered with the dry bones of men who appeared to have fallen in battle. Limhi's people thought this must be the land of Zarahemla, and that their Nephite brethren who dwelt there had been destroyed. But in this they were wrong, for they found with the dead some records engraved on plates of gold, which, when afterwards translated by the power of God, showed that these bones were those of some of the Jaredites who had been slain in war. They evidently missed the land of Zarahemla, having probably traveled to the west of it and passed northward through the Isthmus of Panama.

Shortly after this, a small company, numbering sixteen men, reached them from Zarahemla. Their leader's name was Ammon. He had been sent by king Mosiah to the land of Nephi, to find out what had become of the people who left with Zeniff, Limhi's grandfather. At first, Ammon's men were taken for spies and cast into prison. The next day the mistake was discovered, and Limhi and his people were overjoyed to hear from their friends. Soon plans were laid to effect the escape of the enslaved Nephites, which, under the guidance of Limhi, Ammon and Gideon, was successfully accomplished. The Lamanite guards were made drowsy through a large present of wine, of which they freely drank. While in this condition the Nephites escaped through an unfrequented pass, crossed the wilderness and reached the land of Zarahemla in safety. (B. C. 122). After the arrival of his people in Zarahemla, we hear nothing more of Limhi, save that he and all who accompanied him from Lehi-Nephi were baptized by Alma, the elder, and became members of the church of God.

Manti, Land of. 233 Mary.

MANTI, LAND OF. This land was situated contiguous to the wilderness at the head waters of the Sidon (Alma, 16: 6), and lay on the line of march generally taken by the armies of the Lamanites when they invaded Zarahemla. Its exact boundaries are not defined; indeed, it is altogether probable that they varied considerably at different periods of Nephite history. However, it is evident that it was the most southerly of all the lands inhabited by the Nephites, in the western half of the South American continent, after they had moved from the land of Nephi.

MARY. The mother of Jesus Christ. She is twice mentioned by name in the prophecies of the ancient Nephite worthies. King Benjamin in prophesying to his people of the coming of the Redeemer (B. C. 125) said, "He shall be called Jesus Christ, the Son of God, the Father of heaven and earth, the Creator of all things from the beginning, and his mother shall be called Mary." (Mosiah, 3: 8.) Alma, the younger, in his preaching to the people of Gideon (B. C. 83) declared that Jesus should "be born of Mary * * * * she being a virgin, a precious and chosen vessel, who shall be overshadowed, and conceive by the power of the Holy Ghost, and bring forth a son, yea, even the Son of God." (Alma, 7. 10.) She was also shown to Nephi in a vision (B. C. 600), though not mentioned by him by name. He records: "I beheld the city of Nazareth; and in the city of Nazareth I beheld a virgin, and she was exceedingly fair and white." Of this virgin an angel tells him: "The virgin whom thou seest, is the mother of the Son of God, after the manner of the flesh." Further on he states: "I looked and beheld the virgin again, bearing a child in her arms. And the angel said unto me, Behold the Lamb of God, yea, even the Son of the Eternal Father." (1 Nephi, 11: 13—21).

LUCIFER. The Son of the Morning; Satan. This name appears but once in the Book of Mormon (11 Nephi, 24: 12), in a quotation from the writings of Isaiah.

MADMENAH. A Benjamite village, north of Jerusalem, whose inhabitants were frightened away by the appearance of the armies of Sennacherib. It is only mentioned in the Book of Mormon in a quotation from the writings of Isaiah. (11 Nephi, 20; 31).

MAHAH. One of the sons of Jared, apparently the third. It is presumable that he was born in Western Asia, before the people of Jared commenced their migration to America. Like the rest of his father's family, he was a righteous man; and when offered the kingly authority by the people he refused that honor.

MAHER-SHALAL-HASH-BAZ. A son of Isaiah. His name, which means speed-spoil, was given by Divine revelation, as a token that the "child should not have knowledge to cry, my father, and my mother, before the riches of Damascus and the spoil of Samaria shall be taken away before the king of Assyria."

It is this incident that appears in the Book of Mormon in Nephi's quotations from the writings of Isaiah. (11 Nephi, 18: 1—4).

MALACHI. The prophet of the Jews of that name. His prophecies, as contained in the third and fourth chapters of his book, were quoted to the Nephites by Jesus during his ministrations to them. As Malachi lived between two and three hundred years after Lehi left Jerusalem, the Nephites knew nothing of the glorious things that the Father had revealed to him until Jesus repented them.

MANASSEH. This name is used in two ways in the Book of Mormon: (1) For the kingdom or people of Israel (11 Nephi, 19: 21), in a quotation from the writings of Isaiah; and

Mathoni. 234 Melchizedek.

MATHONI. One of the twelve Disciples, called and chosen by Jesus to minister to the Nephites, at the time of his visit to that people (A. C. 34). Mathoni was present near the temple in the land Bountiful, when Jesus appeared, and was baptized by Nephi on the day following. He is not again mentioned by name in the sacred record. His brother Mathonihah was also one of the Nephite Twelve.

MATHONIHAH. One of the twelve Disciples called and chosen by Jesus to minister to the Nephites at the time of his visit to that people (A. C. 34). Mathonihah was present near the temple in the land Bountiful, when Jesus appeared, and was baptized by Nephi on the day following. He is not again mentioned by name in the sacred record. His brother, Mathoni, was also one of the Nephite Twelve.

MATTHEW. The Jewish Apostle. He is not mentioned in the text of the Book of Mormon; but reference is made to him in the heading of chapters 12, 13 and 14 of III Nephi, as much that appears in these chapters is also found in Matthew, chapters 5, 6 and 7.

MEDES. The people of Media, a country of western Asia, lying to the northwest of Persia. The name occurs but once in the Book of Mormon, in a quotation from the prophecies of Isaiah (11 Nephi, 23: 17).

MELCHIZEDEK. The great high priest, who was king of Salem, and to whom Abraham paid tithes. The Book of Mormon gives many details of his life not contained in the Bible. Among other things we are told "this Melchizedek was a king over the land of Salem; and his people had waxed strong in iniquity and abominations; yea, they had all gone astray; they were full of all manner of wickedness; but Melchizedek, having exercised mighty faith, and received the office of the High Priesthood, according to the holy order

(2) for the son of Joseph, in the statement (Alma, 10: 3) that Lehi was one of this patriarch's descendants.

MANTI. A Nephite military officer of the early days of the Judges. He with three others — Zeram, Amnor and Limher, and their men, — were sent out by Alma to watch the Amlicites after their defeat by the Nephites. (D. C. 87). The next day they returned to camp in great trepidation, and reported that the Amlicites had joined an invading host of the Lamanites in the land Minon, and that together they were pushing with great haste towards the city of Zarahemla. Manti is only mentioned in connection with this incident, but it is not improbable that he was destined to settle the south country, and that the land of Manti was named after him.

MANTI, CITY OF. The chief city of the land of Manti. It was situated near the head-waters of the Sidon, and was the most southerly city of importance in that region. Being an outlying settlement of the Nephites, though strongly fortified, it suffered greatly by the invasions of the Lamanites. In the great war, inaugurated by Amalickiah, it was captured by the Lamanites (some time before B. C. 66), and by them converted into an important base for their operations against the Nephites, both east and west, in B. C. 63, Gid and Teomner, two Nephite generals, recaptured it by stratagem; and Helaman took his Ammonite and other troops there and made it his headquarters. It was not again captured by the Lamanites during that long and disastrous war. In later Lamanite invasions it undoubtedly fell, more than once, into their hands, as it was in the direct line of the course they generally took when entering the Nephite territory.

MANTI, HILL. A hill near the city of Zarahemla, upon which Nehor, the murderer of Gideon, was executed. B. C. 91. (Alma, 1: 15).

Metals. 235 Middoni.

of God, did preach repentance unto his people. And behold, they did repent; and Melchizedek did establish peace in the land in his days; therefore he was called the prince of peace, for he was the king of Salem; and he did reign under his father. Now, there were many before him, and also there were many afterwards, but none were greater; therefore of him they have more particularly made mention." (Alma, 13: 17—19.)

METALS. The metals named in the Book of Mormon are Brass, Copper, Gold, Iron, Lead, Silver, Steel, and Zill.

MICHMASH. A town belonging to the tribe of Benjamin, about 9 miles north of Jerusalem. It is mentioned but once in the Book of Mormon (11 Nephi, 20: 28), in a quotation from the writings of Isaiah.

MIDDONI. A land of the Lamanites. Here Aaron, Muloki, and Ammah were imprisoned, and treated with great cruelty by its sin-hardened inhabitants. Directed by the revelations of God, Ammon, then in the land of Ishmael, determined to go and deliver his brethren. Lamoni, the converted king of that land, decided to accompany him, as he believed he had influence sufficient with Antiomno, king of Middoni, to obtain the release of the imprisoned missionaries. (D. C. 86.) On their way, Ammon and Lamoni met the latter's father, the supreme ruler of all the Lamanites, journeying from the land of Nephi (Lehi-Nephi) to the land of Ishmael. From the circumstance of this meeting it is presumable that Middoni lay somewhere between Ishmael and Nephi, and as it is spoken of as down, it was probably situated in some of the lower valleys, or north towards the wilderness that separated the lands of Nephi and Zarahemla. Arrived at the land of Middoni, Lamoni found favor with Antiomno and procured the release of Aaron and his associates. Though they had at first so cruelly treated the Nephite missionaries, the Lamanites of this land were among those who were converted to the Lord by their ministrations. (Alma, 23: 10.)

MIDIAN. The Midianites, descendants of Midian, the son of Abraham and Keturah. They dwelt principally in the desert north of the peninsula of Arabia. Midian is mentioned but once in the Book of Mormon, in a quotation from the writings of Isaiah. (II Nephi, 20: 26.)

MIDIAN. A land of the Lamanites. It is mentioned but once in the sacred record, and then as the appointed meeting place of the sons of Mosiah and fellow missionaries, who assembled to consult as to the best means to adopt to preserve the converted Lamanites from the murderous persecutions of their fellow countrymen. (B. C. 82.) From Midian the missionaries went to the land of Ishmael, to hold a council with Anti-Lehi-Nephi and Lamoni.

MIGRON. A place disturbed by Sennacherib's approach to Jerusalem. Its exact situation is not known. The name occurs but once in the Book of Mormon (II Nephi, 20: 28), in a quotation from the writings of Isaiah.

MINON. A land of the Nephites, on the west bank of the Sidon, and a day and a half journey south of the city of Zarahemla. (Alma 2: 24.) In B.C. 87 an invading host of the Lamanites were here joined by the defeated followers of Amlici, and as they marched northward they ravaged the country through which they passed, the inhabitants fleeing before them with their families and flocks. Alma came to the rescue of the fugitives, and in a desperate battle defeated the allied armies. Minon is only mentioned in connection with this invasion. Elder Orson Pratt calls it about two days journey south of Zarahemla.

MOAB. The Moabites, descendants of Lot. Their home was the country east of the valley of the Dead Sea. This name only occurs in the Book

of Mormon in a quotation from the words of Isaiah. (II Nephi, 21: 14.)

MOCUM. A sin-stained city, mentioned but once in the Book of Mormon (III Nephi, 9: 7), and then in connection with its destruction at the time of the crucifixion of the Savior. It sank into the earth, and waters came up in its place, that the wickedness and abominations of its inhabitants might be hidden from the sight of Heaven, and that the blood of the prophets and saints might not come up any more before the Lord against them. No clue is given to the region where Mocum was situated.

MORIANCUMER, LAND OF. The place on the shore of the great ocean where Jared and his people tarried four years before crossing to America. It was evidently named after the brother of Jared (Mahonri Moriancumer). Here the Lord Jesus appeared to him and gave him many glorious revelations; and here, by Divine command, the company built the eight barges which carried them across the ocean. We have no direct information in regard to the locality of Moriancumer, but those who believe that the Jaredites traveled eastward through Central Asia, are of the opinion that it was near the mouth of one of the great rivers that flow through the Chinese empire into the Pacific Ocean.

MORIANTON. The founder of the city called by his name, and the leader of its citizens. Morianton appears to have been a wicked, passionate, self-willed, avaricious man, and the first notice we have of him (B. C. 68), grows out of a contention that arose between his people and those of the neighboring city of Lehi. Morianton claimed for his people some of the land lying between the two cities, then in possession of the Lehites, and so determined was he to carry his point, that he neglected all peaceable methods of settling the difficulty, and appealed to

the dread arbitrament of the sword. The people of Lehi, whose cause was just, fled to Moroni, the Nephite commander-in-chief, and asked his help. When Morianton learned of this move, knowing that he was in the wrong, and fearing the strength of Moroni, he persuaded his people to flee to the land northward. He would probably have carried his plan into effect, had it not been for his ungovernable temper. In a fit of passion he cruelly beat one of his maid servants, who ran away to the camp of Moroni and told the latter of the secret intentions of Morianton and his people. Such an exodus was very repugnant to Moroni's feelings and judgment. He feared to have a hostile people in the north, who, in times of war with the Lamanites, could harass the Nephite rear. He therefore detailed Teancum, with an army corps, to head the people of Morianton, and stop their flight northward. This the latter was not able to accomplish until they had reached the borders of Desolation, at the Isthmus of Panama. Here a battle took place, for so great was the power of Morianton over his people, that, by his flattery and wickedness, he filled them with the spirit of stubbornness to such an extent that they forcibly resisted the armies of the Commonwealth. In the battle that ensued, their leader was slain by Teancum, his hosts defeated, and those not slain were taken prisoners and carried back to the camp of Moroni. Here the difficulties were investigated and settled amicably. Upon their covenanting to keep the peace, they were restored to their lands, and a union was effected between them and the citizens of Lehi, who also returned to their possessions.

MORIANTON. A king of the Jaredites. It appears that Riplakish, a monarch of that race, became so obnoxious to his people on account of his tyranny and abominations, that they rose in rebellion, slew him and drove his descendants out

---

239 Morianton, City of.

of the land. After many years, one of these descendants, named Morianton, gathered an army of outcasts and invaded the Jaredite country. The war that followed was an exceedingly severe one and lasted a number of years. One by one the cities of the Jaredites fell into the hands of Morianton, until he had made himself master of the entire country. When established in power, he conciliated the people by lightening their burdens, so that they anointed him king. During his mild though energetic reign the people were greatly prospered, many new cities were built, and the nation grew exceedingly rich. He lived to a very great age, and when too old to hold the reins of government, he abdicated in favor of his son Kim, Morianton surviving this action eight years. His character is thus summarized in the Book of Ether: "he did do justice unto the people, but not unto himself, because of his many whoredoms; wherefore he was cut off from the presence of the Lord."

MORIANTON, CITY OF. The city built by Morianton in the land of the same name. After the settlement of the quarrel (B. C. 68), between its people and those of the land of Lehi, we next read that it was captured by the Lamanite armies under Amalickiah. (B. C. 67.) By B. C. 63 the Lamanites had made it a very strong place, and stationed a heavy garrison therein, with large quantities of provisions. In this year Moroni made preparations to recapture, it but whether he succeeded at that time, or not until later, is not clear from the record. We think it is probable that owing to the rebellion at Zarahemla, headed by Pachus, which demanded Moroni's presence there, that he did not retake Morianton until B. C. 61, when the neighboring city of Lehi was captured, and also all the other cities in the hands of the Lamanites, except Moroni. (Alma, chapter 62.)

Morianton, Land of. 240

Mormon.

MORIANTON, LAND OF. A small section of the Nephite possessions, in the neighborhood of the Caribbean Sea. It was first settled by a man named Morianton in the days of the judges (about B. C. 72). The only thing known of its history is the unrighteous quarrel of its inhabitants with their neighbors, the people of the land of Lehi (B. C. 68), their attempt to escape to the north, and their detention and forced return home by the armies of the Commonwealth. (Alma, chapter 50.)

MORIANTUM, LAND OF. A land of the Nephites, only mentioned once, and then in Mormon's second epistle to his son (Moroni, 9: 9). It appears that towards the close of the last great war between the Nephites and Lamanites, both races had descended to the most horrid, cruel and disgusting practices; and in this the Nephites, if possible, exceeded their foes. Among those who had become utterly degraded, were the people of Moriantum. Mormon records that they had grown like unto wild beasts in their habits; that they first defiled the Lamanitish maidens whom they took prisoners, then slowly tortured them to death, and after they were dead devoured their flesh, and this as a token of bravery. Surely human nature could scarcely descend to greater depths of infamy and cruelty than this.

MORMON. The father of Mormon, and grandfather of Moroni. He appears to have resided in the northern continent until A. C. 322, when he took his son, Mormon, into the land southward. Nothing is known of his private life, and all that we are told of him is that he was a descendant of Nephi. (Mormon, 1: 5); but judging from the great virtue exhibited by the younger Mormon in his boyhood, we are led to believe that he was a man who trained his children in the fear of the Lord, and taught them the truths of the gospel.

241　　Mormon.

MORMON. The last great prophet-general of the Nephite race, but better known to us as the custodian and compiler of the records of his people, and the writer of the greater portion of the work named after him, and known as the Book of Mormon. The father of Mormon, who was a descendant of Nephi, bore the same name, and his illustrious son was born on the northern continent (A. C. 311), but when the latter was eleven years of age they both traveled south to Zarahemla. Before his departure south, Mormon formed the acquaintance of Ammaron, the keeper of the sacred records, which, because of the iniquity of the people, he had hidden in a hill in the land Antum. After he had hidden them up, he informed Mormon, then a child ten years old, of what he had done, and placed the buried treasures in his charge. He instructed Mormon to go, when he was about twenty-four years old, to the hill where they were hid, and take the plates of Nephi and record thereon what he had observed concerning the people. The remainder of the records, etc., he was to leave where they were.

It was in the year 322 A. C. that actual war broke out between the Nephites and Lamanites for the first time since the Redeemer's appearing. A number of battles were fought, in which the armies of the former were victorious. Four years later the savage contest was renewed. In the interim, iniquity had greatly increased. As foretold by the prophets, men's property became slippery, things movable were subject to unaccountable disappearances, and dread and distrust filled the hearts of the disobedient. When the war recommenced, the youthful Mormon, then fifteen years old, was chosen to lead the armies of his nation.

The next year saw disaster follow the Nephite cause. That people retreated before the Lamanites to the north countries. The year following ground. Zarahemla, with its hallowed associations, its glorious temples, where the daily sacrifice was unceasingly offered, its proud palaces, its luxurious homes, its courts of justice, where the chief judge sat in the magnificence of almost kingly authority to administer the law—this, their queen city, the seat of their government, the centre of their civilization, the home of their highest priesthood, was in the hands of their merciless, vandal-like foes. Nor had the danger stopped; with hurried hands the Nephites built a line of defense across the Isthmus of Panama, from sea to sea, for the unnumbered hosts of their conquerors were still pushing forward. This line of fortification was effectual; it stopped the roll of the barbaric tide northward, and the Lamanite commanders rested with the possession of a continent.

In this war the Nephite dissenters took active part against their white brethren, and to this fact, in part, may be attributed the sudden success that shone on the Lamanite arms. But little by little, in succeeding years, the half-repentant Nephites regained their lost ground, until (B. C. 31) the most northerly half of their possessions had again fallen into their hands; but because of their only partial repentance, their leaders had not strength to lead them farther, and the proud city of Zarahemla still remained in the hands of the warriors of Laman.

In the darkest hours of this war, we read that Moronihah did preach many things unto the people because of their iniquity, * * and did prophesy many things, * * and what should come unto them if they did not repent. We thus learn that he, like his father, was not only a great military commander, but a zealous and faithful servant of God, and a prophet. When this third war censed, he had been commander-in-chief of the Nephite forces for about thirty

years, and his name is not again mentioned in the sacred record.

MORONIHAH. A Nephite general who commanded a corps of ten thousand men in the last great struggle between the Nephites and Lamanites. He, with all his command, was slain in the final series of battles in the land Cumorah, when the Nephite nation was annihilated (A. C. 385).

MORONIHAH, CITY OF. One of the great and iniquitous cities of the Nephites destroyed at the time of the Saviour's crucifixion. The earth, during the great convulsions that then occurred, was carried up upon the city; it and its people were buried, and in its place stood a great mountain. Thus were its iniquities and abominations hid from the face of the Lord, and the blood of the prophets and saints came up no more to Him against them (III Nephi, 8: 10, 25; 9: 5). Nothing is written which throws any light on the location of this ill-fated city.

MOSES. The great lawgiver to Israel. Frequent references are made to him in the Book of Mormon. Lehi refers to the prophecy of Joseph, the son of Jacob, of the coming and mission of Moses (II Nephi, 3: 9, 10, 16, 17) Nephi and others make mention of his dividing the waters of the Red Sea (I Nephi, 4: 2; 17: 24—27; Helaman, 8: 11). The ancient Nephite prophets also speak of his foreknowledge of the coming of the Messiah (I Nephi, 22: 20, 21; Mosiah, 13: 33, Helaman, 8: 15, 16); of his smiting the rock for water (II Nephi, 25: 20); of the lifting up of the brazen serpent in the wilderness (Helaman, 8: 14); of his burial by the Lord (Alma, 45: 19). Jesus said to the Nephites, "I am he of whom Moses spake" (III Nephi, 20: 23). The five books of Moses are mentioned (I Nephi, 5: 11), and the law of Moses is spoken of more than forty times.

MOSIAH I. Mosiah resided in the land of

Nephi, and lived there during the latter half of the third century before Christ. Whether he was originally a prophet, priest or king, the historian (Amaleki) does not inform us. Most certainly he was a righteous man, for the Lord made choice of him to guide the obedient Nephites from their native country to a land that he would show them.

The causes that led the Lord to make this call upon the Nephites are not stated, but some of them can be easily surmised. Among such we suggest that:

The aggressive Lamanites were constantly crowding upon them, ravaging their more remote districts, entrapping and enslaving the inhabitants of the outlying settlements, driving off their flocks and herds, and keeping them in a constant state of anxiety and dread, which hindered their progress and stayed the growth of the work of God. The Lord therefore led them to a land of peace.

Again, this course of events, continued for so long a period, had caused much hard-heartedness and stiffneckedness in the midst of the Nephites. Some of the people had remained righteous, some had grown very wicked. To separate these classes the Lord called the faithful and obedient to follow Mosiah to another land.

For a third reason: there was a portion of the house of Israel, a few hundred miles to the north, entirely unknown to their Nephite brethren. These people had sunk very low in true civilization; they were so degraded that they denied the being of their Creator, they had had many wars and contentions among themselves; they had corrupted their language, had no records nor scriptures, and were altogether in a deplorable condition. To save and regenerate this branch of God's covenant people, Mosiah and the Nephites were led to the place where they dwelt.

The statement made by Amaleki regarding this great migration under Mosiah is brief. We are altogether left to our imagination to picture the scenes that occurred at this division of a nation. Nor can we tell how many, preferring home, kindred and friends, and the endearments and associations of their native land, faltered and turned behind, while the faithful started on their journey northward into the untrodden wilderness. Nor are we informed what afterwards became of those who allowed the allurements of the world to prevail. It is most probable that they united with the Lamanites, were absorbed into that race, and, like them, became darkened, bloodthirsty and savage.

The Nephite evacuation of the cities built in the land of Nephi no doubt had a beneficial effect on those portions of the Lamanite race that took possession of them. They thereby became acquainted with some of the comforts and excellences of civilization, and, though very slow to learn, their experience at this time laid the foundation for a slight advance of the arts of peace in their midst.

Mosiah gathered up the willing and obedient, and, as directed by the Lord, started on the journey. Whither they were going they understood not, only they knew that the Lord was leading them. With preachings and prophesyings they crossed the wilderness and passed down into the land of Zarahemla.

On the west bank of the river Sidon the people of Mosiah found a populous city, of whose existence they had never before heard. Its people were a semi-civilized and irreligious race, speaking a strange language, and with many habits and customs different from those of the new comers.

The meeting must have been a perplexing one to both people, brought face to face but unable to understand each other by reason of their different modes of speech. We often read in history of

the irruption of an inferior or more barbarous race into the domains of a more highly civilized one, but it is seldom, as in this case, that the superior race moves in a body, occupies the country and unites with the less enlightened people. It is probable that the first feelings of the old settlers were akin to dismay as they learned of the hosts of the invaders that were marching upon them; but these feelings were soon soothed and an understanding arrived at by which the two people became one nation. We are forced to the conclusion that this arrangement could not have been effected without the direct interposition of Heaven, by and through which both peoples were brought to a united purpose and common understanding.

When the Nephites began to comprehend the language of their new fellow citizens, they found that they were the descendants of a colony which had been led from Jerusalem by the hand of the Lord, in the year that that city was destroyed by the king of Babylon (say B. C. 589). (See Mulek.) At this time their king or ruler was named Zarahemla (about B. C. 200). The reason assigned for their departure from the worship of the true God, their degradation and the corruption of their language, was that their forefathers brought with them from their ancient home in Palestine no records or copies of the holy scriptures, to guide and preserve them from error in their isolated land of adoption.

When the two races joined, it was decided that Mosiah should be the king to the united people, though the Nephites were then the less numerous. This arrangement probably grew out of the fact that though fewer in numbers they were the more civilized and, also being worshipers of the God of Israel, they would not willingly submit to be ruled by those who had no knowledge of His laws.

The education of the people of Zarahemla to the standard of the Nephites, and the work of

harmonizing the two races, were not the task of an hour. It required much wisdom, patience and perseverance. Mosiah gave stability to the new kingdom by his own virtues and wise example, by the just laws he established, and by placing the service of the Lord before all earthly considerations. It is evident that he built a temple in the new land, as its existence is particularly mentioned in the days of his son, king Benjamin, and as the people observed the law of Moses in the matter of sacrifices and offerings, a temple would be one of their very first necessities that to the forms, types, and ceremonies of the Mosaic law were added gospel principles, with a clear and definite understanding of the coming and divine work of the Messiah. Mosiah was not only a divinely inspired leader and king, but he was also a seer. While reigning in Zarahemla a large engraved stone was brought to him, and by the gift and power of God he translated the engravings thereon. They gave an account of the rise, fall and destruction of the great Jaredite nation, from the days of its founders, to the time of their last king, Coriantumer, who himself was discovered by the people of Zarahemla, and lived with them nine moons. When Mosiah died he was succeeded by his son Benjamin.

MOSIAH II. The third king of the Nephites, in the land of Zarahemla, where he was born B. C. 154, he was consecrated king by his father, Benjamin, B. C. 125, and died in Zarahemla, B. C. 91, aged 63 years. He came to the throne under most happy circumstances; he had the full confidence of his subjects, who were a righteous, Godfearing people; the Lamanites were at peace with the Nephites, and internal development and prosperity characterized the condition of his kingdom. Individually he proved to be one of the greatest and best of kings, his whole energies were devoted to the good of his people, who loved him with an intensity of affection scarcely equaled in the annals of any race. In the fourth year of his reign the expedition under *Ammon* started, which resulted in the return to Zarahemla of nearly all the living descendants of the company that left under *Zeniff* to reoccupy the land of Lehi Nephi. The leader of one of these companies was *Alma* the elder, whom Mosiah called to take charge of the church in Zarahemla. Soon after the arrival of these fugitives from the land of Nephi, Mosiah gathered all the people together, and had them made acquainted with the vicissitudes and sorrows through which the new comers had passed since their fathers left Zarahemla. Also taking advantage of the presence of so many of his subjects, he addressed them on such matters as he deemed necessary and desirable. At his request, Alma also taught them. When assembled in large bodies Alma went from one multitude to another, preaching repentance and faith in the Lord; afterwards, by Mosiah's direction, he went through the land, organizing and establishing churches and ordaining priests and teachers over every church. Thus were seven churches established at this time in the land of Zarahemla.

In the course of years, many of the rising generation gave no heed to the word of God. These were mostly such as were too young to enter into covenant with the Lord at the time that Benjamin anointed Mosiah to be his successor. Not only did they themselves reject the doctrines of the atonement, the resurrection and other gospel principles, but they led away many who were members of the Church, and sorely persecuted those who remained faithful to God and His laws. Encouraged by the fact that four of Mosiah's sons, and one of *Alma's*, were leaders in this crusade, they paid no attention to the national law which guaranteed freedom of conscience to all men alike. By Divine interposition,

Mulek, City of.   263   **Muloki.**

of Judea, was carried away captive into Babylon, and that they journeyed in the wilderness and were brought by the hand of the Lord across the great waters. Again we are informed that they landed on the northern continent, in the land afterwards known to the Nephites as the land *Desolation*, and for this reason the Nephites called North America the land of Mulek. This must not be confounded with the country immediately surrounding the city of Mulek, in South America. In after years this colony migrated southward and settled on the River Sidon, where their descendants were afterwards found by the Nephites.

MULEK, CITY OF. A city of the Nephites on the east borders by the sea shore, about a day's journey south of the city Bountiful, and therefore in the northernmost part of South America. It was captured by the Lamanites under Amalickiah (B. C. 67), who placed a Zoramite, named *Jacob*, in command. By stratagem, Moroni, Lehi and Teancum recaptured it (B. C. 64), when Moroni made it Lehi's headquarters. It again fell into the hands of the Lamanites when (B. C. 34-33) they drove the Nephites from all their possessions in the northern continent; but it was one of the first cities retaken by Moronihah, when the tide of victory turned (B. C. 32). It is then mentioned as being one of the cities to which Lehi and Nephi, the sons of Helaman, went forth calling the people to repentance, in that great mission which they commenced in the land of Bountiful and continued to the land of Lehi-Nephi, B. C. 30.

MULEK, LAND OF. The name given by the Nephites to the whole of North America, because *Mulek* landed on this continent, while Lehi brought his colony to the southern continent, to which his descendants gave his name. (Helaman, 6 101).

MULOKI. When (B C. 91) the four sons of

through a holy angel, these young men were turned from the error of their way, and afterwards became strong pillars in the Church, and messengers of salvation to both Nephite and Lamanite. For the four sons of Mosiah (named *Ammon, Aaron, Ommer, and Himni*, not content with their zealous labors among their countrymen, proposed to go and labor among the Lamanites. The good king, like many of his subjects, did not favorably regard this proposal, he feared for the lives of his sons; but having inquired of the Lord and received assurances of Heavenly protection, he gladly let them go.

Mosiah now felt that it was time that the question of the succession to the throne should be settled. In his magnanimity he sent among the people to learn whom they would have for their king. The people chose his son Aaron, but Aaron would not accept the royal power, his heart was set upon the conversion of his fellow-men to the knowledge of the gospel. This refusal troubled the mind of Mosiah; he apprehended difficulties if Aaron at some future time should change his mind and demand his rights. Mosiah therefore issued another address in which he proposed to retain the kingdom during the remainder of his life, after which the Nephites should be governed by judges elected by themselves. In other respects, also, Mosiah consented to newly arrange the affairs of the people; and, it we may so express it, to codify the laws. This code became the constitution of the nation under the rule of the Judges, which limited the powers of the officials and guaranteed the rights of the people. This compilation was acknowledged by the people, whereupon the historian remarks, "Therefore they were obliged to abide by the laws which he had made," and from that time they became supreme throughout the nation. It is stated in another place that this change was made by the direct

Muloki.   264

king Mosiah started on their perilous mission to convert the savage Lamanites to the true faith, they were accompanied by several other elders of the Christian Church, whom they had selected on account of their faith and devotion. Neither the names nor numbers of these co-laborers are given, but two or three are incidentally mentioned in the recital of the history of the mission. Of these Muloki appears the most prominent, and it is only in connection with this mission that his name is mentioned in the Book of Mormon.

When the missionaries, after committing themselves to God, separated on the borders of the Lamanites, Ammon went to the land of Ishmael, Aaron to Jerusalem; where Muloki first went we are not informed. When Aaron was driven out of the land of Jerusalem by reason of the wickedness of its people, he passed over to a neighboring village, styled *Ani-Anti*, where he found Muloki and others laboring with much zeal, but with little success. Finding their efforts unavailing, Aaron, Muloki, Ammah and their companions departed from Ani-Anti and went over into the land of Middoni, where Antiomno was king. Here they labored zealously, though but few hearkened unto their words. Before long the wicked raised the standard of persecution and the three brethren above named were cast into prison, while others fled to the regions round about. The prisoners were treated with extreme cruelty, they were bound with strong cords, which cut into their flesh, they were deprived of proper food, drink and clothing, and otherwise they suffered many afflictions. After many days' confinement, they were set at liberty by *Antiomno*, through the intercession of Lamoni and Ammon; their unfortunate condition having been revealed to the latter by the Lord, with instructions to go and set his brethren at liberty. When Ammon met these faithful brethren, he was greatly grieved, because of their

Mosiah, Sons of   262   **Mulek**

command of Jehovah. But besides being a king, Mosiah was also a seer. The gift of interpreting strange tongues and languages was his. By this gift he translated from the twenty-four plates of gold, found by the people of king Limhi, the record of the Jaredites. So wonder that a man possessed of such gifts, so just and merciful in the administration of the law, so perfect in his private life, should be esteemed more than any man by his subjects, and that they waxed strong in their love towards him. As a king, he was a father to them, but as a prophet, seer and revelator, he was the source from whence Divine wisdom flowed unto them.

His sons having started on their mission to the Lamanites (B. C. 91), Mosiah gave the sacred plates and the associate holy things into the care of the younger Alma, and the same year passed away to the rest of the just.

MOSIAH, SONS OF. The four sons of the second Mosiah, who accomplished the great and successful mission to the Lamanites (B. C. 91 to B. C. 78). Their names were Aaron, Ammon, Ommer and Himni.

MULEK. The infant son of Zedekiah, king of Judea, who was preserved when the rest of his brothers were slain (II Kings, 25. 7) by the king of Babylon. Eleven years after Lehi left Jerusalem the Lord led another colony from that city to America, among whom was Mulek, who, at that time, must have been very young, as his father was only 21 years old when he commenced to reign; and he reigned but eleven years in Jerusalem (II Chronicles, 36. 11; Jeremiah, 52. 1). It is altogether probable that when Mulek attained a proper age he, on account of his lineage, was recognized as king or leader of the colony.

Regarding the journey of this company, all we are told in the Book of Mormon is that they came out of Jerusalem at the time that Zedekiah, king

Nahom.   265   **Nehor.**

wretched, naked, wounded and starved condition. After a season of mutual joy, thanksgiving and congratulation, the elders again separated to renew their labors in the ministry, but to what particular land Muloki went, or among whom he sojourned we have no information.

NAHOM. A place on the line of travel of Lehi and his company through the Arabian desert. Here Ishmael died and was buried. (I Nephi, 16: 34.)

NAPHTALI, LAND OF. The country inhabited by the tribe of Naphtali, in Canaan, afterwards known as Galilee. It is mentioned but once in the Book of Mormon, in a quotation from the ninth chapter of Isaiah. (II Nephi, 19: 1.)

NAZARETH. The city were Jesus spent his childhood. It was shown Nephi in his vision of the coming and birth of our Savior. (I Nephi, 11: 13) It is nowhere else mentioned by name in the Book of Mormon.

NEAS. A grain, kind unknown, mentioned in connection with wheat, barley, and sheum, as being planted by the Nephites on the land of Lehi-Nephi. (Mosiah, 9: 9.)

NEHOR. Could our readers have taken a glimpse at the fair capital of the Nephites in the first year of the Judges (B. C. 91), they would have noticed in its principal street a portly, handsome man, manifesting in his carriage the evidences of great bodily strength, combined with vanity, self-sufficiency and subtlety. They might have observed that his raiment was made of the finest fabrics that the looms of Zarahemla could produce, lavishly embroidered and ornamented with the labors of the cunning workman in silk, in feathers and the precious metals, while at his side hung a richly decorated sword. This man was no king, no governor, no general of the armies of Israel; he was simply Nehor, the successful religious circulation of the hour, to whom the unstable listened and the weak minded flocked.

Nehor's teachings had at any rate the interest of novelty to the Nephites, yet some of his theories were older than himself. They had been rejected in the counsels of heaven before Lucifer, the Son of the Morning, fell. He would save all men in their sins and with their sins; he abolished hell, established a paid order of priests, and taught doctrines so liberal that every man could be a member of his church and yet continue to gratify every vice his nature inclined to. For this liberality of doctrine, Nehor expected in return liberality of support for himself and assistants, in which anticipation he was not disappointed. Many adopted his heresies, his success fired his zeal, and developed his vanity. He was so used to the sycophancy of his converts that he was restive under contradiction, and when Gideon, the aged patriot and teacher in the true Church, one day met him in the streets of Zarahemla and upbraided him for his wicked course, neither respecting his great age nor his many virtues, Nehor drew his sword and smote him till he died. For this wilful and unprovoked crime, the murderer was tried, convicted and afterwards executed. His execution took place on the hill Manti, and, from the way in which his death is spoken of, we imagine that he was hanged.

Though Nehor's shameful life was thus ended, unfortunately his doctrine did not die with him. It was too pleasant to those who desired to gain heaven by a life of sin. Consequently it spread widely through the teachings of his followers. In later year the traitorous Amlicites, the apostate Amalekites, the bloodthirsty Amalonites and Ammonihahites, were all believers in his soul-destroying doctrines. The bloodshed, the misery produced, the treasure expended through the

wickedness and folly of these base creatures, cannot be computed.

NEHOR, CITY OF. A city of the Jaredites It is mentioned but once (Ether, 7:9) and then in the early history of that race. Here Shule gave battle to his brother Corihor, who had usurped the throne, defeated him and restored the kingly authority to their father, Kib.

NEHOR, LAND OF. The land to which Corihor first retired when he rebelled against his father Kib, who reigned in the land of Moron (Ether, 7:4). We are of the opinion that it was not far distant from Moron, and, if so, would be in or near Central America.

NEPHI, THE SON OF LEHI. One of the greatest prophets whose presence ever dignified this earth. He was one of the most lovable of men, true as steel, never wavering, full of integrity, faith and zeal; he loved the Lord with all his heart. It is seldom we find a character in the history of this fallen world that was as perfect or as complete as was that of Nephi. He was naturally a leader, his faith and courage made him so, while his devout humility gave him strength with Heaven. In many respects he resembled Moses; not only was he their law-giver, but a practical teacher of his people in the every-day concerns of life. Like Enoch, he was a prophet, seer and revelator, but in whom were deposited the mysteries of God's dealings with future generations; like Abraham, he was a father to his people; like Melchisedec, he was their king and high priest; like Noah, he was a ship-builder, for which he delivered his family, and like Tubalcain, "an instructor of every artificer in brass and iron." In one respect he was like almost all the prophets, for he was derided, mocked, abused and persecuted by those who should have loved him most, those whose welfare he made his constant labor.

Nephi was the son of Lehi, a devout Israelite,

of the tribe of Manasseh, who resided in Jerusalem; he was born probably about B. C. 617, was married B. C. 600, in the valley of Laman, on the borders of the Red Sea; he lived to a ripe old age, and had a numerous posterity, though of his immediate sons and daughters the Book of Mormon is entirely silent. It is presumable that one of his sons succeeded him under the title of Nephi II, as king of the Nephites.

When, on account of the persecution of the Jews, Lehi was commanded by the Lord to leave Jerusalem, Nephi gladly seconded all his efforts, and became a help and a stay to his father during the many troubles and perplexities of the toilsome journey through the Arabian wilderness. Early in that journey they rested for a time in a little valley bordering on the Red Sea to which Lehi gave the name of Laman. Twice while they tarried there the sons of Lehi were commanded to return to Jerusalem. The first time they went to obtain certain records relating to their tribe, and God's dealings with His people (see Zoram); the second time to invite Ishmael and his family to join them in their migration. When they had accomplished the purpose of their stay in the valley of Laman the Lord commanded them to depart, and provided a guide for their travels in the shape of a Divinely prepared compass, which they called a Liahona. During the whole of the journey, its peace was marred by the rebellious and violent conduct of Lehi's unbelieving and unrepentant sons, of whom Laman was the leader. The first serious outbreak was during the return of Lehi's sons from Jerusalem to the tents of their father with Ishmael and his family. Some of the sons of Ishmael seem to have regretted the step which their father had taken. Possibly, like Laman and Lemuel, they had no faith in the prophecies of the servants of God, who declared that yet a little while and Jerusalem should be destroyed; and Laman and Lemuel

soon impregnated them with that spirit of malice and discontent that they themselves had already so prominently shown. Two of the daughters of Ishmael also manifested this spirit. As usual, the way in which they showed their feelings was by abusing and ill-treating Nephi. He was the special object of their dislike, by reason of his faithfulness to the commandments of God, and because the Lord had shown to him that he should be their ruler.

When the spirit of rebellion first manifested itself, as they journeyed in the wilderness, Nephi rebuked the malcontents in somewhat severe terms. Angry with his words of reproof and entreaty, the rebellious portion of the camp took Nephi and bound him with cords; their intention being to leave him in the wilderness to be devoured by wild beasts. But Nephi in mighty faith prayed to the Lord to deliver him, and that the cords that bound him might be burst. His petitions were answered. No sooner had he offered this prayer than the bands were loosed, and he stood a free man before his brethren.

Again, in the love of his heart, he plead with his tormentors. But they were still filled with the spirit of malice and murder, and once more sought to lay violent hands upon him. However, the wife of Ishmael and one of her daughters, and one son, begged so earnestly for them to desist that at last their hearts were softened, and in sorrow and humility they sought Nephi's forgiveness. This he freely granted without a moment's hesitation; he was but too glad to have them turn from their cruel and wicked course. Still, as they had offended God, as well as injured their brother, Nephi exhorted them to pray unto the Lord for forgiveness; which they did.

This outbreak was but the precursor and type of many others that afterwards troubled the little company. Another, which occurred shortly after,

originated in so apparently trivial an accident as the breaking of Nephi's bow, while in the Arabian desert. It appears that in one of their expeditions for food Nephi, who was their most expert hunter, broke this bow, which was made of fine steel. Because of this misfortune they obtained no food, and, as a result, they became very hungry. Being hungry, they grew quarrelsome and rebellious. To such an extent did this spirit prevail in the camp, that even Lehi so far forgot himself as to murmur against the providences of God. Nephi, ever faithful, alone refrained from complaining against the Lord; he exhorted his brethren, as was his custom in times of trouble and sorrow, to put away the hardness of their hearts and humble themselves before the Lord and then all would be well with them. His words had their effect. Lehi felt truly chastened, and was brought down into the depths of sorrow. When in this condition the word of the Lord came to him, and he was instructed to look upon the Liahona, and read the things that were written thereon. The reproof that was written on the ball was such as to cause Lehi exceedingly, but it also brought relief to the party, as the writing instructed them where food could be obtained. Nephi, having made a bow out of wood, went with it and with a sling and stones, and found the game in the place that the writing had indicated. He slew enough for food for all the company. When he returned to the tents of his people, bearing the beasts he had slain, there was great rejoicing in the hearts of all, and they humbled themselves before the Lord and gave thanks to Him.

When the people of Lehi reached the sea shore they reposed greatly that their tedious wanderings were over; for they had not traveled in a straight line from coast to coast, but had wandered around and about as the Liahona directed

them, which worked according to their faith and faithfulness. Eight years had been spent in taking a journey which, had they been as faithful as they should have been, would only have occupied a few weeks or months.

They pitched their tents by the sea shore, and after many days, the voice of the Lord came unto Nephi, saying, "Arise, and get thee into the mountain." As ever, Nephi obeyed the heavenly word. He went up into the mountain, and there cried unto the Lord. Then the Lord spoke unto him and commanded him to build a ship, after a manner and pattern that He would show him, that the people might be carried across the great waters that lay before them.

Here a difficulty presented itself to the mind of Nephi. He had no tools, and how was it possible to build a ship without the proper instruments. So he laid the matter before the Lord, who, in answer to his prayers, told him where he could find ore with which he might make the tools he needed.

Nephi at once proceeded to carry out the commands of the Lord. With the skins of beasts he made a bellows to blow the fire, but fire as yet he had none, as the Lord had not permitted a fire to be lighted in the wilderness. So he smote two stones together, and their first fire was lighted since the company left the borders of the Red Sea. When his forge was made and his fire was lit, Nephi began to melt the ore that he had obtained to make the tools that he needed.

When his brothers saw that Nephi was about to build a ship, they began to ridicule him. They would give him no help, for they did not believe he was instructed of the Lord. Nephi became very sorrowful because of the hardness of their hearts. When they saw this they were glad, and, tauntingly told him they knew that he was lacking in judgment and could not accomplish so great a work as to build a ship. Then Nephi recounted many things wherein the power of God had been manifested in the deliverance of their fathers; all of which he impressed upon them as a lesson that when God commanded, men should obey without doubt, or without question. Said he, "If God had commanded me to do all things, I could do them. If He should command me that I should say to this water, Be thou earth, it would be earth. Then how much less is it to build one ship than to do the marvelous works of which I have told you."

At first when Nephi held out these great truths to his brethren, they were angry and threatened to throw him into the sea; but the Spirit of God was so powerfully upon him, that they dared not touch him lest they wither; even if he but held out his hand towards them, they received a shock.

After a time the Lord told him to stretch forth his hand again toward his brethren, and that they should not wither; but the power of God should smite them; and this he was commanded to do that they might know that the Lord was their God. So Nephi stretched forth his hand as he was commanded, and the Lord shook them as He had promised. Then they fell down to worship their younger brother, who in times past they had so much abused; but he would not permit them. He said, "I am your brother, even your younger brother, wherefore worship the Lord thy God, and honor thy father and thy mother."

Then the brothers of Nephi worshiped the Lord, and showed their repentance by helping Nephi to build the ship; while he, from time to time, received the word of the Lord as to how he should work its timbers; for he did not work after the manner of the ship-builders of that time, nor after any manner that men were accustomed to.

But he built the ship just as the Lord had shown it to him; and he often went up into the mount and prayed to the Lord, and God showed him many great things.

Now when the vessel was finished, Nephi's brothers saw that it was good, and its workmanship exceedingly fine, therefore they again humbled themselves before Heaven. Then the voice of the Lord came to them and commanded them to go on board, which word they willingly obeyed, and at once put forth to sea. The vessel was then driven by the winds towards the promised land. After they had been sailing prosperously for a number of days, the hearts of Nephi's brothers and of the sons of Ishmael and others grew merry and in their merriment they forgot the Lord. They danced and sang and became very boisterous and rude. This conduct pained Nephi exceedingly, He feared lest God should be angry with them and smite them. Therefore he began to protest with much seriousness against the course they were taking; but they grew angry with him, and his two elder brothers, Laman and Lemuel, took him and bound him. So furious were they that they treated him with great harshness, binding the cords so tightly around his limbs that they caused him much suffering.

Then the Liahona ceased to work. It had been directing the course of the ship thus far, but now that they had rebelled against the Lord it would no longer point the way that they should sail. They were in a dilemma, for not one of them knew which way the ship should be steered. To add to their trouble and perplexity there arose a great and terrible tempest, and the ship was driven back upon the waters for three days; and though they were afraid that the raging waters would engulf their little vessel, yet so hardened were they that they would not loose Nephi.

On the fourth day matters were still worse.

There appeared to be no hope, but that they would be swallowed up in the sea. Then, and not till then, did they seem to understand that the judgments of God were upon them, and that they must unavoidably perish unless they repented. Then they reluctantly loosened the bands which bound Nephi's wrists and ankles, and let him go free. But his limbs, by reason of the way in which he had been bound, were swollen, and he tells us great was the soreness thereof. Nevertheless, in all his afflictions he never murmured.

During the time that Nephi had been thus bound, his father Lehi had begged most earnestly for the release of his son, but the rebels threatened everyone who sought Nephi's release; and his parents who had now grown aged, were brought down to sick beds by reason of their afflictions and came very near to being cast into a watery grave.

When Nephi was freed he took the compass, and it commenced to work as before. He prayed to the Lord, after which the winds ceased to blow; the storm passed away, and there was a great calm. Then Nephi took charge of the ship and guided it in its course towards the promised land, which, after many days it reached in safety.

Arrived on the land of promise, they found it rich in minerals, and fruitful. The little colony at once proceeded to sow the seeds they had brought with them and were delighted to find that they fructified and brought forth abundantly; and all might have been peace and happiness in their midst had it not been for the murderous jealousy of Laman and his associates. After a time, Lehi called his posterity and others together and blessed them. Many and glorious were the promises made by the patriarch to Nephi. Soon after this, Lehi passed away to his eternal reward.

No sooner was Lehi dead than the hatred that rankled in the hearts of Laman and those who sympathized with him seems to have become

intensified. It became evident that the two peoples could not live together in peace. They had nothing in common except that they belonged to the same family. Laman's vindictiveness grew so cruel that Nephi's life was in danger; and, as the readiest way out of the difficulty, Nephi was instructed of the Lord to take those who would listen to his teachings and obey the commandments of God into some other part of the land. Therefore, he gathered together those people who would hearken to him, and, taking that portion of the property that belonged to them, as also the sacred records, the sword of Laban, the Liahona and other treasures, they departed into the wilderness. Those who listened to Nephi and accompanied him on this journey were, besides his own family, his brothers Sam, Jacob and Joseph, his sisters, whose names are not given, and Zoram, with their families. There might have been, possibly, some others, as we are led to infer from the statement in the Book of Mormon, but who they were we are not told.

The distance which Nephi and his people traveled was not, probably, very great; that is, it is not to be measured by thousands of miles, for we find that in a very few years the Lamanites had found out their place of retreat, and were harassing and making war upon them.

The Nephites desired that the land they now possessed should be called the land of Nephi; and this was the name by which it was always afterward known. The people of Nephi made yet another request. It was that Nephi should be their king. This desire did not altogether please him; but for the safety of his people he consented. The kingly power in his hands partook much of the nature of fatherhood. His people were few in numbers, and he looked after their individual interests, guided them in their undertakings, directed them in their labors, and when he found

that there was danger of an attack from the embittered adherents of Laman, he took the sword of Laban, and, using it as a pattern, fashioned other swords for their defense. Being thus prepared for the attacks of their enemies, the Nephites repulsed every time they came to battle.

Nephi also taught his people to be industrious. They were a lonely people, cut off from communication with all the rest of the world, without excitements, and with very few amusements that are common to most peoples. He knew that nothing would be so dangerous to their spiritual welfare, as well as to their health, as to permit them to spend their days in idleness. He, therefore, taught them many kinds of work, the women to take the wool of the sheep and the hair of the llamas and make clothes thereof; while upon the men devolved the labor of building a temple. Holding the Holy Priesthood himself, he consecrated his brothers Jacob and Joseph to be priests also.

Shortly after the arrival of Lehi and his little party on this continent, Nephi received a commandment from the Lord to make certain plates of ore on which to engrave the doings of his people. And a few years later Nephi received further instructions, wherein he was commanded to make other plates upon which also were to be engraven the history of the Nephite people. By them, both these plates were called the plates of Nephi, but they were not used for identically the same purpose. Upon one set of plates was inscribed the religious history of the people, upon the other was given in greater detail the history of their wars, contentions, development and other secular matters.

Some years later, how long we are not told, Nephi anointed another man to be king over his people, and then, having grown old, he died.

So greatly was he beloved by his subjects that the people called the next king, Nephi the second, the next, Nephi the third, and so on. He had been their prophet, priest and king; father, friend and guide; protector, teacher and leader; next to God, their all in all.

NEPHI, THE SON OF HELAMAN.

In Nephi we have one of the greatest prophets that ever trod the earth, or to whom the God of our salvation revealed His glorious will. He lived during the greater portion of the first century before Christ, and disappeared from the knowledge of mankind but a short time before the advent of the Messiah in Bethlehem. He is first referred to in the Book of Mormon (B. C. 44) as the elder of Helaman's two sons, Lehi being the younger. These two brothers appear to have been inseparable during their life; they are almost always mentioned as associated in the great and oft-times perilous labors of the ministry undertaken for the salvation of either Nephites or Lamanites. We have no information with regard to the time of Nephi's birth, but when his father died, in the year B. C. 39, he succeeded him as chief judge, the duties of which office he filled with wisdom and justice for about nine years, when, owing to the wickedness of the people, he resigned that office, and Cezoram was chosen by the people in his stead (B. C. 30).

The years that Nephi judged his people are some of the darkest in Nephite history. Owing to their great pride and iniquity, the Lord left them to themselves, and they became weak like unto the Lamanites, man for man. When war was declared the latter, being much the more numerous, carried everything before them. In vain the Nephites under Moronihah struggled for their homes and their liberties. They were forced back by the hordes of the Lamanites from city to city, from land to land. Not a place could be found in the whole southern continent where the soldiers of the Nephites successfully held their ground. With hurried hands they built a line of defense across the Isthmus of Panama, from sea to sea, for the hosts of their conquerors were still pushing northward. This line of fortifications stopped the roll of the barbaric tide northward, and the Lamanite commanders rested with the conquest of a continent.

These richly deserved misfortunes brought the Nephites partly to their senses—they began to repent. Taking advantage of this change in the state of their feeling, Nephi, Lehi, and their general, Moronihah preached energetically, and uttered many prophecies concerning what would most assuredly come upon them if they did not amend their ways. After a time, Moronihah felt that they had sufficiently humbled themselves for the Lord to measurably be with them, and he once more ventured to lead his warriors against the Lamanites. Step by step they regained their former possessions, until all the most northern settlements had been reoccupied. Further than this Moronihah dared not venture, the conduct of the people was not sufficiently reformed, they had not repented in fulness of heart and purpose. So he waited in the hope of a better and brighter day, when the people would have thoroughly turned from all their besetting sins, and when he, in the strength of the God of Israel, could lead them on to victory. Thus Zarahemla still remained in the hands of the foe.

When Nephi retired from the judgment seat, it was with the intention of devoting his entire time to the preaching of the Gospel. He associated his brother Lehi with him, and commencing at the most northerly settlement on the southern continent—Bountiful—he journeyed and preached throughout all the land southward in the possession of the Nephites. From thence the two

brothers passed onward to Zarahemla, where they found many Nephite dissenters, to whom they proclaimed the word of God in great power. Numbers of these confessed their sins, were baptized unto repentance, and immediately returned to their brethren to repair, if possible, the wrongs they had done, and make such restitution as lay in their power. Numbers of the Lamanites also received the truth gladly, insomuch that eight thousand of them were baptized in Zarahemla and the regions round about.

From Zarahemla, Nephi and Lehi proceeded south to the land of Nephi, where they were captured by an army of the Lamanites, and thrust into the very same prison in which Ammon, Helem and Hem were beforetime confined. Here they were treated with great inhumanity by their savage captors, food was denied them, and it was decided to kill them. When the officers commissioned with the carrying out of this cruel decision arrived at the prison, they found the two prophets encircled about as if by a pillar of fire. This sight filled them with awe; they dared not attempt to execute their orders; they held back from laying hands on the prisoners, lest they should be burned, but they also observed that the two brothers stood unhurt and unterrified in the midst of the ascending flames. Emboldened by the trepidation of the Lamanite officials, Nephi and Lehi stood forth and explained to them that it was by the power of God that this marvelous thing had happened; that it had been manifested that they might learn that no one could harm them, that they were the servants of the Most High, and His almighty arm shielded them. Nor was this all: a sudden earthquake shook the ground, the prison walls tottered to their foundations, a pall of thick darkness covered all whom curiosity or other motives had gathered to the prison. The unburning flame, the tottering walls,

the quivering earth, the impenetrable cloud of blackness, all conspired to fill their hearts with solemn fear and awful dread. They realized the almighty power of God, they were filled with the sense of their own abject insignificance. A voice, the voice of One whom they knew not, sounded in their affrighted ears, once, and again, yea, a third time, and each time that the voice came it was followed by the trembling of the earth and the shaking of the prison walls. All nature quivered at the presence of the Majesty on High, while the heavy, palpable, impenetrable darkness still enshrouded them. From above the voice descended, it was outside the cloud, its tones came not to their quaking hearts with the roar of the pealing thunder, nor was it like the tumultuous flow of angry, raging waters, but it was "a still voice of perfect mildness," almost a whisper, that pierced to their inmost souls. That voice was the voice of the mighty God of Jacob, and He called upon all those who heard Him to repent, and to do His servants no ill, and with the third repetition of this command were added marvelous words of salvation that cannot be uttered by men. And because of the thick pall of darkness that enveloped them, and the fearful dread that filled their hearts, none dared move: fear, astonishment, apprehension of what was to come, had riveted each to the spot on which he stood.

Now among the crowd was a Nephite dissenter, an apostate from the true Church, named Aminadab. This man, happening to turn his face in the direction where the two prophets stood, beheld that their faces shone with a glorious light, and that they were conversing with some one who appeared to be above them, for their eyes were turned heavenward. Aminadab drew the attention of those who surrounded him to this glorious appearance, and the spell that bound them was sufficiently removed to enable them to

turn towards the prisoners and to become witnesses of the fact also. "What do all these things mean?" they anxiously inquired. "They do converse with the angels of God," answered Aminadab. What shall we do that this cloud of darkness, must repent and cry unto the Voice, even until we may be removed? "was their next question. "You shall have faith in Christ," he replied. They did cry unto God with all the energy that their terrifying surroundings inspired, and so continued to supplicate until the cloud was dispersed, when, to their great surprise, they discovered that they also were entombed in a pillar of living fire. Yet this fire did not hurt them, it did not singe their garments, it did not consume the prison walls, but their terror was swept away, and they were filled with a joy that was unspeakable, for the Holy Spirit of God filled their souls, and they broke forth in marvelous words of praise and rejoicing. Again, a pleasant, searching whisper reached their gladdened ears. It said unto them, "Peace, peace be unto you because of your faith in my well-beloved, who was from the foundation of the world." Now there were about 300 souls who heard and saw these things, and they cast up their eyes unto heaven, which was opened to their vision, and holy angels came down and ministered unto them.

The tidings of this glorious appearing were quickly spread near and far in the lands where the Lamanites dwelt, and so powerful was the testimony and so great were the evidences, that the major portion of the people believed, repented and obeyed the Gospel. Then, like all true Saints, they manifested the sincerity of their repentance by works of restitution: they laid down their weapons of war, they cast aside their false traditions, their hatred gave place to love, and they restored to the Nephites Zarahemla and the other lands they had taken from them (B. C. 30). So

great was the reformation in their character, so radical was the change in their habits, that they soon exceeded the Nephites in faith and works of righteousness. It is a lamentable fact that at this time many of the latter had become hardened, impenitent and grossly wicked. But there were those who still remained faithful to the truth, whose hearts greatly rejoiced at the conversion of their former foes. This joy was, the next year, greatly increased by the arrival of many missionaries from among the hitherto darkened and benighted people. The tables were turned, the two races had changed places; Laman was teaching Nephi the ways of holiness and the law of the Lord. And God was abundantly with them, His matchless power attended them; they opened their mouths and He filled them with inspired words of truth. The Holy Spirit sealed their utterances, and many of the Nephites believed. Nor were Nephi and Lehi idle, they were sounding the Gospel trump, long and loud, in lordly Zarahemla and its tributary districts, and then, with many of the Lamanite priesthood, they proceeded to the land northward.

Peace throughout the vast continent from north to south, from the Atlantic to the Pacific, followed this reformation. A Nephite could visit and do business in every part of the wide land, and so could a Lamanite. This goodly peace brought stability, stability brought wealth, wealth engendered pride, pride gave birth to numerous sins, to be followed by contentions, dissensions, and then wars. These evils begat sorrow, sorrow softened their heart to repentance, repentance was followed by the blessing of God which again brought peace, prosperity and, by-and-bye, riches. And at this era of Nephite national life, this is the one external round which their inspired historians are compelled to chronicle. Within four short years of the happy time of universal peace we have just

referred to, the riches of the world had induced stubbornness and rebellion towards God, combined with the insane desire to rob, plunder and murder their fellow-men. If there were a people swift to do evil, they were the Nephites of that generation. In the year B. C. 26, Cezoram, the chief judge, was murdered by an unknown hand, as he sat on the judgment seat, and his son, who succeeded him, suffered in like manner within the year. The Gadianton robbers grew in strength, numerically and morally, and were actually fostered among the Nephites, while the more righteous Lamanites utterly destroyed all that they found within their borders. The one people dwindled in unbelief, the other grew in grace and in the power of God's divine Spirit.

Nephi tarried on the northern continent until the year B. C. 23, when, his teachings and his prophecies having been repelled by its inhabitants, he returned in sorrow to Zarahemla; but he found no comfort there. The Gadianton robbers filled the judgment seats, and perverted the law to their own avarice and lust. The life, the property, the liberty, the virtue of righteous men and women were counted as things of naught, their playthings or their spoil.

Nephi's house in Zarahemla was situated on one of the principal thoroughfares which led to the chief market-place. In his garden, near the highway, he built a tower, whither it was his wont to repair for prayer. On one occasion, shortly after his return from the north, he became so deeply concerned because of the iniquities of the people, that in earnest supplication to the Lord he raised his voice so high that he was heard by the passers-by in the street below. A listening crowd soon gathered, and when the prophet had ended his devotions and become aware of their presence, he commenced to teach them. His words were not sugar-coated, to adapt them to the predilections of his congregation. To the contrary, he boldly rebuked their sins, their murders, their whoredoms, their secret iniquities, at the same time, in the love of the Gospel, entreating, beseeching and pleading with them to amend their lives and do better. He also warned them of the terrible, impending judgments that would inevitably fall upon them if they repented not. His words caused a division among his hearers, some clamoring for his arrest and imprisonment as one who bore false testimony and reviled the law, while others maintained that he spoke the truth and was a prophet. To prove to their sin-darkened minds that the prophetic gift was with him, he told them to send to the hall of judgment, and that there they would find the chief judge murdered, lying in his blood; yet more, that the murderer was the victim's brother. Five of the crowd hastened to prove his words. They hurried to the judgment hall, where they found the chief magistrate in the condition that Nephi had declared. Other citizens, who knew nothing of Nephi's words, having entered the hall and finding the five men there with the dead body, concluded that they were the assassins, and consigned them to prison. And some of the most hardened afterwards charged Nephi with being an accomplice before the act, and that he had arranged the whole affair to obtain influence with the people, so that they would believe and accept his doctrine. On this charge he was bound and imprisoned. By the wisdom that Heaven gave him so abundantly, he was enabled to baffle this attempt on his life, and through his instrumentality the murdered judge's brother having been brought to confess his crime, Nephi was delivered from his traducers and set at liberty. Some of the citizens now acknowledged that he was a prophet, others declared that he was a god, while many remained hardened in their sins. So violent became the contention, that

the people gathered in excited crowds upon the streets, wrangling and disputing about the events of the past two days. In their excitement they entirely forgot Nephi, and left him standing alone in the street. With a sorrowful heart he wended his way homeward; but before he reached there, the voice of the Lord came to him with many words of comfort and commendation. As with others of His servants, the Lord made a covenant with him, that whatsoever he bound on earth should be bound in heaven, and whatsoever he loosed on earth should be loosed in heaven; that he should have power over the elements to bless and to curse; to smite the earth with famine and pestilence and destruction, and that none should have power to hurt him. The Almighty then directed him to return and again raise his cry of repentance in the cities of the Nephites. He obeyed, and lifted up his voice in solemn warning; he went from multitude to multitude, from city to city, from land to land, but without effect. Sometimes, when he thus warned his fellow-men, they sought to imprison and otherwise maltreat him, but the Spirit of God would bear him out of their midst to labor in some other place. In this manner three years passed away; contentions and wars, murder and violence, filled the land.

At last, wearied with beholding so much misery and contention, Nephi prayed that the Lord would not suffer the people to be destroyed by the sword, but rather let a famine desolate the land and, peradventure, bring the people to an understanding of their awful condition, and cause them to humble themselves and repent. God heard and answered his petition, the heavens became as brass over the land, the rains ceased, the earth dried up, the crops failed, the people perished for want of food.

Two years passed (D. C. 19 and 18) and the third came, but still the refreshing rain was with-

held (H. C. 17). During this year the people, humbled by their sufferings, turned towards the Lord. They endeavored to root out iniquity from their midst. They destroyed the Gadianton robber bands, and established the government on a more righteous foundation. Nephi, observing the change in their conduct and feelings, interceded with the Lord in their behalf. His prayers were answered, the welcome rain descended on the parched-up soil, and a bounteous harvest once more crowned the labors of the husbandman (B. C. 16).

The repentant people now regarded Nephi in his true light; they revered him as a great prophet, and for a few short years they listened to his teachings. While they did so they prospered. But the leaven of unrighteousness had too thoroughly permeated the national life for their faithfulness to God to be of long duration. For two, three, or perhaps half a dozen years they would maintain their integrity, and then corruption would seethe, the vile would snatch the reins of government, the good would be oppressed, and contention and war, with all their horrors, would again reign supreme. Thus it was after the three years of famine. For two years there was peace, in the third there began to be much strife (B. C. 13), in the next, the Gadianton bands reappeared, and carried havoc among their more peaceable fellow-countrymen. Going on, year by year, they grew in iniquity and ripened for destruction. For many years Nephi strove to stem the tide of vice. At times partial success warded his unceasing efforts, and he had joy in baptism of some honest souls. But the bulk of the people had rejected the gospel, had no love for its holy principles, and were for its blessings.

Shortly before the birth of Christ, Nephi transferred the plates of brass and other records

---

287 Nephi, the Disciple.

his son Nephi, gave him charge concerning them, and departed from the land of Zarahemla. Whither he went, or what became of him, is hidden from the knowledge of mankind. That he did not return to the dwelling-places of humanity is testified to by his son some ten years afterwards (A.C.9).

Of Nephi's private life and circumstances we can learn but little from the Book of Mormon. It is evident that his public labors as a preacher of righteousness occupied almost his entire time. Two of his sons, Nephi and Timothy, are mentioned by name; these were both chosen by the crucified Redeemer to be members of the Quorum of the Twelve Disciples who ministered among the Nephites. His character is the one that stands pre-eminent in his age; he was of a verity a friend of God, who so acknowledged him, blessed him with as high and glorious privileges as are ever conferred on man, made peculiar and special covenants with him, and gave him revelations daily. His whole history gives evidence of his faith, patience, courage, integrity, humility and zeal. In his long life he saw much sorrow, but God took him to Himself at last.

NEPHI, THE DISCIPLE. Nephi, like his illustrious father, was the leading spirit of the age. Previous to the visit of the crucified Redeemer to the Nephites, he was their high priest and prophet. When the Messiah came to them, and chose twelve Disciples to be special ministers of His name and glory, Nephi was the first that He called, and to him, on various occasions, the Savior immediately directed His conversation and instructions.

Shortly before the birth of our Savior, Nephi received the sacred plates with their appendages from his father, with strict instructions on the same. From that time the elder Nephi was no more seen by mortals, and his son took his place as representative of Jehovah to the inhabitants of the western world.

Nephi, the Disciple. 288

When 600 years had passed since Lehi left Jerusalem, the wicked and perverse raised a great outcry that the prophecies had failed and the believers were deluded, that the delusion was a danger to the state, and those who adhered to it should be slain. They even appointed a day on which to carry out their sanguinary threats should the promised signs not be first given. These were days of anxiety and dread to Nephi. For consolation he sought the Lord in long and fervent prayers. And his prayers received a full and joyous answer. The word of the Lord came to him that that night the looked-for sign should be given, and on the morrow Jesus would come into the world. And so it came to pass. The new star appeared in the heavens, there were two days and a night of undiminished light, and all the people, both the righteous and the evildoers, recognized the sign and accepted its signification; the Lord of Life and Glory was clothed with humanity.

For about thirty years we have no direct statement of the work done by Nephi as a minister of God's word. Those thirty years were a period marked with many vicissitudes in the national and spiritual history of the Nephites. For seventeen years from the time of the birth of our Savior they gradually increased in wickedness; war and desolations afflicted them until, in their extremity, they were brought to repentance. But their repentance did not bring immediate deliverance from earthly troubles—the Gadianton robbers held the upper hand, and it was not until A. C. 21 that, by a signal victory, they freed themselves from their oppressors and invaders. Then followed a slow period of peace and prosperity, with its usual train of consequences—riches, pride, inequal, oppression and varied iniquities, and year by year they grew worse, until A. C. 29. But even then they had not decreased in their lowest; the next

289 Nephi, the Disciple.

year we read of their unjustly and unlawfully condemning to death the prophets who were sent to them. They overrode the laws, filled the country with sedition, and sought to establish a monarchy in the place of the republic. The royalists, however, did not effect their purpose, but they succeeded in breaking up the government. The people then split up and divided into numerous factions, each governed by its peculiar laws and regulations, and having its own chief (A. C. 31).

At this time Nephi is again brought to our notice. He comes forth as a servant of the Most High God, administering the words of eternal life with such power and great authority that none could disbelieve his testimony, for angels ministered to him daily. His cry was faith in the Lord Jesus Christ, repentance and baptism for the remission of sins. Many were the mighty works he performed; he cast out devils and unclean spirits; he healed the sick and even raised the dead. But the wicked were actually angered at these manifestations of God's goodness, and but few were converted. Still, Nephi continued his labors, and at the end of three years he rejoiced in the re-establishment of the Church among the righteous. the organization of the priesthood and the development of the purposes of God. For all this, the greater portion of the people continued to delight in sin; the day of their destruction had come.

Thus passed away thirty and three years. The time had now come for the fulfilment of the prophecy of Samuel, the Lamanite, when there should be darkness over the face of the land for the space of three days. On the fourth day of the first month of the thirty-fourth year, a great and terrible tempest arose, the horrors of which exceeded all others since the deluge. Huge tidal waves swept the coasts, swift cyclones and irresistible hurricanes mowed down forest, wilderness,

city and tower, leaving blank desolation in their
train; the earth trembled to its foundations,
belched forth fire, uprose in giant peaks or sank in
deep abysses. The whole face of the land was
changed by these undescribable commotions.
Some cities were burned, some sank in the depths
of the sea, some were entombed in the earth, while
mountains covered the place where others had
before stood. It is not our intention here to detail
the horrors of the three days of mental and physical darkness that followed the hurricane and the
earthquake, nor to dilate upon the great and
terrible mourning of the people for their kindred
slain, their cities destroyed and their treasures
lost. The mental horror of those black days was
intensified by the fear that they had sinned away
their day of grace, as they realized the tens of
thousands of the dead had done. Then was heard
a voice from heaven, crying, "Wo, wo, wo unto
this people, except they shall repent." That voice
was the voice of the Redeemer, and He recounted
to them the destructions, the tribulations, the
sorrow that had come upon them because of their
abominations, but added the pleasing news that
they who survived had been spared because they
were more righteous than those who had fallen
victims to the fury of the storm. He bore record
of Himself, of His sufferings and death—that He
had given His life as a ransom for the sins of the
world—and many words of counsel and instruction He added to His testimony for their future
guidance. When the voice ceased, there was silence
throughout the land for the space of many hours.
Afterwards the voice of the Savior was again
heard, repeating to the humbled Nephites how
often He would have gathered and spared His
people Israel, but they would not. Thus did the
three days of terror pass away. At its close the
darkness dispersed and the wailing of the people
stopped, for their mourning was turned into praise

and thankfulness unto the Lord Jesus, their
Redeemer.

The horrors of the desolation past was succeeded by the most glorious age in Nephite history. The extreme of misery was followed by a
fulness of joy. The crucified Redeemer himself
appeared and ministered among the people; with
His own voice he explained the beauties and har-
monies of salvation's wondrous plan. The simple,
heart-reaching truths of the everlasting Gospel He
repeated in the same plain and gentle terms in
which He had taught His disciples at Jerusalem,
and even greater truths did He announce and
greater works perform, because of the more
abundant faith of the Nephites. He also organized His Church in their midst, and called
twelve Disciples, who became His special rep-
resentatives and the presiding authorities of
His Church. These are to sit in the great day
of judgment as the judges of the seed of
Nephi, and be themselves judged by the Twelve
Apostles whom He had called from among the
Jews.

First of these Nephite Twelve stood Nephi,
who, by virtue of his seniority, his previous position, or his goodness, or, perhaps, all combined,
was recognized by the Savior on various occasions
as the foremost of his race. Nephi, at this time,
was most probably advanced beyond the middle
age of man, as he had held the records more than
thirty-three years after his father's departure from
this earth, and as that event occurred when the
elder Nephi was quite aged, and Nephi was his
eldest son, it is presumable that, if he were one of
those who died when he was seventy-two years
old, his day on the earth was not a long one after
the departure of his Divine Master.

Though Nephi had himself been baptized, and
had in times past baptized many, yet a new dispensation being now opened, Jesus commanded

the Twelve whom he had chosen to baptize all the
people; He afterwards gave them power and authority to confer the Holy Ghost. Nephi was the
first who was baptized among all the people; he
then baptized the remaining eleven of his Quorum,
which, having been done, they were filled with the
Holy Ghost and with fire; indeed they were encircled around with fire which came down from
heaven, while holy angels ministered to them the
unspeakable things of the kingdom.

After the final departure of the Savior, we
are told but little of Nephi's personal life. His
son, Nephi, appears to have taken charge of the
records almost immediately after these events,
while another son, Jonas, was a member of the
Quorum of the Twelve.

NEPHI, THE SON OF NEPHI, THE
DISCIPLE. This holy man appears to have
arrived at the age of manhood when the Messiah
visited the Nephites, as (if we get a right understanding of the sacred records,) the plates, with
the other holy things, were taken charge of by
him very shortly after that glorious appearing. It
is presumable he was then a young man, as he retained them seventy-six years, or until A. C. 110,
when his son Amos received them. His duty, as
the recorder of the doings of his people, was a
most happy one; he had nothing but good to
relate of their lives and actions, and to record
that perfect peace prevailed on all the vast continent. The Nephites increased in numbers (and
Lamanites there were none), they prospered in
circumstances, they grew in material wealth, all of
which was held in common, according to the order
of God; they colonized and spread far abroad;
they rebuilt their ancient capital and many other
cities, and founded many new ones; but, above all,
they were rich in heavenly treasures, the Holy
Spirit of God reigned in every heart, and illumined
every soul. It was a foretaste of the Millennium

to the whole people of half the world, and when
Nephi died (A. C. 110) this inexpressibly happy,
heavenly state still continued in undiminished
warmth of Divine and brotherly love and strength
of abiding faith. All the generation to which
Nephi belonged entered in at the straight gate,
and walked the narrow way to the Eternal City of
God, not one of them was lost.

NEPHI, CITY OF. The name frequently
given to the city of Lehi-Nephi.

NEPHI, LAND OF. From the days of the
first Mosiah to the era of Christ's advent, South
America was divided into two grand divisions.
These were the land of Zarahemla and the land of
Nephi. During this period, except in times of war,
the Lamanites occupied the land of Nephi, and the
Nephites inhabited the land of Zarahemla. That
these two lands occupied the whole of the southern continent is shown by the statement of the
sacred writer: "Thus the land of Nephi, and the
land of Zarahemla, were nearly surrounded by
water; there being a small neck of land between the land northward and the land southward." The width of this narrow neck of land is
in one place said to have been the distance of a
day and a half's journey for a Nephite. In another
place it is called a day's journey. Perhaps the
places spoken of are not identical, one may have
been slightly to the north of the other, along the
line of the isthmus.

Both the lands of Nephi and Zarahemla were
subdivided, for governmental purposes, into
smaller lands, states or districts. Among the
Nephites, during the latter period, in the days of the republic,
were ruled by local chief judges, subject to the
chief judge of the whole nation; and among the
Lamanites by kings, who were tributary to the
head king, whose seat of government was at the
city of Lehi-Nephi.

The land of Nephi covered a much larger area

of country than did the land of Zarahemla. The
two countries were separated by the wilderness
which extended entirely across the continent from
the shores of the Atlantic Ocean to the Pacific.
The northern edge of this wilderness ran in a line
almost due east and west, and passed near the
head of the river Sidon. All north of this belt of
wilderness was considered the land of Zarahemla;
all south of it was included in the land of Nephi.

The exact place where Lehi and his little
colony first landed on that continent is not stated
in the Book of Mormon; but it is generally
believed among the Latter-day Saints, from a
statement made by the Prophet Joseph, to be
on the coast of Chili, in thirty degrees south
latitude.

In the region where Lehi landed, there he also
died. Soon after his death, Nephi, and those of
the colony who wished to serve the Lord, migrated, by the command of God, to another
country. The reason for this command was the
murderous hatred shown by Laman and Lemuel
towards Nephi and his friends. Nephi and his
company journeyed in the wilderness. By the expression "the wilderness," we understand the
inspired writer to mean the uncultivated and uninhabited portions of the land. The journey of
the Nephites was northward, as is shown by their
later history; but Nephi, in his very brief account
of this migration, says nothing with regard to the
direction in which they traveled. At the end of
many days a land was found which was deemed
suitable for settlement. There the company
pitched their tents, and commenced the tilling of
the soil. In honor of their leader, it was called
the land of Nephi.

No doubt the choice of location was made by
Divine inspiration. It was a highly favored land,
rich in mineral and vegetable productions, and
yielded abundant crops to the labors of the

husbandmen. It appears to have been near some
great waters, the Pacific Ocean or an inland sea,
for Jacob, Nephi's brother, in speaking of the po-
tency of the faith of his people, says, "We truly can
command in the name of Jesus, and the very trees
obey us, or the mountains, or the waves or the
sea." In this happy country the Nephites dwelt,
prospered and increased until they again moved
northward. Perhaps not once, nor twice, they
migrated, but several times; for we hold it to be
inconsistent with the story of the record and with
good judgment to believe that in their first journey
they traveled as far north as they were found four
hundred years afterwards, when they again took
up their line of march, and finally settled in the
land of Zarahemla. In the first place, there was no
necessity for Nephi and his people taking such a
lengthy, tedious and hazardous journey; in the
second place, in their weak condition, it was nigh
unto an impossibility; again, in a few years the
Lamanites had followed and overtaken them.
It is altogether inconsistent to think that that
people, with its racial characteristics, could in so
short a time have accomplished so marvelous a
triumph as to follow, hunt up and attack their
late brethren, if the latter had placed all the distance from Chili to Ecuador between themselves
and their pursuers. When we consider the difficulties of travel through the trackless wilderness, the
obstacles interposed by nature, the lack of railroads
or other guides to indicate where the Nephites had
gone, it seems out of the question to imagine that
in twenty years or so, the shiftless, unenterprising
Lamanites had accomplished such a feat. To the
contrary, we believe that Nephi and those with
him traveled until they considered themselves safe,
then settled down in a spot which they deemed
desirable. By and by the Lamanites came upon
them, the Nephites defended themselves as long
as they could, and when they could do so no

longer they again moved to the northward. Their
early history was one of frequent wars; and as
the Lord used the Lamanites as thorns in their
sides when they turned from Him, we judge for this
reason, and that they were found so far north in
the days of Amaleki and Mosiah, that the savage
descendants of Laman had frequently defeated
them and driven them farther and farther away
from the land of their first possession.

The inquiry will naturally arise, as a result of
these suggestions: In what portion of the South
American continent lay the home of the Nephites
in the days of Mosiah? This cannot be answered
authoritatively. We are nowhere told its exact
situation. Still, there are many references in the
Book of Mormon from which we can judge, to
some extent, of its location. Apostle Orson Pratt
suggested that it was in the country we now call
Ecuador.

We believe that the lands occupied by the
Nephites before they went down into the land of
Zarahemla were situated among the table-lands or
high valleys of the Andes, much as Utah is located
in the bosom of the Rocky Mountains and mountain
chains. For these reasons:

First—They were lands rich in minerals, which
all through the American continents are found
most abundantly in mountainous regions.

Secondly, the climate of the torrid low lands,
almost directly under the equator, would be intol-
erable for its heat, and deadly in its humidity;
while the country in the high valleys and table-
lands would be excellently adapted to human life,
especially (we may presume) before the great upheavals and convulsions that marked the death
of the Redeemer.

It is also probable that in their journeys the
Nephites would follow the most available route,
rather than plunge into the dense, untrodden,
primeval forests of the wilderness; the home of

etc., making the journey, in two separate stages
in twenty-two days. It is scarcely supposable
that they traveled in a direct line; mountains,
rivers and swamps would render the journey somewhat circuitous or winding. But even supposing
that they did advance in an almost direct line
from point to point, it would only make the
distance between Nephi and Zarahemla 220 miles,
if they traveled ten miles a day; 330, if they
traveled fifteen miles; and 440 if they journeyed
twenty miles a day.

Zarahemla was situated on the Sidon, certainly a considerable distance from its head waters,
as other lands and cities such as Minon and
Manti are mentioned as lying far above it. If
we measure the distance from such a point southward, either 200, 300 or 400 miles, all these
measurements will bring us into the country now
called Ecuador.

We are of the opinion that the land of Lehi-
Nephi was situated in one of the higher valleys,
or extensive plateaus of the Andes. In the first
place, admitting it was in Ecuador, it would lie
almost immediately under the equator, and the
lowlands would be unbearable for an industrious population on account of the great heat; as
well as exceedingly unhealthy.

Again, the crops which the Nephites raised
most abundantly—barley and wheat—are not those
that flourish in a tropical climate, but can be
grown most advantageously in a temperate region.

It was also a land rich in mineral wealth,
which is not probable would have been the case
if it had been situated among the wide-spreading
alluvial plains east of the Andes.

It is likewise spoken of as a hilly or mountainous country. The hill north of the land of
Shilom is frequently mentioned in the historical
narrative.

For another reason, the expression "up" is

all manner of savage animals, venomous snakes
and poisonous reptiles, where a road would have
to be cut every foot of the way through the
most luxuriant and gigantic tropical vegetation
to be found on the face of the globe. Therefore
we regard its accessibility as another reason for
believing that the Nephites did not leave the great
backbone of the continent to descend into the
unexplored depths of the region whose character
they aptly sum up in the one word, wilderness.

It must be remembered that there were two
lands called by the name of Nephi. The one was
a limited district immediately surrounding the city
of Lehi-Nephi or Nephi. There Mosiah and the
Nephites dwelt, about two hundred years before
Christ. The other land of Nephi occupied the
whole of the continent south of the great wilderness. This wilderness formed its northern boundary, and its frontier thereon ran in a straight
course from the east to the west sea, or, to use
our modern geographical names, in a straight
line from the Atlantic to the Pacific Ocean.

As this wilderness, though of great length
east and west, was but a narrow strip north
and south, and its northern edge ran close to
the head waters of the River Sidon (or Magdalena), it is evident that the land of Nephi covered by far the greater portion of South America.
Within its wide boundaries was situated the original land of Nephi, as well as many other lands
called by various local names.

It is very obvious how there grew to be these
two lands of Nephi. At first, the small district
around the capital city comprised all the territory
occupied by the Nephites. As they spread out,
whatever valley, plain, etc., they reclaimed from
the wilderness was considered a part of that
land; and thus, year by year, its borders grew
wider and wider, while for convenience sake or
govermental purposes, the newly built cities and

almost always used when reference is made to
persons going towards the land of Nephi. Not
only did they travel from Zarahemla up the Sidon
and across the wilderness to Nephi, but also up
from the land of Ishmael and other portions of
the land of Nephi to the city of Nephi and its
surroundings in contradistinction to this, persons leaving Nephi went down to the land of
Zarahemla and other places.

The only time in which the word down is
used, when referring to parties going towards
Nephi, is when certain persons came down to the
city from off the hill mentioned above.

In the second generation the Nephites began
to grow numerous, and iniquity made its appearance among them. It was then that Jacob, their
priest, prophesied: The time speedily cometh, that
except ye repent, they [the Lamanites] shall possess the land of your inheritance, and the Lord
God will lead away the righteous out from among
you. This prophecy was completely fulfilled, if
not on previous occasions, about 300 years or
so afterwards, when Mosiah, by the command
of God, led the righteous Nephites out of the land
of their inheritance—the land of Nephi—down into
the land of Zarahemla.

From that time the land of Nephi was possessed and ruled by the posterity of Laman, Lemuel and Ishmael; or by Nephite apostates, who,
with superior cunning, worked themselves on to
the Lamanite throne.

During the era that the Nephites dwelt in the
land of Nephi they built several cities. These the
Lamanites eagerly took possession of when Mosiah and his people vacated them. Reference to
them is found in the record of Zeniff's return from
Zarahemla, and reoccupancy, by treaty with the
Lamanites, of a portion of the old Nephite home,
known as Lehi-Nephi and Shilom.

Our next information regarding the condition

the land surrounding were called by varied names,
according to the wishes of the people, most
frequently after the leader of the out-going colony
or founder of the city. To distinguish the smaller
land of Nephi from the whole country, it is sometimes called the land of Lehi-Nephi.

We have stated that the small land of Nephi
was a very limited district. We think this is
easily proven. It was so limited in extent that
we are told king Noah built a tower near the
temple so high that he could stand upon the top
thereof and overlook not only the land of Lehi-
Nephi where it was built, but also the land of
Shilom and the land of Shemlon, which last
named land was possessed by the Lamanites. No
matter how high the tower, the land of Lehi-
Nephi must have been comparatively small to have
enabled a man to overlook all three lands from
the top of one building.

It was on the borders of this land, in the
forest of Mormon, that Alma used to hide himself. It was there he gathered the believers in
his teachings, baptized them in the waters of Mormon, and organized the Church of Jesus Christ.
From the waters of Mormon, to Zarahemla it
was twenty-two days' actual travel for an emi-
grant train.

Alma having been warned of the Lord fled
with his people into the wilderness which divided the lands of Nephi and Zarahemla. They
journeyed for eight days when they rested and
commenced to build a city, which they called
Helam. Being afterwards compelled to leave this
city, on account of the persecutions of the Lamanites and Amulonites, they again took their
journey northward, and reached the homes of the
main body of the Nephites in Zarahemla in about
fourteen days.

Here we have a people encumbered and de-
layed by flocks and herds, heavily laden with grain,

of the land of Nephi is glenned from the history
of the mission of the sons of king Mosiah to the
Lamanites in that region. This mission began
when Mosiah then divided into several distinct
kingdoms, each ruled by its own king, but all subject to the head monarch, whose court was at
Nephi. The lands specially mentioned in connection with this mission are those of Nephi, Middoni, Ishmael, Shilom, Shemlon, Helam, Amulon
and Jerusalem.

NEPHIHAH. The second chief judge of the
Nephite republic. Of his birth and early life nothing
is said, but at the time of his elevation to the
chief judgeship he is called "a wise man who was
among the elders of the church." It appears that
when Alma found the combined duties of chief
judge and president of the church too excessive
for one man to properly perform, he selected
Nephihah as his successor in the first named
office (B. C. 83) and that this selection was rati-
fied by the voice of the people. The principal
events that occured among the Nephites during
Nephihah's judgeship were:

The destruction of Ammonihah by the Lamanites (B. C. 81).

The Ammonites established in Jershon (B.C.77).

The defection of the Zoramites and the invasion of the Lamanites under Zarahemnah (B.C.74).

The rebellion under Amalickiah and the Lamanite attack on Ammonihah and Noah (B.C.73).

Contention between the people of Lehi and
Morianton (B. C. 68).

The years that Nephihah judged the Nephites
were of great material progress. Many new cities
were founded, and a wide stretch of country
reclaimed from the wilderness. He passed away
to the realms of the blest in B. C. 68, having,
according to the sacred historian, "filled the judgment seat with perfect uprightness before God."

Alma and such great confidence in him that he desired to intrust him with the sacred records. This
honor and responsibility Nephihah declined, and
Alma conferred these treasures upon his son Helaman. Nephihah was succeeded in the judgment
seat by his son Pahoran.

NEPHIHAH, CITY OF. We fancy there
were two cities of this name: one situated on
the southern frontier, some distance east of Manti
and the Sidon (Alma, 56: 25); the other on the
Atlantic seaboard, north of Moroni (Alma, 50:
14). Of this latter city it is written that in the
year B. C. 72 the Nephites began a foundation
for a city between the city of Moroni and the city
of Aaron, joining the city of Aaron and Moroni;
and they called the name of the city or land, Nephihah. This is the region again referred to in
chapters 51, 59 and 62 of the Book of Alma. It
was captured by the Lamanites B. C. 67 and retained by them until B. C. 61, when Moroni
retook it by a night surprise. Elder Orson Pratt,
in a footnote to chapter 56, draws attention to
the fact that the Nephihah there mentioned is not
the one spoken of in the other chapters.

NEPHIHAH, PLAINS OF. Plains near
that city of Nephihah mentioned in Alma, ch. 62.
Here Moroni desired the Lamanites to meet him in
battle, but they, knowing the great courage of the
Nephites and the greatness of their numbers, kept
within the walls of the city.

NEPHIHAH, LAND OF. The region on
the Atlantic seaboard immediately surrounding
the city of the same name. It appears to have
been bounded by the land of Moroni on the south,
while that of Aaron was contiguous in another
quarter (probably north).

NEPHITES, THE. A people descended from
Manasseh, the son of Joseph, named after Nephi,
the fourth son of Lehi, who, in connection with
the Lamanites, occupied the American continent

from about B. C. 590 to A. C. 385, when they were
destroyed by the latter race. Originally they were
the descendants of Nephi, Sam, Jacob, Joseph, and
Zoram, but in later ages the distinction was one of
religion and government more than of pedigree;
hosts of the two peoples having, at different times,
seceded from their own races and fused and inter-
mixed with the other.

NEUM. A Hebrew prophet, quoted by Nephi
(1 Nephi, 19: 10). He prophesied that the Son of
God should be crucified.

NIMRAH. A Jaredite, the son of Akish
Out of jealousy Akish had starved to death one of
his sons, a brother of Nimrah, and the latter being
angry with his father, gathered a small number of
men and fled to the exiled king, Omer, who had established himself on the Atlantic Coast, probably
in the region we call New England. What afterwards became of Nimrah we are not told. (Ether,
9: 8, 9.)

NIMROD. An early Jaredite prince, the son
of Cohor. In his days the kingdom was a divided
one, Shule reigning over one portion and Cohor
over the other. Cohor, desiring to obtain un-
divided dominion, gave battle to Shule, was
defeated and slain. Nimrod, recognizing the
superior rights of Shule surrendered the region his
father had ruled over to that monarch. For this
act and for his faithful allegiance, Nimrod found
favor in the eyes of Shule, and he had authority
given him to do "according to his desires" in the
latter's kingdom. (Ether, 7: 22.)

NIMROD, VALLEY OF. A valley in Mesopotamia, or in the adjacent regions, called after
the mighty hunter who founded the Babylonian
empire. There the Jaredites assembled and organized for their journey. In this valley, also, the
Lord talked with the brother of Jared, and commanded that the company should go forth into
that region where man had never yet been; but the

brother of Jared did not at that time see the
Lord, for He was hidden from him in a cloud.
(Ether, 2.)

NOAH. The son of Zeniff and second king
over the Nephite colony which returned from
Zarahemla to the land of Lehi-Nephi. Unlike his
father, he was not a righteous man, but gave
way to drunkenness and harlotry, and, as is often
the case with monarchs of his disposition, grievously oppressed his people. He surrounded himself with creatures after his own heart, and placed
the holy priesthood in the hands of men who
were as corrupt as himself. He greatly beautified
the temple in the city of Lehi-Nephi, which he be-
fouled with his debaucheries; while the cost of
the rich adornment with which he lavishly ornamented it was wrung from his unwilling subjects
in a tax of one-fifth of all they possessed. Not
only did he greatly beautify the temple, but he
built himself a magnificent palace, and erected
many other costly buildings in the city of Lehi-
Nephi, and in the neighboring valley of Shilom.
He also built two very high watch towers, one of
which stood near the temple, and the other on the
hill to the north of the land of Shilom. Later, he
planted many vineyards and made an abundance
of wine, which resulted in him and his people
becoming drunkards.

Noah had not been long on the throne before
small marauding bands of Lamanites began to
harass the Nephites and drive off their flocks. The
king set guards around his possessions to keep the
Lamanites off, but he did not post them in sufficient numbers, and they were slain or driven
away. He finally sent his armies and drove the
Lamanites back. This victory made him and his
people conceited and boastful, and developed a delight in them to shed the blood of the Lamanites.
At this time, (about B. C. 150,) a prophet,
named Abinadi, appeared among them, and pre-

dicted that they would be brought into bondage
to their enemies unless they repented of their
wickedness. The king and the people were very
angry with Abinadi, and sought to take his life.
Two years after he came among them in disguise.
This time he uttered, in the name of the Lord, very
terrible prophecies against Noah and his people,
all of which were fulfilled in a very few years. But
the people would not heed Abinadi, and the more
he exposed their iniquities the more furious raged
their anger against him. They finally took him,
bound him, and hurried him, with railing accusations, before the king. There the priests began to
cross-question him, that they might confuse him
and cause him to say something that would give
them a pretext for slaying him. This conduct
gave Abinadi the chance in turn to question his
accusers, by which he exposed their deceit and
iniquity; and it also enabled him to explain many
of the principles of the gospel of life and salvation.
His teachings were, however, exactly what Noah's
infidel priests did not want. They charged Abinadi with having reviled the king, and on this
charge-obtained Noah's consent for his execution.
And, finally, Abinadi was cruelly tortured and
burned to death by his fellow citizens in the sin-
stained city of Lehi-Nephi.

Abinadi's cruel death was, in the providences
of the Lord, made the means of establishing the
church of Christ among Noah's subjects. One of
the young priests, named Alma, was converted by
the prophet's teachings; he wrote them down and
taught them to others. A church was organized
on the outskirts of the city, but, in a little while,
the movement reached the ears of the king, and
he sent his soldiers to capture the believers. Being
warned of the Lord, the latter fled and escaped
their pursuers.

Soon after the return of Noah's army from
their unsuccessful attempt to capture Alma and

his people, a great division grew up among that
monarch's subjects. They were heartily tired of
his tyranny and his debaucheries. One of those
most dissatisfied was an officer of the king's army
named Gideon. In the disturbances that now
arose between Noah and his people, Gideon sought
to slay the king. But Noah fled to the tower near
the temple. From its top he beheld an advancing
host of the Lamanites. Pleading with Gideon for
his life, he ordered his people to flee. They did so,
but being encumbered with their families, the
Lamanites soon overtook them and began to slay
them. The craven-hearted king then commanded
his men to leave the women and children to the
mercy of their savage foes and flee into the wilderness. Some obeyed, while others refused. Those
who followed Noah soon grew ashamed of their
cowardice and desired to return to meet the Lamanites to avenge the slaughter of their wives and
little ones, or perish as they had done. King Noah
objected, and his unworthy priests sustained him.
At this, the soldiers grew exceedingly angry; all
love for him as a man was crushed out, all respect
for him as a monarch was lost; they took him and
burned him to death, as he had done Abinadi, and
would have sacrificed the priests in the same way
had they not fled from them. They then turned
their faces towards Lehi-Nephi and were overjoyed
to meet some messengers who bore the welcome
tidings that the Lamanites had spared the lives
of those who had been left behind, though they
held them in bondage. Noah was succeeded by his
son Limhi.

NOAH. An early Jaredite leader, the son of
Corihor and the father of Cohor. Noah rebelled
against king Shule, and against his own father,
drawing from their allegiance all his brothers and
many of the people. When sufficiently strong, he
attacked and defeated Shule, and took possession
and reigned over the land of the Jaredites' first

inheritance, probably Moron, (near the land known
to the Nephites as Desolation). A second time he
attacked Shule, defeated and captured him, and
carried him to Moron. It was Noah's intention
to put Shule to death, but before he could do so
some of the sons of Shule crept into the house of
Noah by night and slew him. They then broke
down the door of the prison in which their father
was confined, liberated him and restored him to
his throne, while Cohor reigned over that portion
of the land originally conquered by his father,
Noah. (Ether, 7: 20.)

NOAH. The Bible Patriarch. His name is
mentioned four times in the Book of Mormon—
once in the promise (Alma, 10: 22) that the
people should not again be destroyed by a flood;
twice in a quotation, by the Savior, of Isaiah, 54:
9; and once in the statement that the Jaredite
barges "were tight like unto the ark of Noah."
(Ether, 6: 7.)

NOAH, CITY OF. One of the western cities
of the Nephites, not far from Ammonihah. After
destroying the latter city (B. C. 81), the Lamanites came around by the borders of Noah, slew
a number and took many prisoners. These captives were afterwards liberated by the Nephite
general, Zoram, and restored to their homes. This
city was strongly fortified by Moroni so that
when the armies of Amalickiah attempted to
carry it by assault (B. C. 73), being unable to force
the gates, they endeavored to dig down the wall
built by Moroni; but in this vain attempt they
left more than a thousand dead and wounded in
the ditch surrounding it, while the Nephites had
not one soldier slain, and only about fifty were
wounded. (Alma, 49.)

NOAH, LAND OF. A region in the land of
Zarahemla, contiguous to Ammonihah, between the
river Sidon and the Pacific Ocean. We are of the
opinion that it was situated in the wilderness that

bordered en that great sea. It was unsuccessfully invaded by the Lamanites in B.C. 81 and B.C 73; but doubtless fell into their hands in the days of Moroniliah (about B. C. 34), when the whole of South America fell into the hands of Laman's savage soldiery.

NOB. A sacerdotal city in the tribe of Benjamin, situated not far from Jerusalem. It is only mentioned in the Book of Mormon in Nephi's transcription of the writings of Isaiah (II Nephi, 20:32).

OGATH. A place in North America not far from the hill Ramah (Cumorah), and consequently in the modern State of New York (Ether, 15:10). Here Shiz, for four years, gathered those of the Jaredites, men, women, and children, who sympathized with his cause, preparatory to the final contest which ended in the utter destruction of the Jaredite race.

OMER. A righteous, but unfortunate king of the early Jaredites. He was the son of Shule, and the father of a prince named Jared. Jared rebelled against his father and by his flatteries led away the people of half the kingdom. He then gave battle to his father and took him prisoner, holding him in servitude half his days. While thus in bondage Omer begat several children, among whom were two sons, named Esrom and Coriantumr. When these young men grew to manhood they espoused the cause of their father, raised an army, attacked the forces of Jared by night, and utterly routed them. Jared obtained his life by renouncing his rights to the throne, and Omer was reinstated in the kingly authority. Jared, greatly chagrined at the loss of the royal power, entered into secret combination with Akish, a friend of Omer, to assassinate the king and restore Jared to the throne. Their attempt was partially successful. Omer was driven from the throne, but, being warned by the Lord in

a dream, he fled, with the faithful portion of his family, to the far off North Atlantic sea-board, passing in his journey the hill Shim, where the Nephite records were in after ages hid, and the hill Cumorah. From the direction of his journey we are justified in believing that the land Ablom, where he established himself, was on the New England coast. From time to time, others joined Omer, while the Jaredite people were rent by intestine wars, which ended in their almost entire destruction. Then Omer returned with his followers and reigned over the remnant of a once numerous people. He lived to be exceedingly old, and two years before his death he anointed his son Emer to reign in his stead. His days were many and full of sorrow.

OMNER. One of the sons, apparently the third, of king Mosiah II. With his brothers, in early life, he appears to have been an unbeliever in the gospel, and an enemy to the people of God's church; with them he was brought to an understanding of his position by the appearance of an angel. He then, with the rest who witnessed this heavenly visitation, went abroad among the Nephites, endeavoring, by his diligence, zeal and self-abnegation, to atone for the wrongs he had before time committed. In D. C. 91, he formed one of the party who went to the land of Nephi to convert the Lamanites, and remained in that mission until its close, suffered in all its privations and persecutions and rejoiced abundantly in its triumphs. Of his individual labors in that mission little is said, though the inference may be drawn that he spent a considerable portion of the time with and assisted his brother Aaron in his labors and ministrations. He returned with his fellow missionaries to Zarahemla in B. C. 78. In later years (B. C. 75), he accompanied Alma and others to the land of Antionum, to minister among the apostate Zoramites.

OMNER, CITY OF. A city of the Nephites on the east borders by the sea shore, in other words, a seaport town on the South Atlantic Ocean or Caribbean Sea. It was probably named after Omner, the son of Mosiah, and, if so, we are justified, from the custom of the Nephites, in believing that he was its founder. It fell into the hands of the Lamanites in B. C 67 (Alma. 51:26), and undoubtedly again in B. C. 35 (or about that time), though it is not then mentioned by name.

OMNI. A Nephite prophet, son of Jarom, and a descendant of Jacob, the younger brother of Nephi. He lived in the land of Nephi, and was the custodian of the plates of Nephi from the 239th to the 283d year of the Nephite annals, or 44 years. He characterizes himself as a wicked man, who had not kept the commandments and statutes of the Lord as he ought to have done, but had been principally engaged in defending his people from the constantly recurring onslaught of the Lamanites. The history of his times he sums up in one short sentence: "And it came to pass that 276 years had passed away [from the time Lehi left Jerusalem] and we had many seasons of peace and we had many seasons of serious war and bloodshed." Having kept the plates according to the commandments of his fathers, he conferred them upon his son Amaron. (B. C. 318.)

ONIDAH, HILL. A hill in the land of Antionum, from which Alma, the younger, preached to the Zoramites (B C. 75) (Alma, 32: 4).

ONIDAH, PLACE. The gathering place of the dissatisfied Lamanites, led by Lehonti, who refused to give heed to the king's proclamation of war against the Nephites (B. C. 73). Thither the malcontents were followed by Amalickiah and an army. By the latter's strategy and plotting he obtained an interview with Lehonti on Mount Antipas, and arranged to surrender his troops. Onidah is called "the place of arms," and may

possibly be the hill Onidah in the land of Antionum, though we are of the opinion that it was not, it being within the borders of the Lamanite possessions. (Alma, 47: 5.)

ONIHAH, CITY OF. One of the wicked cities swallowed up in the earth during the great cataclysms that, on this continent, bore record of the death of the Redeemer. When the convulsions were ended, a stagnant lake occupied the place where this city stood; it and all its unstained inhabitants were destroyed. This city is nowhere mentioned except in the statement of its destruction. (III Nephi, 9: 7.)

OPHIR. The Bible land of gold. Its locality has not been determined. Some suppose it to have been in India, some in Arabia, some in eastern Africa. It is named but once in the Book of Mormon (II Nephi, 23: 12), in a quotation from the prophecies of Isaiah.

OREB, ROCK OF. The spot, east of the Jordan, where thousands of the Midianites fell by the hands of the Ephraimites. It is mentioned but once in the Book of Mormon, in Nephi's quotations from the prophecies of Isaiah. (II Nephi, 20: 26.)

ORIHAH. The youngest of Jared's four sons and the first king of the Jaredites. When Jared and his brother had grown old and desired to have the wishes of their people before they went down to their graves, the people desired to be ruled by a king. This idea was displeasing to their leaders, but they ultimately consented to one being chosen. All the sons of Jared and of his brother refused this dignity, until Orihah was named and he accepted the kingly honor. He reigned in righteousness, executing judgment in justice, walking humbly before Heaven, and instructing his subjects in the ways of the Lord. He lived to a very great age, was the father of thirty-one children, twenty-three of whom were sons, and

when he died he was succeeded on the throne by his son Kib. The Jaredites prospered and multiplied greatly under his wise and beneficent reign.

PAANCHI. A son of Pahoran, the elder, who, upon the death of his father, aspired to the vacant judgment seat. When the choice of the Nephite people fell on his brother, Pahoran, the younger, Paanchi, raised the standard of revolt, in which he was sustained by the sympathies of a large body of the people. Before he could put his revolutionary intentions into action he was arrested, tried and condemned to death (B. C. 52). This prompt action excited great anger among his followers, and they employed an assassin named Kishkumen, who was a prominent man among them, to murder the new Chief Judge. This he successfully accomplished without discovery. It was among the dissatisfied and turbulent followers of Paanchi that the Gadianton robbers appear to have had their origin.

PACHUS. During the entire continuance of the Nephite Commonwealth there appear to have been very many of the Nephites to whom the pomp and glamour of royalty had uncontrollable fascinations. Such we find ever ready to support Amlici, Pachus, Jacob or any other man who put forth claims to the kingly authority. This feeling, probably, with some, had its origin in the pleasant remembrance of the happy days of the good kings Benjamin and Mosiah, but we fear it was too often attributable to a selfish ambition which saw personal aggrandizement or exalted position in the restoration of the monarchy. None of these outbreaks appear to have gained greater temporary success than that which was led by Pachus (B. C. 62).

The time chosen for this rebellion was one admirably suited for its unholy purposes. The Nephites were weakened by the long continuance of one of their most bloody wars with the Lamanites,

in which the audacity of the enemy had resulted in the loss of many cities. This state of affairs naturally caused discontent, which was increased by the subtlety of the traitors, who used all their influence to weaken the hands of the government, at the same time, doubtless, contrasting the glories of the monarchy with the misfortunes of the republic. These wiles had their effect, the king-men rose in power, took possession of the city of Zarahemla, withheld reinforcements and provisions from the national troops on the battlefield, and drove the Chief Judge, Pahoran, out of the capital. The latter retired across the Sidon to the city of Gideon.

Pachus was then recognized as king of the Nephites. Thereupon he opened communications with the Lamanites, by which he agreed to hold Zarahemla against the forces of the republic, while the Lamanites continued the warfare on the Atlantic coast and in the southwest. In this way, the contracting parties expected to conquer the patriot forces.

When Pahoran reached Gideon, he issued a proclamation to the people in the regions around about to gather to the defense of their common liberties. This appeal was so heartily responded to, that the king-men were afraid to risk the issue of battle outside of Zarahemla. Such was the situation when Pahoran wrote to Moroni, the commander-in-chief of the armies of the Commonwealth, to come to his rescue. Moroni, who was fighting on the Atlantic seaboard, promptly obeyed. Gathering up volunteers as he marched, he quickly arrived at Gideon, where he joined his forces to those of Pahoran, and unitedly they marched into the land of Zarahemla. A battle ensued in which the royalists were defeated and king Pachus was slain. As a natural consequence, Pahoran was reinstated in the judgment seat, and for a short time the Nephite Commonwealth was free from internal dissension.

The trials of the captured king-men then commenced. Those found guilty of treason were executed, or were allowed the privilege of joining the armies in the field and fighting for the liberties of the people. Many embraced this offer, while others preferred to die with the lost cause, rather than take up arms in defense of the government they hated.

PACUMENI. At the death of Pahoran, the elder, the Nephite Chief Judge, three of his sons contended for the successorship. The people chose *Pahoran, the younger.* To this choice Pacumeni assented, while the other brother, *Paanchi,* rose in rebellion. Shortly after, Pahoran was assassinated by *Kishkumen,* a follower of Paanchi, when Pacumeni was chosen by the people to fill the vacant judgment seat. All this occurred in the fortieth year of the Judges, or B. C. 52.

In the year following, the Lamanites gathered an innumerable army and invaded the land of Zarahemla. Their commander was named *Coriantumr.* He led his vast hosts directly towards the Nephite capital, which he surprised and captured, the Nephites still suffering from the effects of the late divisions and contentions. This was the first time, so far as we have any record, that the city of Zarahemla fell into the hands of the Lamanites. So suddenly did Coriantumr when he found the city had been surprised, the watch slain, and its streets filled with hostile troops, but he was overtaken before he could pass beyond the walls and was smitten, by the hands of Coriantumr, "against the wall, insomuch that he died."

PAGAG. The eldest son of the brother of Jared. When it was decided to establish a monarchy on the new land to which the Lord had led the Jaredites, Pagag was the first choice of the people for king. But he resolutely refused the honor, sensing, perhaps, the evils which would follow the adoption of this form of government. The people

desired that his father should compel him to be king, but he would not do so, and commanded that they should constrain no man to be their king. The result was that all Pagag's brothers and three of the four sons of Jared followed his example, and when chosen refused to accept the proffered dignity; at last, *Orihah,* the fourth son of Jared, accepted. Nothing more is said of Pagag in the Book of Mormon, but from his action in this matter we judge him to have been a wise and God-fearing man. (Ether, 6: 25.)

PAHORAN, THE ELDER. The third chief judge of the Nephite republic. He succeeded his father, Nephihah, on the judgment seat, B. C. 68, and held that exalted position until his death in B. C. 53, when he was succeeded by his son, Pahoran. The days that Pahoran judged the people were full of tumult and war. No sooner was he placed on the judgment seat than great contentions arose between the royalists and republicans. There was quite a number of the people who desired to restore the monarchy, but they were not as numerous as those who desired to maintain the existing form of government. Being outvoted, the king-men resolved to take up arms against the hosts of the Lamanites under Amalickiah, who were then invading the lands of the Nephites. Full power being given to *Moroni,* the Nephite general, to deal with these rebels, he marched against them with his forces, and in the conflict that followed 4,000 of the royalists were slain, while many of their leaders were captured and cast into prison. The remainder submitted, joined their countrymen in opposing the Lamanite hosts, and gave full allegiance to the republican government. In the meantime, the Nephites having been weakened by their internal dissensions, Amalickiah marched triumphantly northward, capturing city after city, along the Atlantic seaboard, while his brother Ammoron conducted a

victorious campaign in the southwest. The calamities brought on by this royalist defection lasted many years, for the war was not ended until B. C. 61, and for many years afterwards its evil effects, in the condition of the people, were widely manifest. Even while the war continued, a second royalist uprising occurred. *Pachus,* the leader, drove Pahoran from the judgment seat and obtained control in Zarahemla. The chief judge retired to Gideon. Shortly afterwards (B. C. 62), Moroni came to the assistance of Pahoran, and their united forces gave battle to the rebels, in which encounter Pachus was slain and his followers defeated. This ended the second attempt to re-establish the kingly form of government during Pahoran's judgeship. After the termination of the war with the Lamanites, every effort was put forth to counteract the demoralization which the long-continued struggle had induced. *Helaman,* and other leaders in the priesthood, went forth among the people preaching the word and organizing the churches; while Pahoran and his associates gave their attention to restoring civil order. A few years later (B. C. 55), the colonization of the northern continent began, which was continued with increasing numbers of emigrants during the succeeding years. In B. C. 53, dissension again had place among the Nephites, numbers went over to the Lamanites and stirred up strife. An invasion followed, which was speedily repulsed by the forces of *Moronihah,* the son of Moroni. The character of Pahoran is best shown in his epistle to Moroni (Alma, ch. 61). He was evidently a wise judge, a faithful servant of God, and a loyal citizen of the republic. He also seems to have possessed the characteristics of patience, mildness and forgiveness to a marked degree, but was not lacking in courage, zeal or determination.

PAHORAN, THE YOUNGER. At the death of Pahoran, the first Chief Judge of that

name who ruled the Nephites, a contention arose among three of his sons (Pahoran, Paanchi, and Pacumeni,) as to which of them should succeed him. As is usual in such cases, each one had his followers, causing much dissension, trouble and confusion among the Nephites. (B. C. 52.) The question was decided by the votes of the citizens of the republic, who chose Pahoran to be chief judge and governor over the people of Nephi. In this decision Pacumeni acquiesced, but Paanchi raised the standard of revolt.

Pahoran retained the judgment seat but a very short time. He was foully assassinated, when in the execution of his duty, by one *Kishkumen,* a leader among the Gadianton robbers, and an adherent of the Paanchi faction. So speedy was the flight of the murderer, and so well was he disguised, that he was not captured.

These things all took place in the fortieth year of the Nephite judges, and Pacumeni was appointed to fill the place rendered vacant by the murder of Pahoran.

The only noteworthy event that took place during his short rule was the commencement of the organization of that terrible band, the Gadianton robbers.

PALESTINA. A poetical name for the Holy Land which occurs twice in the Book of Mormon (II Nephi, 24: 29, 31), in a quotation from the writings of Isaiah.

PATHROS. A region of upper Egypt. It is mentioned once in the Book of Mormon (II Nephi, 21:11) in a quotation from the prophecies of Isaiah.

PEKAH. The eighteenth king of the kingdom of Israel. He was originally a captain of king Pekahiah, but he murdered his master and seized the throne. After a reign of about thirteen years he was put to death by Hoshea, the son of Elah. (About B. C. 740.) His name is once used

in the Book of Mormon, in a transcription from the writings of Isaiah (II Nephi, 17: 1).

PHARAOH. The title of the supreme ruler of ancient Egypt. The individual monarch spoken of in the Book of Mormon is the one in whose reign the Hebrews were delivered from the bondage of the Egyptians, under Moses and Aaron. His name is mentioned twice (I Nephi, 4: 2; 17: 27,) and on both occasions in connection with the destruction of his armies in the Red Sea.

PHILISTINES. The Bible people of that name. They had settled in Palestine as early as the days of Abraham. In later times they grew to be the constant enemies of the Israelites. They are mentioned five times in the Book of Mormon (II Nephi, 12: 6, 19; 12; 21: 14), always in quotations from the writings of Isaiah.

RAHAB. Said to be a poetical name for Egypt. It occurs but once in the Book of Mormon, in a quotation from the writings of Isaiah. (II Nephi, 8: 9.)

RAMAH HILL. The Jaredite name for the Hill *Cumorah.* In its immediate vicinity both the Jaredite and Nephite peoples were destroyed.

RAMATH. A city of the tribe of Simeon. It is mentioned (II Nephi, 20: 29) in a quotation from the writings of Isaiah

RAMEUMPTOM. The name given by the Zoramite apostates to the elevated place in their synagogues, whence they offered up their vainglorious and hypocritical prayers. Alma states the word means a holy stand. It resembles, in its roots, Hebrew, and also Egyptian, in a remarkable manner. Ramoth, high (as Ramoth Gilead), elevated; a place where one can see and be seen; or, in a figurative sense, sublime or exalted. Uptom has probably its root in the Hebrew word translated threshold, as we are told that the Philistine's god, Dagon, had a threshold in Ashdod (see I Samuel, 5: 4, 5). Words with this root are

quite numerous in the Bible. Thus we see how Rameumptom means a high place to stand upon, a holy stand.

RED SEA. This sea is mentioned by name thirteen times in the Book of Mormon. Of these thirteen, eight passages are associated with the destruction of the armies of Pharaoh in the days of Moses, the other five occur in connection with the travels of Lehi and his company from Jerusalem (B. C. 600) to its upper waters, and their encampment on its shores, with the incidents that took place while they tarried there. The continuation of their journey therefrom is mentioned in I Nephi, 16: 14.

REMALIA. The father of Pekah, king of Israel. His name is mentioned five times in the Book of Mormon (II Nephi, Chap. 17 and 18), in quotations from the prophecies of Isaiah.

REZIN. A king of Damascus, contemporary with Pekah, king of Israel. His name occurs five times in the Book of Mormon, in quotations from the prophecies of Isaiah. (II Nephi, 17: 1, 4, 8; 18: 6; 19: 11.)

RIPLAH, HILL. A hill on the east side of the river Sidon, in the neighborhood of the land of Manti. Here a severe battle was fought between the Nephites and Lamanites (B. C. 74). The former were commanded by Moroni and Lehi, and the latter by Zarahemnah. The loss was so great on both sides that the dead were not counted. The battle ended in the surrender of the Lamanites, who, having given up their arms, and covenanted that they would never again come to war against the Nephites, were permitted to depart unto the wilderness.

RIPLAKISH. An unrighteous king of the Jaredites. He greatly afflicted his people by imposing upon them grievously heavy taxes, and when they could not, or would not pay these exactions he cast them into prison, where he compelled them to labor continually to sustain him in his whoredoms and abominations; and in the erection of costly and magnificent edifices that conduced to his luxury; if any prisoner refused to labor he was put to death. In this way he greatly adorned his kingdom, but he also filled it with prisons. For forty-two years the people groaned under his oppressions, when they rose in their anger, slew Riplakish and drove his descendants out of the land. What form of government immediately followed is uncertain, we have no information on this point, but we are told that after many years one of his descendants, named *Morianton*, established himself as king.

RIPLIANCUM. Supposed by some to be the lake Ontario, but evidently one of that great chain of lakes. Its meaning is said to be, "large, or to excel all." (Ether, 15:8.) Near its waters the opposing Jaredite armies, commanded by Coriantumr and Shiz, camped, and afterwards fought an exceedingly sore battle, in which the latter was defeated and driven southward towards the hill Ramah, or Cumorah.

SALEM. The city or country over which Melchizedek reigned. It is only in connection with this circumstance that Salem is mentioned in the Book of Mormon. (Alma, 13:17, 18.)

SAM. An Israelite of the tribe of Manasseh. He was the third son of *Lehi* and Sariah, and was born and brought up in Jerusalem. He accompanied his parents in their exodus from that city (B. C. 600), and was priveleged, with them, to reach the promised land. He does not appear to have been a leading spirit, but was obedient and faithful, and in almost every case sided with the right and followed the teachings of his father and the counsels of his more fervent brother, Nephi. For this he suffered the anger and abuse of his elder brothers, who sometimes resorted to personal violence when matters did not go to suit

them. When the colony divided, after the death of Lehi, Sam and his family joined their fortunes to those of Nephi Of Sam's birth and death we have no record. He married one of the daughters of Ishmael while the party was encamped in the valley of Lemuel, on the borders of the Red Sea.

SAMARIA. The chief city of the kingdom of Israel, and figuratively the people of that kingdom. It is mentioned seven times in the Book of Mormon, always in quotations from the writings of Isaiah (II Nephi, 17:9; 18:4, 19:9; 20:9, 10, 11).

SAMUEL, THE LAMANITE. The condition of society in the days of Samuel was somewhat peculiar. (B. C. 6.) The Nephites and Lamanites had, so far as righteousness was concerned, to a great extent changed places. The former were puffed up with worldly pride, were full of vain boastings, envyings, strifes, malice, persecutions, murders and all manner of iniquities. They cast out, stoned and slew the servants of God, while they encouraged, exalted and rewarded the false teachers who flattered them in their vileness. They reveled in all the luxury that the fatness of the land brought forth; they were ostentatious in the use of gold and silver and precious things; but their hearts never turned in thankfulness to the great Giver of all those bounties. The majority of the Lamanites, on the contrary, walked circumspectly before God, they were full of faith and integrity, were zealous in the work of converting their fellows, and kept the commandments, statutes and judgments of the Lord, according to the law of Moses.

Such was the condition of affairs when the Lamanite prophet, Samuel, appeared among the citizens of Zarahemla, and for many days preached repentance in their midst. Their eyes were blind and their ears were deaf, sin filled their souls, and in their anger they cast him out. But the work of his mission was not yet accomplished. As he was

preparing to return to his own country, a holy angel visited him and proclaimed the voice of the Lord; that voice said that he should turn back and prophesy to the people of Zarahemla, the things that should come into his heart.

He returned to the city, but was refused admission at its gates. The iniquitous dwellers therein had no desire to have their peace disturbed by the voice of Divine threatenings. But the prophet had the word of the Lord burning within him, and could not be restrained. He mounted the walls of the city, and from this conspicuous vantage ground, with outstretched hands and loud voice, he proclaimed to the wicked the unwelcome tidings of their coming destruction. Many listened to his proclamation, some few were pricked in their hearts, repented of their evil deeds, and sought the prophet *Nephi*, that they might be baptized. Others were angry, they gathered up the stones in the roadway and hurled them at Samuel, they drew forth their bows and shot arrows at him, but to no effect; the protecting power of God was around him, and he could not be harmed. When some beheld how wonderfully the prophet was preserved, it was a testimony to them that God was with him, and they also sought Nephi, confessing their sins. But the great body of the populace grew more enraged at the want of success that attended their murderous efforts. They called upon their captains to seize and bind him. Following the wild, satanic cry of the multitude, the officers attempted to take him, but he cast himself down and fled to his own country, where he began to preach and prophesy among his own people. And from that time the voice of Samuel was never again heard among the children of Nephi, but in later years Jesus, Nephi, Mormon and others quoted his prophecies or referred to his testimony.

Nearly all the events, great and glorious,

Samuel.   323   Sariah.

terrible and heartrending, of which Samuel prophesied, were fulfilled before the inspired historians of the Book of Mormon sealed up his record. Prominent among these predictions were the signs that should occur at the advent of our Savior; the two days and a night of continued light, and the appearance of a new star in the heavens, that should mark His birth at Bethlehem, even to the exact year when these things should take place; also the convulsions, the storms, the earthquakes that should attend His crucifixion, and the resurrection of many of the Saints that should follow His resurrection. He also foretold, with great clearness and minuteness, that in subsequent years the Nephites should grow in iniquity, and because of their wickedness, their treasures, their tools, their swords, etc., should become slippery, and magic and its like should abound, and within four hundred years, the Nephite race should be destroyed. To the fulfilment of these prophecies Nephi, Mormon and Moroni bear record.

SAMUEL. The Israelitish prophet. He is mentioned but once in the Book of Mormon, and then by the Savior, who said to the Nephites: "All the prophets from Samuel, and those that follow after, as many as have spoken, have testified of me." (III Nephi, 20:24.)

SARIAH. The wife of Abraham. She is mentioned but once in the Book of Mormon, in a quotation from the writings of Isaiah. (II Nephi, 8:2.)

SARIAH. The wife of *Lehi*. She was the mother of six sons and some daughters, the number of the latter is not given in the Book of Mormon. But very little is said of Sariah in the sacred record; she is only mentioned by name five times, but we are of the opinion, from the incidental references made to her, that she did not possess very great faith in the mission of her husband, or in the fulfilment of his prophecies; she rather regarded him as a visionary man, who was leading her and

her children into trouble and danger by his dreams and revelations, and consequently was prone to murmur when any difficulty arose. Four of her sons were grown to manhood when she left Jerusalem (B. C. 600), the other two were born during the little company's eight years' journey in the wilderness. When Sariah's daughters were born is very uncertain, they are so spoken of at the time their parents left Jerusalem, nor is their birth afterwards mentioned. We are told nine or ten years after the company's departure from the Holy City, when it was on the ocean, that Lehi and Sariah were well stricken with years, so we think it quite possible that Lehi's daughters were born at Jerusalem. This is made more probable when we remember that Nephi, the youngest of the four sons, would probably be about twenty years old when his younger brothers were born. It seems reasonable, when we consider the age of Sariah, that it was during this lapse of twenty years, and not later, that his sisters came into the world.

Of Sariah's birth and death we have no record, nor to what tribe of Israel she belonged. She lived to reach the promised land, and, being then aged and worn out by the difficulties and privations of the journey through the Arabian wilderness, very probably passed into her grave before her husband.

SAUL. The name of this king only appears in the Book of Mormon in a quotation from the writings of Isaiah (II Nephi, 20:29), and in connection with the town of Gibeah, the residence of Saul, to distinguish that place from other towns in Palestine of the same name.

SEANTUM. A Nephite of importance, who belonged to the Gadianton bands. His brother, *Seezoram*, also a Gadianton, was Chief Judge, and Seantum, in his conscienceless ambition, with his own hand slew his brother, in order that he might attain to this dignity (B. C. 23). His crime was exposed by *Nephi*, through the inspiration of the

---

Sebus, Waters of.   325   Seezoram.

Spirit of God, and when he was charged with the murder, and blood was found on his garments, he first denied, but afterwards confessed that he was guilty. We are not informed whether or not he suffered the consequences of his crime, but it is highly probable that, owing to his influence and the prevailing iniquity of the people, he escaped punishment.

SEBUS, WATERS OF. A watering place in the Land of *Ishmael*, which, in the time of *Lamoni*, was used to water the king's flocks. On its banks occurred the conflict between *Ammon*, the son of Mosiah, and the Lamanite robbers, who sought to scatter the royal cattle.

SEEZORAM. A member of the Gadianton band, elected by the Nephites, during the times of their degeneracy, to be their Chief Judge. The date of his election is not given, but he probably succeeded the son of *Cezoram*, who was assassinated. (B. C. 26.) Seezoram himself was murdered in the year B. C. 23, in the city of Zarahemla, by his brother Seantum, who desired to obtain the chief judgeship.

The three years preceding the death of Seezoram are dark ones in the history of the Nephites. The people were rapidly growing in iniquity — they gave succor and support to the Gadianton bands, whose members held the chief offices in the gift of the people. Justice was travestied; the law was administered in the interest of the wicked and of those who would bribe or buy the judges; while the righteous were persecuted, abused and robbed in its name. It thus became an engine of oppression to the good or unfortunate, and an instrument to aid and protect the vile and the influential in all their evildoing.

The prophet *Nephi* was the first who informed the people of the death of their chief magistrate. He was preaching from a tower in his garden at the time the foul deed was perpetrated. By the spirit of revelation he told his hearers what had been done, five of them hastened to the judgment hall and found it was as the prophet had declared. So thunderstruck were they that they swooned, in which condition they were discovered by others, with the murdered Seezoram lying before them. When they recovered, they found themselves in prison, charged with the crime, and Nephi was also arrested, because of his prophecy, charged as an accessory before the fact. The confession of Seantum, that he was the guilty one, brought about the release of all those who had been imprisoned, and the five unfortunate accused were converted to the Lord.

Of Seezoram's life, acts or character we have no record; it is probable, nay, we must almost necessarily believe, that he was a leader in iniquity, or it would have been impossible for him to have attained his exalted position through the votes of the sin-stained majority.

SETH. A Jaredite prince, the son of king Shiblom, who, in the war in which his father was slain, was brought into captivity, and so held all the rest of his life. His son, Ahah, regained the kingdom. Of Seth's character we have no details.

SHARED. A Jaredite military commander opposed to Coriantumr during a part of the great series of wars which ended in the destruction of that race. Nothing is said of him until he comes to the front as the leader of an army which gave battle to Coriantumr and defeated him. This appears to have been a lengthy campaign, and not one solitary fight, for we are told that "in the third year he (Shared) did bring him into captivity. And the sons of Coriantumr, in the fourth year, did heat Shared, and did obtain the kingdom again unto their father." The war, at this period, would seem to have grown beyond the control of the great leaders, and to have degenerated into a condition of affairs in which every man's hand was

against his neighbor, and mobs, instead of disciplined armies, carried bloodshed and devastation far and wide, throughout the land. Bands of brigands and robbers committed all manner of outrages, and the country was a scene of anarchy and horror from one end to the other. After a time, Coriantumr, being exceedingly angry, gathered his forces and met Shared in the valley of Gilgal. The fight, which lasted three days, was a desperate and stubborn one. Shared was beaten and retreated as far as the plains of Heshlon, where he again withstood Coriantumr, and this time was victorious, driving his foes back to their former battle ground—the valley of Gilgal. Here another fierce battle was fought, in which Shared was slain and his troops defeated. In after years, Gilead, a brother of Shared's, took his place and continued the bitter conflict with Coriantumr.

SHAZER. A place in the Arabian desert, where Lehi and his colony rested while the hunters of the party procured a supply of food (B. C. 600).

SHEARJASHUB. The son of Isaiah, the prophet, mentioned only in a quotation from his writings. (II Nephi, 17: 3.)

SHELEM. A mountain to which the Jaredites gave this name because of its exceeding height, situated not far from the great ocean which they were about to cross. It was upon this mountain that the Savior touched with His finger the sixteen stones which were to give light in the barges built to carry them to the promised land; and here He showed Himself to the brother of Jared and revealed to him the great truths regarding His coming to the earth in the flesh. (Ether, ch. 3, 4.)

SHEM. A Nephite general, who commanded a corps of ten thousand men in the last great struggle between the Nephites and the Lamanites. He, with all his command, was slain in the final series of battles in the land Cumorah, when the Nephite nation was annihilated. (A. C. 385.)

SHEM, CITY OF. A city on the northern continent, north of Aaron and Jashon. To this city the Nephites, under Mormon, were driven by the Lamanites and Gadiantons (A. C. 345). Here, however, they made a stand and fortified the city. Encouraged by the earnest pleadings of their commander, 30,000 of them gave battle to 50,000 Lamanites, and defeated them. The Nephites followed up their victory with such decisive action that the enemy were driven continually southward, until (A. C. 350) a treaty was entered into, by the terms of which the Nephites retained possession of the whole of North America and the Lamanites held the southern continent.

SHEM, LAND OF. The region immediately surrounding the City of Shem. It appears to have been situated considerably to the north

SHEMLON, LAND OF. A region contiguous to Lehi-Nephi, apparently a neighboring valley. It was a portion of the Nephite domain until their exodus to Zarahemla under the first Mosiah, when the Lamanites took possession of it, and ever afterwards retained it. They did not cede it to the people of Zeniff, as they did the neighboring lands of Lehi-Nephi and Shilom. Shemlon was so near the city of Lehi-Nephi that it could be overlooked from the high tower built near the temple by king Noah. It was in this land that the abduction of the daughters of the Lamanites, by the priests of Noah, occurred, which led to a new and other disastrous consequences, and later produced so many indirect results in the history of the Lamanites. At the time of the mission of the four sons of Mosiah, all the Lamanites of this land were converted to the Lord.

SHEMNON. One of the twelve Nephite Disciples, called and chosen by Jesus at the time of His visit to that people (A. C. 34). Shemnon was present near the temple in the land Bountiful when Jesus appeared, and was baptized by Nephi on the

day following. He is not again mentioned by name in the sacred record

SHEREM. The first of the many Anti-Christs, who, at various times, appeared among the Nephites and endeavored by their teachings to lead the people from the principles of the Gospel. He appeared in the land of Nephi towards the close of the life of Jacob, the son of Lehi, and openly taught that there would be no Christ nor necessity for atonement. He was a type of many who came after, for no matter how these apostates differed on lesser matters, they almost universally denied the coming of the Savior, and taught that the faith of the Nephites in His appearing was a snare and a delusion. Sherem was a man of many words, much given to flattery, and well acquainted with the language of his nation, and withal very zealous in spreading his pernicious doctrines, so much so that he was successful in misleading many. Full of deceit and presumption, he contended with Jacob, denied the Christ and blasphemously called for a sign. A sign was given him. On Jacob's praying to the Lord, Sherem was smitten to the earth by the power of God, and though he was nourished for many days he eventually died. The day before his death he called the people together and acknowledged his iniquity and iniquity. He confessed and told the people plainly that he had been deceived by the power of the devil, and had lied unto God. He died with the terrible thought haunting him that he had committed the unpardonable sin. His confession and death wrought mightily among the people; schism ceased for the time being, and the unity of the church was re-established.

SHERRIZAH. A fortified city mentioned by Mormon in his second epistle to his son Moroni. It was the scene of horrible brutalities during the great war between the Nephites under Mormon, and the Lamanites commanded by king Aaron.

When the Lamanites captured the tower of Sherrizah they led their female prisoners on the flesh of their husbands and fathers, and tortured them by withholding sufficient water to quench their thirst. The contending forces also carried away all the provisions, leaving the aged and the children to starve. Mormon says, "the sufferings of our women and our children upon all the face of this land, doth exceed anything; yea, tongue cannot tell, neither can it be written."

SHEUM. A kind of grain. This name is singularly like the Hebrew shum (garlic), as found in Numbers, 11: 5. Sheum is spoken of as being planted by the Nephites, in connection with wheat, barley and neas in the land of Lehi-Nephi (Mosiah, 9: 9).

SHEZ. A king of the Jaredites, the son of Heth. By reason of the great wickedness of the Jaredites in the days of Heth, the Lord permitted a severe famine to come upon them, by which the far greater portion of the people were destroyed. Of the royal family, all perished except Shez, who, when the crops again began to grow, commenced to build up this desolate race. He was a virtuous man, and taught his people righteousness, and the sun of prosperity shone upon them. His peace, however, was marred by the treason of his son Shez, who rebelled against him. This son, however, was slain by a robber, and peace was restored. In the later years of his lengthy reign, Shez built many cities, and the rapidly increasing people spread out in various directions. This monarch lived to an exceeding old age, was blessed with numerous children, and when he died was succeeded on the throne by his son Riplakish, who was apparently the youngest of his family. (Ether, 10: 1—4.)

SHEZ. A Jaredite prince, the eldest son of the king of the same name. He rose in rebellion against his father, but while thus traitorously

engaged, a robber killed him in the endeavor to obtain some of his riches, which the Book of Ether informs us were great. (Ether, 10: 3.)

SHIBLOM, or SHIBLON. The son of Com; one of the later monarchs of the Jaredites. In his day, because of the iniquity of the people, many prophets appeared and foretold the woes that would mark the extinction of the race. Wars and grievous calamities also marked the reign of Shiblom. First, his brother inaugurated a bloody civil war, which extended throughout all the land. The wicked combinations, such as the Gadianton robbers of the Nephites, did their part to render an archy more complete. Famines and pestilence followed rapine, until "there was a great destruction, such an one as never had been known upon the face of the earth." In the extreme of their misery and degradation, the people began to repent and then the Lord had mercy upon them. Finally, Shiblom was slain and Seth, his son, was brought into captivity. Of Shiblom's private character we have no record; but his rebellious brother issued the infamous mandate that all the prophets who prophesied of the destruction of the people should be put to death. (Ether, 11: 4—9.)

SHIBLOM. A Nephite general, who commanded a corps of ten thousand men in the last great struggle between the Nephites and the Lamanites. He, with all his command, was slain in the final series of battles in the land Cumorah, when the Nephite nation was annihilated. (A. C. 385.)

SHIBLON, THE SON OF ALMA. Shiblon "was a just man, and he did walk uprightly before God, and he did observe to do good continually, to keep the commandments of the Lord his God." Such is the high encomium passed upon the character of this son of Alma, by the sacred historian of the Book of Mormon. Shiblon, like his brothers Helaman and Corianton, is first mentioned in the sacred pages in connection with the Zoramite mission. Of his birth and childhood we know nothing, but he was yet in his youth when his father called him to be one of the missionaries to the land of Antionum (B. C. 75). Like the rest of his fellow-servants of the Lord, he received the Holy Spirit under the hands of his father, and then went forth in the spirit and might of his calling to proclaim the Gospel to the misguided and stiff-necked Zoramites. He labored in their midst with energy, faith and patience, much to the joy of Alma, who, in the commandments he afterwards gave to his sons, commends Shiblon's course in the following language: "I say unto you, my son, that I have had great joy in thee already because of thy faithfulness, and thy diligence, and thy patience, and thy long-suffering among the people of the Zoramites. For I know that thou wast in bonds; yea and I also knew that thou wast stoned for the word's sake; and thou didst bear all these things in patience, because the Lord was with thee; and now thou knowest that the Lord did deliver thee." These words of Alma are the only intimation that we have of the persecutions and sufferings endured by Shiblon at the hands of the followers of Zoram. The life of Shiblon appears to have been almost constantly occupied with the duties of his priesthood. We do not read of him acting in any secular capacity, though it is presumable that like his father and the rest of his brethren, he labored with his hands to sustain himself during the short periods that intervened between his numerous missions. After the death of his father he was intimately associated with his elder brother, Helaman, and appears to have stood next to him in authority in the Church. We have no account of him taking part as a military officer (as did Helaman), in the long-continued war that succeeded the apostasy of Amalickiah, but after the war was ended (B. C. 60), he ably seconded Hela-

man's efforts to re-establish the Church and set it in order At Helaman's death, Shiblon took possession of the "sacred things" (B. C. 57). These he held until his death, which happened four years afterwards (B. C. 53); shortly before which event he conferred them upon his nephew, Helaman, the son of his elder brother.

The four years preceding Shiblon's death are principally noteworthy for the commencement of the Nephite migration to the northern continent. It was during this period that Hagoth established his ship-building yards on the borders of the land Bountiful.

In the year that Shiblon died the Lamanites made another incursion into the lands of the Nephites, but were quickly driven back to their own country after suffering great loss.

Shiblon must have died a comparatively young man. He was styled a youth when he went with his father to labor among the Zoramites, and died twenty-two years after.

SHILOAH, WATERS OF. A stream mentioned in a quotation from the writings of Isaiah. It is said to be the Siloam of the New Testament. (II Nephi, 18: 6.)

SHILOM, CITY OF. The chief, and, possibly, only city in the land of Shilom. It was built by the Nephites before the exodus under Mosiah I. When that migration took place, the Lamanites occupied it, but let it fall into decay. When the Nephites, under Zeniff, regained possession of the land, they repaired its delapidated walls and buildings, and king Noah greatly enlarged and beautified it.

SHILOM, LAND OF. A small district, probably a valley, contiguous to the land of Lehi-Nephi, and apparently immediately north of it. It seems to have been on the direct road from Zarahemla to Lehi-Nephi, as Zeniff and his colony passed through it when they came from Zarahemla

(about B. C. 200). So also did Ammon and his party (B. C. 122). When Limhi and his people escaped from the Lamanites, to avoid observation, they took a circuitous route around Shilom into the wilderness. A hill to the north of Shilom is mentioned several times, and it appears to have been a very conspicuous feature of the landscape. We are informed that it was a place of resort for the Nephites before they left that region under the guidance of Mosiah I. Later, king Noah built a high tower thereon. After the people of Limhi had escaped (B. C. 122), the Lamanites reoccupied this land; and shortly after, Amulon and his associate priests were made teachers of the people residing therein. In the days of the mission of the four sons of king Mosiah to the Lamanites, all the inhabitants of this land were converted to the Lord.

SHIM, HILL. A hill in the land Antum (in North America), wherein Ammaron deposited unto the Lord all the sacred writings of the Nephites. (A. C. 321.) He instructed Mormon to go to this hill, when he should be 24 years old, take out the plates of Nephi and engrave thereon "all the things" that he had observed concerning the Nephites. The remainder of the plates he was to leave where they were Mormon carried out these instructions, and in later years (A. C. 376), seeing that the Lamanites were about to overthrow the land, he removed all the records which Ammaron had hidden, to a safer place—the Hill Cumorah. A hill Shim is also mentioned in the Book of Ether, (Ether, 9: 3), as lying on the line of travel of the fugitive king Omer, between Moron and Ahlom, which we are of the opinion is the same hill as that in which the records of the Nephites were hidden.

SHIMNILON. A Lamanite city in the land of Nephi; its locality is not given. Many of its citizens were converted to the Lord under the teachings of the sons of Mosiah (Alma, 23: 12, 13).

---

laid down their arms and migrated to the land of Jershon (B. C. 78).

SHINAR. Supposed to be the name by which the Hebrews originally designated Lower Mesopotamia. It is mentioned but once in the Book of Mormon (II Nephi, 21: 11), is a quotation from the writings of Isaiah.

SHIZ. The last of the great military commanders opposed to Coriantumr in the final war between the Jaredite factions. Shiz was the brother of Lib, another mighty warrior who did battle with Coriantumr. In one of the many engagements fought during this series of wars, Lib was slain, when Shiz took command of his forces and routed Coriantumr, following him in quick pursuit from the plains of Agosh, where the battle took place, to the sea shore. His march was one of horror and terror to the people. As he swiftly pressed forward, he destroyed everything within his reach, burning the cities and slaying their inhabitants, sparing neither man, woman nor child, as he swept along, and a cry of despair went up through all the land, "Who can stand before the army of Shiz? Behold, he sweepeth the earth before him!" So rapid were the movements of the contending armies, that the slain remained unburied, and the stench from their bodies filled the air with pestilence. Those yet alive hastened to join one or the other of the contending hosts, either from predilection or because they were forced into the ranks Shiz was filled with the spirit of murderous revenge. He swore he would avenge the blood of his brother, whom Coriantumr had slain. When he caught up with the latter's armies, the fierce himself upon them with all the energy that hatred inspires. The battle lasted three days and ended in the repulse of Shiz, whose warriors fled to the land of Corihor, sweeping off the inhabitants of the lands they passed through who would not join them.

In the valley of Corihor, Coriantumr again sought battle. He challenged Shiz, from the hill Comnor, by the sound of the trumpet, and Shiz was in no temper to disregard the challenge. Twice he attacked his over-confident foe, with the horde of men, women and children who followed his banner, and twice he was repulsed. On the third occasion he bore so heavily upon Coriantumr that the latter was wounded and fainted from the loss of blood. Their leader stricken, his motley following of old and young fell back; but Shiz was in no condition to take advantage of his victory. Both had lost so heavily that they were unable to renew the contest. Two millions of men, with their wives and children, had already fallen in this inhuman, relentless war.

At this point the heart of Coriantumr was touched with the miseries of his people, and he wrote to Shiz, stating that he would surrender the kingdom if the lives of his people could be spared. Shiz's brutal soul was yet untouched; he replied that if Coriantumr would give himself up so that he (Shiz) might slay him with his own sword, he would spare the lives of the people. To this proposal Coriantumr would not accede. With rekindled anger and hatred the two hosts prepared for renewed hostilities. Shiz was victorious in the first battle, and the enemy retired to the neighborhood of the great lakes. Another furious conflict followed, and Coriantumr triumphed, while Shiz retreated southward, to a place called Ogath, near the hill Ramah. Here the two commanders gathered their hosts for the final struggle. All, hale and grandsire, men and maid, had to join one side or the other. The spirit of bloody vengeance filled every heart. Into the trembling hands of age and the feeble grasp of infancy alike, were thrust the sword and spear, while shield and breastplate defended the body strong enough to bear their weights. When once

begun, the dwindling fight kept on from day to day, while night was made hideous by the yells and lamentations, the curses and oaths of the survivors, who were frenzied with anger, even as a man is drunken with wine. Thus they fought, struggled and fell, until one night there remained of all the race but fifty-two of the people of Coriantumr and sixty-nine of the followers of Shiz. But they rested not. The next evening, thirty-two of the adherents of Shiz confronted twenty-seven of Coriantumr's. Next day the battle was continued, until the remnants grew faint from exertion and loss of blood. After three hours' desperate fighting the men of Coriantumr attempted to flee, but Shiz and his warriors prevented them. And so they continued until the two commanders remained alone on the field, all their followers having being slain, and Shiz himself had fainted. Then Coriantumr, having rested to gain sufficient strength, smote off the head of Shiz, who in his dying throes raised himself on his hands and knees as if to renew the contest, fell over, struggled for breath and died.

SHULE. One of the early kings of the Jaredites. He was the son of Kib, born to him in his old age, while he was in captivity, he having been deposed by an elder son named Corihor. When Shule grew to manhood he became mighty in judgment and bodily strength, and being angry with his brother Corihor for rebelling against their father, he raised an army, armed them with swords made by himself, gave battle to his brother at a city named Nebor, defeated the latter's forces and restored their father to the throne. Kib, being very aged, placed the sovereign power in the hands of Shule who reigned in righteousness and extended the borders of his growing people in all directions. Corihor, repentant of his former treason, received many favors from Shule and was placed in high power in the nation, the trusts whereof he faithfully performed. But as he had rebelled against his father in his early days, so in like manner one of his sons, named Noah, rebelled against him and against the king, and in this rebellion drew away all his brothers. At first, Noah was successful. He obtained possession of the land of the Jaredites' first inheritance, called by them Moron, and reigned king in that region of Central America. Again he attacked Shule; and this time took him prisoner, carrying him captive to Moron, with the intention of putting him to death. But before he had carried out his bloodthirsty design, his cousins, the sons of Shule, broke into his house and killed the usurper. They then went to the prison where their father was held, released him from his confinement, and replaced him on the throne of that part of the country not retained by the son of Noah. There were now two kingdoms, both of which were growing, while that one under the government of Shule "did prosper exceedingly and waxed great." After a time, Cohor, the son of Noah, commenced war with Shule, in which he was deservedly unsuccessful, and in the conflict that ensued he was slain. His son Nimrod, knowing the unrighteousness of his father's cause, restored Noah's kingdom to Shule, so that the latter again, as in the beginning, reigned over the whole of the Jaredite race. For this act of magnanimity Shule bestowed great favors upon Nimrod, who did in the whole kingdom "according to his desires."

Though the people were highly prospered at this time, they gave way to idolatry, and grew hard in their hearts. This, no doubt, was intensified by the bad example of the royal family and the miseries and cruelties of the wars which their quarrels induced. During Shule's days the Lord sent many prophets to the Jaredites, who warned the people of His impending judgments. For a time these prophets were rejected and reviled. But Shule made a law that the prophets should have

Sion.   341

harlot. Its meaning is the land of the deserters or apostates. It was situated at the extreme edge of the Nephite possessions, and on the borders of the Lamanites, beyond, that is south or southeast of Antionum, the headquarters of the Zoramites. In this remote land, far from the Nephite capital, outside the reach of the rigors of the law of Moses, the enticing Isabel could carry on her vile calling with the greatest safety and impunity.

SION. This name appears once in the Book of Mormon, in a quotation from the writings of Isaiah. (II Nephi, 22: 6.) (See Zion.)

SODOM. The city destroyed by fire from heaven. It is named twice in the Book of Mormon in quotations from the writings of Isaiah (II Nephi, 13: 9; 23: 19).

SOLOMON. The name of this great king is mentioned seven times in the Book of Mormon. Three times in connection with the temple he built. Three times in connection with the temple he built (Jacob, 1. 15; 2: 23, 24.) And once by the Redeemer in the well-known passage in which he compares the lilies of the field with the glory of Solomon. (II Nephi, 13: 29.)

STONES, PRECIOUS. The precious stones named in the Book of Mormon are agates, carbuncles, sapphires and pearls. All, except the last named, in quotations from the Bible.

SYRIA. This country is named five times in the Book of Mormon (II Nephi, 17: 1−8), always in quotations from the writings of Isaiah.

SYRIANS. The people of Syria. They are mentioned but once in the Book of Mormon (II Nephi, 19: 12), in a quotation from Isaiah.

TABAEL, SON OF. A warrior who is not identified. He lived in the days of Ahaz, king of Judah. His name only appears in the Book of Mormon in a quotation from the writings of Isaiah. (II Nephi, 17: 6).

free access wherever they wished to go, and further decreed a punishment for all those who persecuted and reviled them. The preaching of these holy men eventually brought the Jaredites to repentance, and because of their penitence the Lord spared them and turned away His judgments, and the people prospered again. In his old age Shule begat Omer, who succeeded him on the throne. Shule's days were full of trouble and sorrow, but he reigned in righteousness, was faithful to the Lord, and executed judgment in justice towards his subjects. We are of the opinion that Shule was a contemporary of the Patriarch Abraham.

SHURR, VALLEY OF. A valley in North America, described as being near the hill Comnor. It was here that three desperate battles were fought between Shiz and Coriantumr, towards the close of the final war which resulted in the utter destruction of the Jaredite race.

SIDOM. This place is only mentioned in the 15th chap. of Alma. When the persecuted members of the true church were driven out of Ammonihah by its vicious citizens, they fled to Sidom (B. C. 82), it being apparently not far distant from Ammonihah.

SIDON, RIVER. The most important river in Nephite history; known to-day as the Magdalena. It runs northward through the United States of Colombia and empties into the Caribbean Sea. In the days of the Nephites it formed an important factor in their civilization, as many of their largest cities were built on its banks, and its valleys were the most densely populated of any part of the country. Near its head waters was Manti, the chief city of the south, and further north were Gideon and Zarahemla. It was also the grand trunk road to the land of Nephi, and along its banks poured the hosts of the dark-skinned Lamanites when they forced their way into the land of Zarahemla. Among the most important events

Tarshish.   342

TARSHISH. A country or city mentioned in the Bible, whose locality is undetermined. It is named once in the Book of Mormon (II Nephi, 12: 16), in a quotation from the prophecies of Isaiah.

TEANCUM. One of the bravest, most disinterested and most illustrious soldiers who served the Nephite Commonwealth. Of his life we are told nothing until he is presented to us as one of Moroni's lieutenants.

Teancum appears to have had command of the Nephite army of the north, and to have had committed to him the defense of the Land Bountiful and the Isthmus of Panama. His first exploit to which our attention is drawn was the defeat of the dissatisfied people of the hot-headed Morianton, who, having unjustly quarreled with their neighbors, the people of the City of Lehi, and being apparently aware of the unrighteousness of their cause, determined to migrate to the land northward, and there establish an independent government. Such a movement being evidently dangerous to the peace and stability of the Republic, Moroni determined to prevent the accomplishment of their scheme. He dispatched Teancum at the head of a body of troops to head them off. This the gallant officer succeeded in doing, but not until they had reached the isthmus, where a stubbornly-fought battle ensued, in which Teancum slew Morianton with his own hand, and compelled the surrender of his followers. (B. C. 68.) The prisoners were brought back, the grievances of the two peoples were investigated, a union between them brought about, and both were restored to their own lands.

In the following year (B. C. 67), Amalickiah, the apostate Nephite who reigned over the Lamanites, commenced his devastating invasion of the Atlantic provinces of the Nephites. Commencing at Moroni, on the extreme southeast, he gradually advanced northward, capturing and garrisoning

that occurred in its immediate neighborhood were:

The Amlicites defeated at the hill Amnihu, B. C. 87.

Two invading armies of the Lamanites defeated, one on its west bank, the other on the east, B. C. 87.

The Lamanites defeated at the hill Riplah, B. C. 74.

Manti captured by the Lamanites, (about) B. C. 68.

Manti reoccupied by the Nephites, B. C. 63.

The Lamanites invade Zarahemla, capture the capital and advance northward, but are finally driven back, B. C. 51.

The Lamanites again invade Zarahemla, B. C. 35.

The Lamanites obtain possession of the whole of South America. B. C. 33.

The Lamanites, being converted, restore to the Nephites Zarahemla and the lands they had wrested from them, B. C. 30.

The Nephites, under Lachoneus, all gather to the lands of Zarahemla and Bountiful, A. C. 17.

The Nephites return to their homes on both continents, A. C. 26.

Zarahemla and other cities destroyed during the great storms and earthquakes that attended the crucifixion of the Redeemer, A. C. 34.

SINAI. The mountain where the Lord delivered unto Moses the Ten Commandments. It is named twice in the Book of Mormon: (1) In Abinadi's reproof of the apostate priests of king Noah. (Mosiah, 12: 33). (2) In the statement that Abinadi's face shone with exceeding lustre as Moses' did while in the mount of Sinai. (Mosiah, 13: 5.)

SINIM. A land, supposed by some to be the southern part of China. It is mentioned but once in the Book of Mormon, in a quotation from the writings of Isaiah. (I Nephi, 21: 12.)

SIRON, LAND OF. The home of Isabel, the

Teancum.   343

all the Nephite cities along the coast, until toward the close of the year, he reached the borders of the land Bountiful, driving the forces of the Republic before him. At this point he was met by Teancum and a corps of veterans renowned for their courage, skill and discipline. The Lamanite leader endeavored to force his way to the Isthmus with the intention of occupying the northern continent. In this he was foiled, for the trained valor of Teancum's warriors was too much for that of Amalickiah's half-savage hordes. All day the fight lasted, and at night the worn-out soldiery camped in close proximity, the Lamanites on the sea beach, and the Nephites on the borders of the land Bountiful.

When night had closed and all was still, Teancum, accompanied by one soldier, stole out of his own camp into that of the enemy. He sought the tent of Amalickiah, and when he found it he slew the Lamanite king with his javelin, then quickly returning, he aroused his troops and kept them on the alert all night, fearing that when the foe found they had lost their chief they would make a sudden attack on the Nephites; but it did not so happen. Amalickiah's death was not discovered until the morning, and then his followers hastily retreated to Mulek, where they shut themselves up. Each commander now felt only sufficiently strong to act on the defensive, and Teancum employed his soldiery in vigorously strengthening the fortifications of the land Bountiful and the Isthmus which formed the natural northern boundary of that land. Moroni likewise desired him to harrass and scourge the enemy whenever opportunity offered, but they kept too closely within their fortifications for much to be done in that way. This state of mutual watching, without any aggressive movements, continued for some time. Once Teancum, by Moroni's direction, made reconnaissance in force towards Mulek, but he found it too strongly fortified to warrant an attempt to capture it by assault. He therefore retired to Bountiful and awaited Moroni's arrival, that officer being now conducting operations in the southwest. Moroni did not rejoin Teancum until the end of the year B. C. 65.

At the commencement of the next year a grand council of war was held at the Nephite headquarters. Efforts had been made to induce the Lamanites to come out and fight on the open plains between Mulek and Bountiful, but their leaders very prudently declined. It was therefore decided to make an effort to draw them out by stratagem. The Nephite army was divided into three divisions, commanded by Moroni, Lehi and Teancum respectively. Teancum advanced with a small body of men near to the walls of Mulek. The Lamanites, noticing his weakness, sallied forth to capture him. He retreated rapidly northward along the sea beach, in well-feigned trepidation. The enemy followed in hot pursuit. When they neared Bountiful, Lehi and his men marched out, covered the retreat, and confronted the now fatigued legions of Laman. Jacob, their leader, ordered a retreat to Mulek; Lehi leisurely advanced, till they reached the place where Moroni's command blockaded the road, then both Nephite commanders met the Lamanites in the shock of battle, front and rear. The Lamanites were disastrously defeated, Jacob was killed and Mulek fell into the hands of the Nephites. This was the turning point in the war, for from this time the patriots gradually regained their lost cities.

We have no details of the services of Teancum in the brilliant campaign that followed, during which the tide of victory rolled resistlessly down the Atlantic shore. We will therefore simply say that at last the soldiers of Ammoron were driven out of every Nephite city on the Atlantic seaboard, except the outlying one, called Moroni, where the

his brother Nephi, with the authority of the holy priesthood which he held, came to where the martyr lay, and in the power of Jesus' name, he raised Timothy from the dead. (A. C. 31.)

After the tribulations that ceased that marked the advent of the Lord of life and glory, Nephi and Timothy, with many others, assembled at the Temple that was in the land Bountiful. There the Lord Jesus Christ appeared and ministered to them. He called Nephi to him, then eleven others, and gave them authority to baptize the people. Of these twelve, Timothy was one, and is mentioned next in order to his brother Nephi in the list given by the inspired historian.

After Jesus had chosen the Twelve, He commenced to teach the people the principles of the fulness of the Gospel. So He continued day by day until all was revealed, either to the multitude or to the Twelve, that was necessary for the eternal salvation of the obedient.

After the final departure of Jesus, the Disciples went forth in the midst of the people in the lands that had not been blessed with the personal visit of the Savior, to them they declared the glad message of life eternal; in the name of Jesus they baptized them, and by His authority they conferred the Holy Ghost. So abundantly and so gloriously did the power of God rest with these servants of God, that they raised the dead, healed the sick, gave sight to the eyes of the blind and strength to the limbs of the lame; the deaf heard, the dumb spake, and all manner of miracles were performed, and all in the name of Jesus. Two years after His ascension, every part of the vast continent, where Nephite or Lamanite dwelt, had heard the message, and so abundant was the Disciples' success, that every soul was converted unto the Lord, and in their integrity to God they never faltered.

Timothy is not again mentioned by name in the Book of Mormon.

whole of the invading host was massed for a final desperate stand, and around which Moroni, with hurried and lengthened marches, had concentrated his warriors.

It was the night before an expected decisive battle, and the Nephite officers and soldiery were too worn out to either devise stratagems or execute them. Teancum alone was in a condition of unrest. He remembered with intense bitterness all the bloodshed, woes, hardships, famine, etc., that had been brought about in this great and lasting war between the two races, which he rightly attributed to the infamous ambition of Amalickiah and Ammoron. In his anger he stole forth into the enemy's camp, let himself over the walls of the city, sought out the king's tent, and when he had found the object of his search, he cast a javelin at him, which pierced him near the heart; but, unlike Amalickiah, Ammoron's death was not instantaneous, he had time to awaken his servant before he expired. The alarm was given, the guards started in pursuit, Teancum was overtaken, caught and slain. On the morrow, Moroni attacked the Lamanites, defeated them with great slaughter, captured the city, and drove them entirely out of Nephite territory. (B. C. 61.)

TEANCUM, CITY OF. A city mentioned only in connection with the final struggle between the Nephites and Lamanites (Mormon, 4: 3-14.) It lay near the sea (probably the Pacific Ocean), a little north of the city of Desolation. When the Lamanites captured Desolation (A. C. 363) the remnants of the Nephites fled to Teancum. The next year the Lamanites attacked the city but were repulsed. They came against it again in A. C. 366-7 and drove the Nephites out, taking many women and children prisoners, whom they sacrificed to their idol gods.

TEOMER. A prominent Nephite military officer in the days of the Judges. In the war brought

TREES. The trees mentioned in the Book of Mormon are the cedar, fir, oak, olive, sycamore and teil. The vine is also named.

TUBALOTH. A king of the Lamanites who waged war against the Nephites in the days of the Judges. He was of Nephite extraction being the son of Ammoron, the brother of Amalickiah, and a descendant of Zoram the servant of Laban. His father was killed by the Nephite general Teancum (B. C. 61), and it is probable that he succeeded his father on the throne, though he is not mentioned by name until ten years afterwards (B. C. 51). The death of Ammoron ended one of the most disastrous and long-continued wars that had ever devastated the lands of the Nephites, and appears to have been terminated by the Lamanites from sheer exhaustion. It was not until eight years afterwards that they again invaded the territory of their traditional enemies, when they were driven back to their own lands with great loss. Two years later, Tubaloth gathered and equipped an immense army, which he placed under a general named Corinacumer, who, disregarding the old tactics, marched directly to the city of Zarahemla, which he surprised and captured, and then continued his march northward towards the land Bountiful. But he was out-generaled and utterly defeated by the Nephites, he himself being slain; the remnants of his army were allowed by Moronihah to return to their own land. So disastrous was this campaign, that for sixteen years Nephite soil was free from the tread of the invader. We have no means of telling if Tubaloth was still king when the Lamanites recommenced hostilities in B. C. 35.

URIAH. A high priest in the reign of Ahaz. He is mentioned in the Book of Mormon in a quotation from the writings of Isaiah (II Nephi, 18:2).

UZZIAH. A wise and righteous king of Judah (B. C. 809-757?) He is mentioned twice in the

on by the treason and ambition of Amalickiah, he served under Helaman in the army of the southwest. Teomer took a prominent part in the siege and recapture of the city of Manti (B. C. 63), at which time he had command of one of the divisions of the Nephite army. When the Lamanites within the city, fearing that the besieging Nephite army would cut them off from their supplies, made a sortie and endeavored to drive them away, the main body of Helaman's troops retreated, while Gid and his men, and Teomer with his command, who were hid in the wilderness, fell in the Lamanite rear, cut off communication between the advancing army and the city, and then unexpectedly fell on the very small guard which the Lamanite commander had incautiously left to take care of Manti. The guard was easily overpowered, and Gid and Teomer obtained and retained possession of the city; during which time the main body of the Lamanites were out-generaled by Helaman, who led them afar off into the wilderness, and then by a rapid counter march, during the night, reached Manti before them.

TIMOTHY. It is but little we are told in the Book of Mormon of the life or labors of this devoted servant of the Lord, this uncompromising preacher of righteousness. His days, before the coming of the Savior, were spent in proclaiming the saving truths of the Gospel, in declaring unto the Nephites that the kingdom of heaven was at hand, and in rebuking their constantly increasing depravity. His words cut like a two-edged sword, they laid bare the iniquities of their corrupt rulers and unjust judges, their seditious lawyers and idolatrous priests, as well as of the degraded rabble; he spared none whose deeds were evil. Angered at the unwelcome recital of their abounding crimes, the vile populace stoned him till he died, that they might no longer hear the sound of his reproving voice. But his work on earth was not yet finished;

Book of Mormon (II Nephi, 16: 1; 17: 1), in connection with the writings of Isaiah.

ZARAHEMLA. When Mosiah I led the more righteous portion of the Nephites northward from the land of Lehi-Nephi. (About B. C. 200), he found on the west bank of the river Sidon a city inhabited by a partly civilized and irreligious people, whose language he could not understand. They were ruled by a chief or king named Zarahemla. When the two races began to understand each other it was found that the people of Zarahemla were the descendants of a colony which was led by the Lord out of Jerusalem in the year when that city was destroyed by the king of Babylon (B. C. 589). After wandering in the wilderness they were brought across the great waters and landed in the southern portion of the North American continent. In after years they migrated southward to the place where they were found by Mosiah. Among the members of the original colony was Mulek, the youngest son of king Zedekiah; and it is presumable that most of them were of the house of Judah.

Of the history of the colony for nearly four hundred years we know next to nothing. It is summed up in the few following words: "And at the time that Mosiah discovered them, they had become exceedingly numerous. Nevertheless, they had had many wars and serious contentions, and had fallen by the sword from time to time; and their language had become corrupted; and they had brought no records with them; and they denied the being of their Creator; and Mosiah, nor the people of Mosiah, could understand them." (Omni, 1: 17.)

ZARAHEMLA, CITY OF. The capital of the Nephite nation, from about 200 years B. C. to A. C. 30, when the Commonwealth was disrupted and the people divided into tribes. This city was situated on the west bank of the Sidon river, and was originally built by the descendants of the people of Mulek, who left Jerusalem. B. C. 589. Zarahemla appears to have been their leader at the time the Nephites, led by Mosiah I, discovered them, and as the city was named after him it is probable that it had not been built long before the arrival of the latter people. After the advent of the Nephites, the two peoples united in one nation, and this city became the seat of their government, the residence of their chief judges and high priests, and the centre of their civilization. In it was also built a temple to the God of Israel. During the days of the Judges, nearly every event of importance to the whole nation took place or originated in this city. It was the headquarters of the royalists or "king-men", whose attempts to restore a monarchy led to so many contentions and so much sorrow, and so frequently ended in bloodshed. It was captured by the Lamanites in B. C. 51, and again in B. C. 35 and was then held by them until B. C. 30.

In B. C. 6, Samuel, the Lamanite, appeared upon the walls of Zarahemla, and prophesied of many wondrous events yet in the future. Among them he foretold its destruction by fire from heaven, in consequence of the great wickedness of the major portion of its inhabitants. (Helaman, 13:12-14.) In accordance with this prophecy Zarahemla was destroyed during the great convulsions of nature that attended the sacrifice of the Lord Jesus. It was afterwards rebuilt, but we are not informed if it was again recognized as the chief city of the nation, though from its admirable position and past associations, it is quite probable that it was.

ZARAHEMLA, LAND OF. As there were two lands of Nephi, the greater and the lesser, so, for exactly the same reasons, there were two lands of Zarahemla; the one occupying the whole of

South America, from the great wilderness, which formed its southern border, northward to the land Bountiful; the other, the district immediately surrounding the capital city, which bore the same name

That there was a Zarahemla within Zarahemla is shown by various passages in which persons are spoken of as journeying to the land of Zarahemla, when they were already within the borders of the greater land of that name. For instance, Minon, on the river Sidon, is said to have been situated above the land of Zarahemla (Alma 2:24); again, Alma took Amulek and came over to the land of Zarahemla from Sidom (Alma, 15:18). While in many other places, notably where the boundaries of the possessions of the Nephites are given, the name Zarahemla is applied to the whole of the lands of that people, even sometimes including Bountiful, which is generally spoken of separately.

In the days of the first Mosiah and his son, king Benjamin, the greater portion of the Nephites appear to have been located in and immediately around the city of Zarahemla. King Benjamin, when about to resign the royal authority into the hands of his son Mosiah, commanded him to gather his people together, for, he adds, on the morrow I shall proclaim unto this my people out of mine own mouth, that thou art a king and a ruler over this people (Mosiah, 1:10). The proclamation was sent forth and the people were gathered in an unnumbered host; a thing that could not have been done in so short a time had their habitations been widely scattered over an extended territory.

In the reign of the younger Mosiah, the people spread out in all directions, and colonies were planted in distant regions. This vigorous policy was continued, only on a much larger scale, during the days of the Judges. We suggest that the lands

or cities included within the borders of the land of Zarahemla, in the days of the Judges, were:

In the extreme north, the land of Bountiful, which extended southward from the Isthmus of Panama. On its southern frontier lay the land of Jershon

On the river Sidon: Zarahemla, Minon, Gideon and Manti.

In the interior, eastward of the Sidon: Antiomum, Siron, and Nephihah.

On the shores of the Atlantic Ocean and Caribbean Sea: Mulek, Morianton, Lehi, Omner, Gid, Aaron and Moroni.

In the interior west of the Sidon: Melek, Aaron, Noah, Ammonihah and Sidom.

Between the upper waters of the Sidon and the Pacific Ocean: Cumeni, Antiparah, Judea and Zeezrom.

ZEBULUN. One of the Twelve Tribes of Israel. Reference is made to the land of Zebulun (II Nephi, 19:1), in a quotation from the writings of Isaiah.

ZECHARIAH. An Israelite of whom nothing personally is known. His name is mentioned (II Nephi, 18:2), in a quotation from the writings of Isaiah, where he is spoken of as a "faithful witness to record."

ZEDEKIAH. One of the twelve Disciples called and chosen by Jesus to minister to the Nephites at the time of his visit to that people (A. C. 34). Zedekiah was present near the temple in the land Bountiful, when Jesus appeared, and was baptized by Nephi on the day following. He is not mentioned again in the sacred record.

ZEDEKIAH. The last king of Judah. In the first year of his reign, Lehi and his family left Jerusalem. Zedekiah's name occurs eight times in the Book of Mormon, five of which are connected with Lehi's departure, the other three relate to the monarch's posterity. The killing of the sons

of Zedekiah by the king of Babylon is spoken of in Helaman, 8:21.

ZEEZROM. A distinguished lawyer in the corrupt city of Ammonihah, at the time that Alma and Amulek ministered to its unrepentant people (B. C. 82). Zeezrom led the opposition to the servants of God, and by his subtlety, ingenuity and boldness endeavored to make it appear that they had contradicted themselves in their preaching, and had also spoken disrespectfully of their country's laws. At last, however, he began to feel the power of God, and when he did so he was not so hardened that he was not willing to acknowledge it. At this, his former admirers turned against him, and having reviled and maltreated him, drove him out of the city with other converts. The fugitives fled to a neighboring city, called Sidom, where Zeezrom, overwhelmed with the realization of his iniquity, fell sick of a fever. At last, the glad tidings reached his ears that Alma and Amulek were safe, for he had feared that through his iniquities they had been slain. No sooner did they reach Sidom than he sent for them, for his heart began to take courage. When they entered his presence, he imploringly stretched forth his hands and besought them to heal him. Alma questioned him regarding his faith in Christ, and finding that the good seed had germinated in his bosom and brought forth fruit, this mighty High Priest cried unto the Lord, "O Lord our God, have mercy on this man, and heal him according to his faith, which is in Christ." When Alma had said these words, Zeezrom leaped upon his feet and walked, to the great astonishment of all who witnessed it. Alma then baptized the repentant lawyer, who began from that hour forth to preach the glorious message of eternal salvation. His energy, his wisdom, his learning, his talents were now used towards the upbuilding of the kingdom of God, with as much zeal as he had

before labored for corruptible riches and worldly fame. From this time forth Zeezrom became a preacher of righteousness, laboring under the direction of Alma, who then presided over the Church of Christ throughout all the land; and we next hear of him ministering to the people in the land of Melek. In later years, he accompanied Alma in his mission to the Zoramites. After this we are told no more of his personal history, but his name and teachings are more than once referred to by later servants of God.

ZEEZROM. A Nephite city on their southwest frontier, probably a short distance west of Manti. In the great war between the Nephite commonwealth and Amalickiah, Zeezrom fell into the hands of the Lamanites. It was in their possession when Helaman arrived in that region with his army of young Ammonites (B. C. 66). This is the only time that this city is mentioned by name, but it doubtless was captured by the Lamanites more than once in their successful invasions of Zarahemla in later years.

ZEMNARIHAH. A chief captain of the armies of the Gadianton robbers who, in A. C. 21, came up on all sides in great force and laid siege to the people of Nephi. This system of warfare was, however, unsuccessful, as the Nephites, who were gathered with their flocks, herds, provisions, etc., into one land, had laid up large stores of provisions, while the robbers had to subsist upon the game they could kill in the wilderness. The Nephites, therefore, adopted a policy of constantly harrassing the robbers, making sorties by day and by night in unexpected places, and inflicting great loss upon the forces of Zemnarihah. The results of this policy grew so disastrous that the robbers ultimately changed their tactics and made an effort to reach the land northward, but being enfeebled by want of food they were not able to act with sufficient rapidity. The Nephite general,

Gidgiddoni, being apprised of their intention, headed them off on the north and cut off their retreat on the south. Finding themselves hemmed in, the robbers capitulated, and those who did not do so were slain. Among the prisoners was Zemnarihah, whom the Nephites hung on the top of a tree until he was dead, after which the tree was felled to the earth. The robbers who had been captured were cast into prison, and by and by the word of God was preached to them. Those who repented and covenanted to murder and rob no more were liberated, while those who remained obstinate on account of their iniquities, all classes became brutal, sensual and devilish, and such a one, we are compelled to conclude, was Zeezrom, from the brief account given of his treatment of the weak and suffering of his own nation.

ZENEPHI. A Nephite general who lived in the fourth century of the Christian era. He commanded an army in the war with the Lamanites, at the time that Mormon was commander-in-chief of the Nephite forces. He is mentioned but once in the sacred record, and then by Mormon in his second epistle to his son Moroni, when detailing the terrible condition of the people through the brutal manner in which the war was being conducted on both sides. The Spirit of the Lord having been withdrawn from both Nephites and Lamanites on account of their iniquities, all classes became brutal, sensual and devilish, and such a one, we are compelled to conclude, was Zeezrom.

ZENIFF. The first of the three kings who reigned over the colony of Nephites who returned from Zarahemla and established themselves in the land of Lehi-Nephi, about B. C. 200.

Zeniff and his people, having left Zarahemla, traveled southward towards the land of Nephi. The blessings of the Lord were not greatly with them, for they did not seek Him nor advise to His will. In the wilderness they lost their way, and suffered from famine and many afflictions; but after many days they reached the neighborhood of the city of Lehi-Nephi, the former home of their race. Here Zeniff chose four of his company, and accompanied by them went to the king of the Lamanites. This monarch, whose name was Laman, received them with the appearance of kindness. He made a treaty with them, and gave them the lands of Lehi-Nephi and Shilom to dwell in. He also caused his own people to remove out of these cities and the surrounding country, that Zeniff's people might have full possession. King Laman was in reality not as friendly as he pretended to be. His object was to get the industrious Nephites to settle in the midst of his people, and then by his superior numbers to make them his slaves; for his own subjects were a lazy, unprogressive race.

As soon as Zeniff and his followers occupied their new possessions they went to work to build houses and to repair the walls of the city; for the idle Lamanites had suffered them to fall into decay. They also commenced to till the ground, and to plant all manner of seeds of grain, vegetables and fruit therein. Soon, through their thrift and industry, they began to prosper and multiply. This caused king Laman to grow uneasy. He desired to bring them into bondage that his people might reap the benefits of the labors of the Nephites. But they were growing so rapidly that he feared that if he did not soon put a stop to their increase they would be the stronger of the two people. To prevent this he began to stir up the hearts of his people in anger against the Nephites. He succeeded so well that in the thirteenth year of Zeniff's reign in the land of Lehi-Nephi a numerous host of Lamanites suddenly fell upon his people, while they were feeding and watering their flocks, and began to slay them. They also carried off some of their flocks, and the corn from their fields.

Those of the Nephites who were not slain or overtaken fled to Zeniff. As quickly as he could he armed his people with bows and arrows, swords and cimeters, clubs and slings, and with such other weapons as they could invent. Thus armed they went forth in the strength of the Lord to meet the enemy, for in their hour of peril they had cried mightily unto Him, and He heard their cries and answered their prayers.

Thus strengthened they met their foes. The battle was an obstinate and a bloody one. It lasted all day and all night. At last the Lamanites were driven back, with a loss of 3,043 warriors, while the people of Zeniff had to mourn the death of 279 of their brethren. After this, there was peace in the land for many years.

During this time of peace Zeniff taught his people to be very industrious. He caused his men to till the ground and raise all kinds of fruit and grain. The women he had spin and make cloth for clothing, fine linen, etc. In this way, for twenty-two years, they prospered and had uninterrupted peace.

At this time the old king Laman died, and his son succeeded him upon the throne. Like many young princes, he desired to distinguish himself in war. So he gathered a numerous host of the Lamanites, and having armed them in the same manner as the Nephites, he led them to the north of the land of Shemlon, which lay near the land of Nephi-Lehi.

When Zeniff learned of the approach of young king Laman's armies, he caused the women and children of his people to hide in the wilderness; but every man, young or old, who was able to bear arms was placed in the ranks to go out against the foe. Zeniff himself was an aged man, but he still continued to command his forces and led them in person to battle. Strengthened by the faith Zeniff implanted in their hearts, the Nephites gained a great victory; and so numerous were the slain of the Lamanites that they were

not counted. After this there was peace again in the land. Shortly after this Zeniff died, and, unfortunately for his kingdom, chose for his successor an unworthy son, named Noah.

ZENOCH, or ZENOCK. A prophet of Israel, of whose personal history, or to what age he belonged, we know nothing. His writings were familiar to the Nephites, as he is quoted by Nephi. (I Nephi, 19: 10), Alma, (Alma, 33: 15), Amulek, (Alma, 34: 7), Nephi, (Helaman, 8: 20), and Mormon (III Nephi, 10: 16).

ZENOS. A Hebrew prophet, often quoted by the Nephite servants of God. All we are told of his personal history is that he was slain because he testified boldly of what God revealed to him. That he was a man greatly blessed of the Lord with the spirit of prophecy is shown by that wonderful and almost incomparable parable of the Vineyard, given at length by Jacob (Jacob, chap. 5). His prophecies are also quoted by Nephi, (I Nephi, 19: 10, 12, 16), Alma, (Alma, 33: 3, 13, 15), Amulek, (Alma, 34: 7), Samuel, the Lamanite, (Helaman, 15: 11), and Mormon (III Nephi, 10: 16).

ZERAHEMNAH. A Lamanite general, who commanded the forces of that people, who, at the request of the apostate Zoramites occupied Antionum with the intention of attacking the Ammonites in the land of Jershon. Like most of the commanding officers of the Lamanite armies of that age, he was a Nephite dissenter (B. C. 74.) Zerahemnah, finding that Moroni, the Nephite commander was too well prepared for their attack on the land of Jershon, retired through Antionum into the wilderness, where they changed direction and marched towards the head-waters of the river Sidon, with the intention of taking possession of the land of Manti. But Moroni was too vigilant to allow his enemies to slip away without knowing what had become of them. He had

his spies watch the movements of Zerahemnah's forces, and in the meanwhile sent to Alma to inquire the mind and will of the Lord with regard to his future course. The word of the Lord was given to Alma, and he informed Moroni's messengers of the movements of the Lamanites. The young general, with becoming prudence, then divided his army. One corps he left to protect Jershon, and with the remainder he advanced by rapid marches towards Manti, by the most direct route. On his arrival he at once mustered all the men who could bear arms into his forces, to help in the defense of their liberties against the advancing foe. So rapid had been his movements and so prompt had been the response to his call that when the Lamanites reached the neighborhood of the Sidon he was prepared for their coming. The battle which was fought when the opposing armies met was one of the most stubborn and bloody in Nephite history. Never from the beginning had the Lamanites been known to fight with such exceeding great strength and courage. Time after time their hosts rushed upon the well-ordered ranks of the Nephites, and notwithstanding the latter's armor they clove in their heads and cut off their arms. But the cost of these charges to their own numbers was terrible. The battle began at a hill called Riplah, and afterwards extended to both banks of the Sidon. At one time a lull took place in the carnage, and Moroni, who had no pleasure in shedding blood, made an offer of such terms of surrender as he considered the circumstances warranted. But Zerahemnah and other captains of the Lamanite hosts rejected the offer and urged their warriors to renewed resistance. So the battle recommenced with unabated fury. At last, however, Zerahemnah himself, to prevent the total annihilation of his armies, consented to the proposed terms of surrender and entered into the required covenant of peace. So

great were the losses on both sides that the dead were not counted. After this fearful battle, we read no more of Zerahemnah.

ZERAM. One of four Nephite officers, sent with their men, by Alma, from the valley of Gideon to watch the movements of the defeated Amlicites, the evening after the great battle fought by Alma and the armies of the Nephites at the hill Amnihu, on the east side of the river Sidon (B. C. 87). The next day they returned in great haste and reported that they had followed the Amlicites, until the latter had joined, in the land of Minon, a numerous host of Lamanites, who were driving the Nephite inhabitants before them and marching rapidly towards the city of Zarahemla.

ZERIN, MOUNT. A mountain of which we know nothing except what is contained in the following passage: For the brother of Jared said unto the mountain Zerin, remove, and it was removed. (Ether, 12: 30.)

ZIFF. A metal, kind unknown, used by the artificers of king Noah in the land of Lehi-Nephi (Mosiah, 11: 3, 8). The word ziff means, in the Hebrew, metallic brightness. (The word is used in Daniel, 2; 31, also in Isaiah, 30: 22, where it means overlaying metal.)

ZION. This word occurs forty-four times in the Book of Mormon; nearly always in quotations from Isaiah, or in references thereto.

ZORAM. The servant of Laban (B. C. 600), afterwards the friend of Nephi. When Nephi had slain Laban near his house at Jerusalem, he went into the dead man's residence, and assuming the voice of Laban commanded Zoram, who had the keys of the treasury, to bring the records he needed. It being night, Zoram was deceived, and quickly obeyed. Then Nephi commanded Zoram to follow him with the records to his brethren. This Zoram did, supposing that the brethren to whom Nephi alluded, were the elders of the Jews.

Nephi and Zoram took their course to the place where Nephi's brothers had secreted themselves outside the walls of Jerusalem. When the latter saw them coming they were greatly afraid, for they did not recognize their brother, dressed in the armor of Laban. They thought that he had been killed and that these men were coming to slay them also; so they fled before them. Nephi, perceiving the difficulty, called to them in his own voice. While this arrested their flight, on the other hand it alarmed Zoram. He would have returned in terror to Jerusalem and, no doubt, have spread the alarm, if Nephi had not caught hold of him, given him assurances of good will and made a covenant with him that if he would be faithful to Nephi and his brethren he should be a free man like unto them; for it appears that Zoram was a bond-servant, most probably an Israelite who had fallen into debt, and, as provided by the law of Moses, was serving Laban till that debt was paid by his services. This covenant Zoram faithfully kept. He went down with the sons of Lehi into the wilderness, and he and his posterity were numbered with the people of Nephi ever afterward. In the valley of Lemuel, Zoram married the eldest daughter of Ishmael. When Lehi, previous to his death, blessed his posterity he also extended his blessings to Zoram. Though with some conspicuous men of later Nephite history—Amalickiah, Ammoron, Tubaloth, for instance—were his descendants; neither have we any record of his death.

ZORAM. A righteous, God-fearing Nephite general in the days of the judges. When the apostate chief captain of their armies at the time of the Lamanite capture of Ammonihah (B. C. 81). Knowing that Alma, the younger, the high priest, had the spirit of revelation, he and his sons, Lehi and Aha, went and inquired the mind and will of the Lord as to the direction the Nephite forces should take in their endeavor to rescue the prisoners captured by the invaders. Alma inquired of the Lord and received an answer that the Lamanites would cross the Sidon in the south wilderness, beyond the borders of Manti. Alma then told Zoram: "There shall ye meet them, on the east of the river Sidon, and there will the Lord deliver unto thee thy brethren who have been taken captive by the Lamanites." Following these instructions, Zoram and his sons led the Nephite armies across the Sidon and marched into the south wilderness on the east side of the river. There they came upon the enemy, scattered them and drove them further into the wilderness. They also rescued all the Nephite prisoners and restored them to their own lands. We read nothing more of Zoram after this campaign.

ZORAM. A Nephite apostate of the time of the Republic. He was the founder of the sect of the Zoramites, and established them in the land of Antionum. Of his birth, death or personal history we are told nothing. He was alive at the time that Alma and his co-laborers visited and endeavored to reclaim his deluded followers. (B. C. 75.)

ZORAMITES. A family of the Nephites. They were the descendants of Zoram, the servant of Laban, and received their blessings with and were joined to the posterity of Nephi.

ZORAMITES. An apostate sect of the Nephites, who took their name from one Zoram, their leader. They occupied the land of Antionum, where they flourished, B. C. 75.

In the various apostasies, partial or total, that from time to time disgraced the Nephites, there is one characteristic that seems universal to them, however much they differed on minor points. It was the denial of the coming of the Savior in the flesh, and of the necessity of His atonement for the sins of the world. This was the evil one's strong point in his efforts to mislead the ancient Nephites. Thus it was with the Zoramites. They bowed down to idols, denied the coming of Christ, declared the doctrine of the atonement to be a foolish tradition, and misinterpreted the teachings of holy scripture with regard to the being of God. Their declaration of faith was: "Holy, holy God; we believe that thou art God, and we believe that thou art holy, and that thou wast a spirit, and that thou art a spirit, and that thou wilt be a spirit forever." Moreover, they claimed to be a chosen and a holy people, separated from their fellowmen, and elected of God to eternal salvation, while all around were predestined to be cast down to hell. This creed naturally resulted in its adherents and advocates being puffed up in vanity and consumed with pride. They became haughty, uncharitable and tyrannical, and oppressors of their poorer neighbors. Their strange medley of religious ideas gave birth to corresponding vagaries of worship. Being elected to be God's holy children, they had no need of prayer. Once a week they assembled in their synagogues and went through an empty form, which was a little prayer, a little praise and considerable self-glorification. Having done this, they never mentioned God or holy things again throughout the week; indeed, it was a portion of their creed that their synagogues were the only places in which it was lawful to talk or think of religious matters.

Their ceremonies were as absurd as their creed. In the centre of each of their synagogues was erected a holy stand, called rameumptom, which stood high above the congregation; the top being only large enough for one person to stand upon. Each worshiper mounted to this top, stretched out his hands toward heaven, and, in a loud voice, repeated their set form of worship. Having done this, he descended and another took his place, and so on, until all who desired to go through the mummery had satisfied their consciences or gratified their pride.

When the tidings of this defection reached Alma, he proceeded to the land Antionum. He was accompanied by his two younger sons, three of the sons of king Mosiah, also by Amulek and Zeezrom. To his anxiety to bring these dissenters back from the error of their ways, was added the fear that if they remained in their wickedness they would join the Lamanites and bring trouble upon their more faithful fellow citizens by urging the renewal of war.

On the arrival of Alma and his fellow-laborers at the seat of this apostasy, they at once commenced their ministrations. They taught in the synagogues and preached in the streets. They visited the people from house to house, using every possible effort to bring these misguided dissenters to an understanding of their perilous condition. Many of the poor and humble received the word of God, while the majority rejected it with contemptuous scorn. Some of the missionaries were maltreated. Shiblon, the son of Alma, was imprisoned and stoned for the truth's sake, while others fared but little better.

Having done all the good they could, the missionaries withdrew to Jershon, into which land the believing Zoramites were soon after driven by their unrepentant fellows. There they found a safe asylum among the Ammonites, who, regardless of the entreaties and afterwards the threats of those who remained in Antionum, shielded and comforted them. The Zoramites then affiliated with the Lamanites, and an army of the latter race, commanded by Zerahemnah, entered Antionum and attempted to drive the Ammonites out of Jershon. In this they were not successful, and, eventually, after a most desperate conflict, they were forced back into their own lands. It appears that the Zoramites accompanied them, as many of the Lamanite military leaders are afterwards spoken of as belonging to that sect.

www.ingramcontent.com/pod-product-compliance
Lightning Source LLC
Chambersburg PA
CBHW031746090426
42739CB00008B/898